BLOOD ON THE STREETS

Anthony Galvin is the author of several true-crime books, including *The Cruellest Cut: Irish Women Who Kill*, *Family Feud: Gangland Limerick Exposed* and the forthcoming *Ring of Death: Famous Kerry Murders*. A former journalist, he lives in County Cork and has two children.

BLOOD
ON THE STREETS
A MURDEROUS HISTORY OF LIMERICK

ANTHONY GALVIN

MAINSTREAM
PUBLISHING

EDINBURGH AND LONDON

First published in Great Britain in 2013 by
MAINSTREAM PUBLISHING COMPANY
(EDINBURGH) LTD
7 Albany Street
Edinburgh EH1 3UG

ISBN 9781780575865

A catalogue record for this book is available
from the British Library

Printed in Great Britain by
CPI Group (UK) Ltd, Croydon, CR0 4YY

1 3 5 7 9 10 8 6 4 2

CONTENTS

INTRODUCTION

WHEN STEVE COLLINS decided to leave Limerick in March 2012, everyone's initial reaction was one of relief; now he was safe from the constant threat of a bullet in the back. Then we all felt a surge of anger – the gangs had won.

Steve Collins is a businessman whose son Roy was gunned down because he had testified against a member of the McCarthy-Dundon gang. His only crime was that he had done what any other decent citizen should do – stand up to the crooks.

Initially, the family became a thorn in the side of the gangs, constantly reminding people that the streets were not safe as long as the scum ruled parts of the city. But finally the strain of constantly living with a Garda patrol following them, having to look over their shoulders when they were out, checking under their car for bombs in the morning, grew too much. Roy Collins' parents went into the witness protection programme and were relocated out of the country. In a final show of solidarity for the family torn apart by the vicious mobsters, the state agreed to buy their pub, giving them a substantial fund to begin their new life.

That is modern Limerick: a city in the grip of a vicious drugs war that has destroyed countless lives.

*

Murder is a sordid business.

As a teenager, I loved poring over true-crime books and magazines, but that was a very sanitised version of murder. It is only when you stand on a lonely street corner and you can see the rough canvas on the ground covering the last mortal remains of someone's son or daughter that you truly realise how awful murder is. Crime scenes are often grimy, dirty and wet. Gardaí stand around keeping the few onlookers away. Grieving friends and relatives exchange sad glances. Everyone waits until the pathologist gets there and carries out the initial investigation, after which the body can be removed and made respectable for the funeral.

The glamour of Hollywood is nowhere to be seen.

I remember the first murder I covered as a junior reporter on the *Limerick Leader*. It was a Friday morning in 1990, bright and sunny. The news came in that around 7.30 a.m. a man had been stabbed to death in Moyross, one of the rougher areas of the city. While others worked the phones, I was sent out with a photographer to talk to the neighbours.

When we arrived, I got out and approached a few people. Most expressed their sympathy, but would not go on the record. Then I found a man who was eagerly telling everyone his story. He had seen the stabbing and had been the first on hand to offer assistance. He had cradled the dying man and put his coat under the man's head. I scribbled furiously as he talked. Then I asked the key question – would he mind if I quoted him?

'I don't give a fuck,' he laughed. He was clearly relishing his central role that morning.

I also spoke to a garda at the door of the dead man's house, who told me that the murder was the result of a love triangle. The Gardaí had called on the victim the night before to warn him that someone might be out for him. He had clearly ignored the warning and answered the door to his killer without a thought.

Gardaí won't talk to you at a crime scene any more. Michael McDowell, in his tenure as Minister for Justice, put an end to any of that sort of cooperation. But this was the good old days. I got back to the newsroom and began typing furiously. It was my first front-page lead – a milestone in any journalist's career.

That would be enough to make it stand out for me, but there was a sequel. The man who had seen it all happen had a change of heart. He decided he would rather not have talked to the newspaper. By that stage, it was too late; the paper was on the streets. The *Limerick Leader* is a daily, and I had made that morning's edition.

The man called into the office and accosted me. What happened next could have come out of a Keystone Kops movie. He attacked me with an umbrella. I ended up running around the reception of the paper, avoiding his blows and trying to keep a straight face. He was half my size; I could have broken him with a sneeze.

Most murders don't have a funny side. I have sat with grieving parents who feel their lives are over after seeing a cherished son gunned down. I have sat in courts listening to bleak accounts of friends who have fallen out with murderous consequences. There is too much sorrow and raw emotion for murder ever to be glamorous.

And Limerick has had more than its fair share of murders. The city has gained an unenviable reputation for violence. In the late '80s, it became known as Stab City, thanks to a number of high-profile murders. Then the gang wars broke out at the end of the '90s. Initially, the Keane-Collopy gang were pitted against the Ryan gang. Then the McCarthy-Dundon gang began to throw their weight about, using automatic guns to gain dominance over their rivals. The death toll from the gang wars quickly hit double figures – and included several innocent people caught in the crossfire.

*

When it came to writing this book, I faced a difficult question. It wasn't what to include but what to leave out. In the end, I decided not to concentrate exclusively on the gangland killings, because Limerick is about more than the gangs.

BLOOD ON THE STREETS

Limerick is the third-biggest city in the state. It is sports mad, and the people are friendly and welcoming. There is a thriving arts and culture scene, and some of the local bands have risen to national prominence. It is a great place to live. True, the gangs have taken control of some of the estates. But the decent people are still there, still in the majority. There is still hope.

One thing about Limerick has always impressed me: the efficiency of the Gardaí. In other parts of Ireland, you might get away with murder, but not there. The detection rate is very high. It is thanks to the hard work and talent of the Gardaí that many of the people in the stories that follow ended up behind bars.

It is to those unrelenting investigators – and the families of the victims – that I dedicate the following pages.

1

THE LAST MAN HANGED IN IRELAND

Michael Manning

A DAY OF drunken pub-crawling led to his downfall. On 18 November 1953, after consuming enough for a week, Michael Manning was making his way home to his young wife, who was expecting their first child. But he had been drinking since lunchtime, and alcohol lowers the inhibitions.

When he saw a slim woman ahead of him on the dark road, a few miles from the city centre, Manning thought he could have his way with her. He sped up and dragged the woman into the bushes. He fought against the struggling woman – a nurse in her 60s – tearing her clothes and ripping her panties off her. He attempted to rape her. In the course of the assault, he needed to quieten her, so he punched her in the face and stuffed her mouth with grass.

When he was finally disturbed by the car lights of a concerned citizen, he ran. He left the elderly nurse in the field. By the time help arrived, she was dead.

Michael Manning was arrested that night, woken in his bed by a team of gardaí. Still recovering from his excesses of the night before, he immediately admitted his involvement.

'It was the drink,' he offered by way of excuse.

It could have ended differently. Nurse Catherine Cooper could have struggled to freedom. Someone could have stumbled on the scene a bit earlier and saved her life. Or Manning might have staggered home without encountering anyone who triggered his alcohol-driven lust. It was a completely random attack on a stranger.

But nothing had interrupted Manning, and when the gardaí woke him up, he learnt that the woman he had tried to rape had died as a result of his attack.

Naively, he asked the gardaí when he would be back home. He never came home. He never got to see his child. Michael Manning was the last man hanged in Ireland.

*

Hanging is the quickest and one of the most humane ways to execute a prisoner. The British, who believed they brought civilisation to every corner of the globe during the glory days of the empire, favoured the noose over all other methods.

Across the Channel in France, they preferred beheading. In fact, they turned it into a very efficient process with the invention of the guillotine, a sliding blade that fell from a height and severed the neck in one clean blow. Its inventor had reason to be glad of its efficiency; he was one of its first victims. But even Gallic efficiency had the potential to go wrong. If the prisoner was mis-positioned, the blade could strike him in the shoulders and it would take a second or even a third attempt to dispatch the howling convict.

And there is a second problem with beheading someone. According to medical knowledge, when someone is beheaded suddenly it takes a few seconds for that fact to register with the brain. Once the blade slices cleanly through the flesh and bones of the neck and the head falls into the waiting basket, there is a period of roughly eight seconds in which the brain remains conscious, before the falling blood pressure produces a faint, followed by brain death roughly four or five minutes later as a result of oxygen starvation.

For those eight seconds, the condemned person is fully aware of all that is going on; he sees the baying crowd, feels the cold steel meet flesh and is conscious of the blow to his nose as his head falls face first into the dirt.

Henry VIII used to love beheading people. If he liked them – like second wife Anne Boleyn – he would bring over an expert swordsman from France to do the job cleanly. But if he didn't, then the job went to one of the regular hacks based at the Tower of London. And Henry did not like Margaret Pole, the Countess of Salisbury. In 1541, he condemned the 67-year-old widow to the axe.

She was terrified and struggled as the executioner tried to position her neck on the block. As a result, the first blow went astray, striking her firmly on the shoulder. With a screech, the old lady sprang up and ran into the crowd of 150 horrified onlookers near Tower Green, within the Tower of London complex. The executioner followed her, raining blows on the frail woman until she fell to the ground.

She was then dragged back to the block, where the executioner finally dispatched her. But it took 11 blows before she died.

Spain favoured garrotting over beheading – choking someone to death with a rope or chain. This was used as a method of execution up to the 1970s. The garrottings were held in public until the end of the nineteenth century, then were done behind prison walls. Eventually, they refined the method so that as the strap tightened around the victim's neck, choking or strangling him to death, an iron spike was also pushed into the back of the neck, eventually breaking the neck and instantly ending the condemned man's agony. The last garrottings were carried out in 1974 in Malaga, when two men were executed for shooting policemen.

The USA opted for 'Old Sparky' – the electric chair – for many decades. One of the cruellest execution methods ever devised, it frequently took a considerable length of time to dispatch a prisoner. Some executions took several minutes, with the prisoner writhing in agony as jolt after jolt of electricity was driven through his skull. More than once, the scalp of the condemned man caught fire during the process, all under the gleeful eye of the room full of spectators who are always invited to be witnesses to an American execution. The electric chair is used only very rarely today.

It has been a tradition of jurisprudence that justice not only must be done, it must also be seen to have been done. Many nations have made the executions of prisoners public events. For centuries, huge crowds would gather for a hanging at Execution Dock on the Thames or at Tyburn (near Hyde Park). When hangings were moved inside the prisons, large crowds would gather outside to be first to hear the grisly news. In Paris, the daily beheadings during the height of the Revolution attracted huge throngs and were festive occasions, with crowds jeering at the condemned aristocrats.

I spoke to a Ugandan taxi driver who gleefully told me about the school tour he was taken on when he was 12. The entire class was bussed to a football stadium to witness the execution of a number of political opponents of Idi Amin. The driver told me cheerfully that after the first volley of shots all the prisoners fell in a heap on the grass of the stadium. Then, bloodied and weakened, one slowly stood up from the bodies. So the soldiers shot at him again. He fell but rose once more. It took a third volley to finish him off. All the time, the schoolboys were cheering loudly for him.

Such a spectacle would be inconceivable in Ireland.

Ireland has always had an uneasy relationship with capital punishment, and we never turned it into a public spectacle. Perhaps it was the legacy of colonisation by the British, which gave us a collective memory of public executions as a mark of oppression. Whatever the reason, from the foundation of the state, executions were carried out behind closed doors.

From the beginning, we chose the most humane method available, which was hanging. When the length of the noose is calculated correctly for the weight of the prisoner, hanging results in the neck snapping, and death is instantaneous. A miscalculation will result in too great a fall – which will snap off the head – or too small a fall, which will result in the prisoner slowly choking to death. But in the mid-nineteenth century hanging became a precise art, and such mistakes were almost unheard of. No execution in the history of the Irish state has ever been botched. During times of war (the Civil War and the Second World War), firing squads were occasionally used, but most of the Irish prisoners condemned to death since the formation of the state have faced the noose.

Initially, the legislators wanted to make Ireland a country free from the death penalty. The draft version of the 1922 constitution included a ban on capital punishment. But the Civil War began and the Dáil did not adopt this measure. During the Civil War, there were 81 executions, mostly of captured anti-Treaty fighters.

After the Civil War, life returned to normal. The question of capital punishment was not revisited, but the state failed to appoint an executioner. Instead, a British executioner was hired to carry out any hangings in Dublin. At one point, an Irish man was selected to be trained as a hangman. He travelled to London but got drunk and failed to perform his duties, and the state decided to continue the arrangement of bringing over a British hangman.

Between the end of the Civil War and 1954, 35 people were executed in Mountjoy prison. They included just one woman. She was Annie Walsh, convicted with her nephew of murdering her elderly husband in 1925. Each blamed the other, but the jury convicted them both.

One of the hangmen brought over from the UK was the famous Albert Pierrepoint. A part-time executioner, he was underpaid and had to run a grocery store, and later a pub, to make ends meet. He was glad of the Dublin nixers.

Many sentences were commuted to life in prison. In 1948, William Gambon was executed for killing his friend in a drunken fight. But it was six years before Pierrepoint was needed again – for the last time.

Michael Manning was the last man hanged in Ireland. He was executed for the murder of an elderly nurse on the outskirts of

Limerick on a bleak November evening in 1953. Although the family of the victim pleaded for clemency, his sentence was not commuted and he paid the ultimate price.

The sentence of death for murder remained on the statute books for another decade, until Justice Minister Charlie Haughey introduced the Criminal Justice Act of 1964. This eliminated the death penalty for most offences. Now people could be executed only for treason, certain military offences and capital murders – for example, murders of foreign diplomats, on-duty gardaí or prison officers.

But in reality the death penalty was gone even by that stage. Between 1923 and 1964, 40 people had their death sentences commuted to life in prison – more than were executed. In the decade between the hanging of Michael Manning and the new act, every single death sentence had been commuted.

In the years following the 1964 Act, 11 people were sentenced to death. All 11 saw those sentences commuted to life in prison. For most of those, life meant 40 years without parole, as opposed to a normal life sentence, which was less than 15 years.

The Criminal Justice Act of 1990, brought in by the Fianna Fáil and Progressive Democrat coalition, abolished the death penalty for all offences. There had been mounting political pressure for such a move for a decade. In a referendum in 2001, the Irish people voted overwhelmingly to insert a clause in their constitution which prevents the death penalty ever being reintroduced in the country. Michael Manning will forever be the last man hanged in Ireland.

*

Michael Manning grew up in Limerick in the '30s, a bastion of poverty and deprivation best described in Frank McCourt's bestselling memoir *Angela's Ashes*. Limerick was a large provincial town rather than a city back then, with a busy port on the Shannon estuary. The airport in Shannon – a huge driver of economic growth for the past 50 years – was not even in the planning stages. The city serviced a rural hinterland and the big industry was bacon curing. Shaw's, O'Mara's and Matheson's were the three big bacon curers, and a lot of people were employed in that industry.

Manning was born in 1929, the year of the Wall Street Crash and the beginning of the Great Depression. But the depression in Limerick had no beginning and seemed to have no end in sight. It was a dark, dank and dreary city, with narrow streets and run-down tenements. 'The lanes', the slum district described so well by McCourt, were a warren of narrow streets and poor houses around Barrington Street and off O'Connell Avenue. Often several people would share a room or two, and there was no electricity. Sanitation was basic; the toilet was a shed out the back, usually shared among several households.

People were poor, but so were their neighbours, and everyone got along as best they could. Manning grew up on the opposite side of town, around Rhebogue, a district on the outskirts of Limerick near the main Dublin Road. His father was what was known as a carman, or carter. He ferried goods about the city on a horse and cart. This was in the days before cars and trucks became commonplace, and most goods were still transported the old-fashioned way.

Manning's father, John, was self-employed and worked hard. He did quite well for himself and eventually moved out of the city, buying an acre of land at Garden Hill, near Castleconnell. The family home in Rhebogue went to another of his sons, Patrick.

Castleconnell is a leafy little village on the banks of the river about seven miles east of the city – then, as now, a sleepy backwater. Michael was John's eldest son. There were seven surviving children in the family.

Michael attended the local primary school, but his schooling ended at the age of 15. This was quite common back then – in fact, Michael probably got more education than most. Many left school by 12. John quickly got his son involved in the family business; Michael spent his days on the cart as his father's helper. He also helped around the small farm.

In 1952, at the age of 23, Michael married a local girl, Joan Madden. She was from Moore's Lane, near the centre of the city. It was just off Clare Street, and less than a five-minute walk from O'Connell Street, the main shopping street at the heart of the city. The happy young couple moved into a small house just five doors up from Joan's parents.

They quickly settled into married life. Michael continued to ply his trade, while Joan stayed at home and minded their little house. But now Michael was moving up in the world. To celebrate his wedding, his father had set his eldest son up in business on his own. He had given Michael a horse and cart. Michael was no longer the helper; he was a self-employed carman in his own right.

There were odd jobs all over the city, but in the early '50s the main work of the carmen was in the city docks. The Shannon is Ireland's biggest river, and goods came downriver from as far away as Athlone in one direction and from the UK and the Continent up the estuary in the other. The docks were always busy. Goods had to be unloaded, then transported up to the railway station, about a half a mile away. There were also plenty of warehouses along the banks of the river. The carmen, with their laden carts, were familiar figures in the square mile at the heart of the city, from the banks of the river up through Henry Street, O'Connell Street and Catherine Street, and on to the railway station. The area that encompassed the station, the river and the docks was their stamping-ground, and they guarded their business diligently.

Michael Manning quickly became a familiar figure. A friendly and easy-going man, he became known as much for his distinctive headgear as anything. Everyone wore a hat in those days, but no one wore a hat like Manning's. Variously described as a cowboy hat, a clown's hat and a Baden Powell, the closest thing to it today is the high hat worn by members of the Canadian Mounties. No one knows where he got it, but the distinctive hat made him instantly recognisable. It was a key part of his eventual downfall.

By the early '50s, cars were becoming a familiar sight on the city streets. Trucks were plying their trade between all the main towns. But they made no inroads on the docks. Limerick harbour commissioners had once tried to link the railway and the docks. They drew up elaborate plans for a line to come from the station down less than a mile to the river. The Department of Industry and Commerce were to fund the investment, which was backed by the Limerick Chamber of Commerce. The job was even tendered out, to the Siemens-Bauunion engineering company, which had built the massive power station at Ardnacrusha.

But the Limerick Hired Carmen's Society, a sort of union that represented Michael Manning and his colleagues, opposed the elaborate plans and they were shelved. The carmen had established their right to a monopoly on the transport of goods from the docks to the railway station. Michael Manning appeared to be set up for life.

In the long days of summer, with the sun smiling from a cloudless sky, it was a good life. In November, it was a lot tougher. The days were shorter, but the working day was just as long. Manning was up early on the morning of 18 November 1953. He collected his distinctive dapple-grey mare from the field where he kept it, harnessed up the cart and set off for the docks. He had a full morning of work to do, and he had to get a move on because he was taking the afternoon off to run an errand for his father.

Manning trotted onto Clare Street, rounded the bend where it merged with Rutland Street then followed on to O'Connell Street. The quickest way to get to the docks was to continue down O'Connell Street until Mallow Street crossed it, then head down Mallow Street to the Dock Road. John Bourke was working with Manning that morning and, for a change, they were not running to the railway station. It was a simple job: a coal boat had docked and they were drawing the coal to Sutton's Yard, further up the docks. As the ship was unloaded, the two men tossed the bags of coal onto the cart and, when it was full, they trundled the short distance to the coal yard, where they unloaded.

Then it was back to the ship for another load.

It took all morning to unload the boat, but the job was done by 12.30 p.m. It was time for a break. Back then, 'lunch' was unheard of. People stopped in the middle of the day for their dinner, then had a light supper in the evening. Newly married, Manning generally went home for his dinner. But this day he chose to have a few drinks instead. He was well known in the local pubs and enjoyed his pint.

Bourke, at 49 old enough to be Manning's father, usually did not drink with the younger man. But he decided to join him that afternoon. Manning only planned on drinking a few pints. He had a busy afternoon ahead of him. He was going to collect a load of cement and lime and transport it the seven miles out to his father's farm, for use in building a garage.

The two men went halfway back to Manning's home, stopping at Denmark Street in the city centre. They went into O'Brien's pub and had a few pints of stout. Some other carmen were there, and it was a sociable occasion. In subsequent statements to the Gardaí, Manning forgot to mention these early-afternoon drinks. He and Bourke had four pints apiece, then left the pub at two o'clock.

Manning headed the short distance home, where his pregnant wife Joan was waiting with his dinner. He ate fast, knowing that in a few hours daylight would be fading. He left his home on Moore's Lane at 2.30 p.m. to pick up the materials for his father. He headed for William Street and stopped at O'Neill's Hardware Store. An assistant helped him load four sacks of cement and four of lime onto the back of the cart. It was now three o'clock and the sun was low in the sky.

He was ready to set off when a man from O'Brien's bar, Michael Flaherty, passed by. Flaherty had missed his bus home and was at a loose end. He invited Manning to come for another drink. Manning took a look at the darkening sky but decided to take a chance. He joined Flaherty in nearby Kirby's pub, leaving his horse and the loaded cart on the street, for what would be an epic pub crawl.

According to depositions taken in the District Court, Manning later told gardaí:

> I left home at half past two in the afternoon and went to Thomas O'Neill's, where I collected a quarter of a ton of cement and four bags of lime. I then went into John Kirby's licensed premises where I had two pints of stout. Michael O'Flaherty had two drinks with me.
>
> I went from that to the public house at the Pike, just at the pump, where I had two glasses of stout, also with Flaherty. I went across then to Hayes's Munster Fair Tavern where I was refused drink, as the girl in the bar said we had too much drink. Flaherty was with me then also.
>
> We went back to the public house where we had been before and the barman who had served us previously refused to give us more drink. He said we had enough drink taken. Flaherty was inclined to sing a song. We then went to Ryan's Public House, where we had a glass of stout each, and only for Flaherty knowing the barman we would not have got those drinks.

Publicans are not known for their civic concern or care for their drinkers, so if the men were refused drink in two premises and struggled to get served in a third, they must have been quite intoxicated. Publican John Kirby remembered serving both men two drinks in his pub. At that stage, he was of the view they were sober. As the day wore on, other witnesses thought differently.

Joseph Dillon, a painter and decorator who saw them enter Merrick's Bar on Blackboy Pike, said they were pulling and pushing each other and cod-acting on the street. William Merrick, the publican, said they appeared to 'have had a few drinks taken'. He served them one round, but refused them a second, telling them to go home.

They didn't go home. According to Joseph Dillon, still painting in the neighbourhood, their next stop was a petrol station on Blackboy Pike. They pulled up to one of the pumps in the

BLOOD ON THE STREETS

forecourt and called for three gallons of petrol. Michael Fahy, the proprietor, laughed and replied, 'The petrol you lads want is selling in the Tavern bar.'

By this point, several pints had been consumed and much of the remaining daylight wasted. Manning suddenly realised he had left it too late to run the supplies out to Castleconnell. He told Flaherty that he would leave the job until the following day. They got onto the cart and began trundling down Mulgrave Street, back towards the city centre.

But a few minutes later a bus passed them, furiously honking its horn. The driver was gesticulating, and when Manning turned he saw that one of the cement bags had fallen off the cart without their noticing. The bag had burst, spilling cement all over the road. The two men pulled over, then found an old coal bag and went back to see how much of the cement they could salvage. Having scooped most of the mess into the bag, they threw it on the back of the cart, then continued on to Upper William Street. It was now 5.15 p.m. and Manning was right back where he had started from three and a half hours earlier.

Flaherty hopped on a passing cart and got a lift home. But Manning did not go home. Quite drunk by now, he had another change of mind and decided it was not too late after all to complete his delivery. He turned around and began heading back out on the road he had come in on. He was going to Castleconnell with his load.

His route took him out on the Dublin Road. He stopped briefly at his brother's house at Rhebogue, then continued on to the suburb of Castletroy. Back then, before the University of Limerick turned it into student-land, Castletroy was a very desirable address. There were big houses with spacious gardens, the residences of professionals and the monied classes. From there, he drove through the village of Annacotty, then turned down the narrow road towards Castleconnell. Between half-six and seven, several people spotted Manning, with his distinctive Mountie hat, on the road towards Castletroy.

He eventually arrived at his father's house, hours later than expected and in pitch darkness. It was 7.30 p.m. He quickly unloaded the sacks. They asked him in for tea, but he declined. He lingered just a quarter of an hour, then turned and began the journey home. It had been a long day, and tea was not on his mind. Manning wanted another drink.

He pulled into Quilty's pub in Annacotty and had a few pints with a man he met there. It was 8.30 p.m. when he left.

As he told the Gardaí:

> I went to my father's house at Garden Hill on the Newport Road, where I delivered my load. I did not remain there longer than about ten minutes or a quarter of an hour. It was about a quarter to eight then and dark at the time. It was getting dark when I was leaving Limerick to go out to my father's. After leaving my father's I drove back towards Limerick, and on the way I went into Paddy Quilty's public house at Annacotty, where I had a pint and a half with Paddy Collins.
>
> I drove from Quilty's to Martin O'Brien's of Newcastle, where I put the horse into grass and left the cart and the harness in the field. I walked in then towards Limerick.

Martin O'Brien's was not another pub. It was one of the few stops that day that did not involve drink. Manning rented a field from O'Brien, and that was where he left his horse and cart. This was a departure from his usual practice. He normally finished his day back at his brother's house in Rhebogue, near the River Groody. This is on the outskirts of the city, and he left his cart there overnight, leading the horse to the rented field. Then he would take his bicycle and cycle home to his wife, who was waiting patiently at Moore's Lane.

That night, he didn't bother with the bike. He abandoned the horse and cart in the field and began the walk home, a distance of perhaps three miles. It was after nine and Manning had consumed so much drink he was barely aware of what he was doing.

*

Earlier that day, an elderly nurse had set out on her own journey, a journey that would put her on a collision course with the drunken Manning.

Catherine Cooper was born in 1890 and lived through the birth of the state. She was a native of west Clare, growing up on a farm at Burrane, near Killimer. Now Killimer is the site of a ferry crossing from Clare to Kerry. Back then it was an area of rolling agricultural land overlooking the Shannon estuary a few miles from Kilrush. Catherine's brother Percy was an IRA veteran of the War of Independence, and the family were well respected. He still lived near the family farm.

The family were descended from Maire Ruadh O'Brien, the famous Red Mary who married one of Cromwell's officers to preserve her estates and her Burren stronghold of Lemenagh Castle, between Corofin and Kilfenora.

Catherine and one of her sisters, Clara, had left Clare as young women, following the emigration trail to London. Both trained as nurses, then worked for 20 years in Kidderminster Hospital. Kidderminster is a small Midlands town about 20 miles from Birmingham, and not far from the Welsh border. It was a far cry from the lights of London, being more like a smaller version of Limerick. Catherine was a good nurse and rose to the senior ranks in the hospital. She was highly thought of.

But romance never blossomed for the tiny nurse, and as she reached her mid-40s Britain was changing. Europe was on a war footing, and it was becoming obvious that Britain would be sucked into the conflict. Both sisters decided to return to neutral Ireland before the war broke out. Clara found work as a clerk with Thomas Cook Travel in Dublin. Catherine found a job not too far from where she grew up. Limerick was a bit bigger than Kidderminster, but not the bustling city it is today. Back then there were a number of hospitals in the city. Barrington's Hospital, facing the river very close to where Michael Manning lived, had been established in 1831. It closed in 1988, but reopened as Limerick's only private hospital.

Ms Cooper was employed as a 'home sister' attached to the

hospital. That meant that she toured the city making house calls to people – expectant mothers, elderly patients, convalescents and so on. As she was constantly engaged in her rounds of visitations to the sick and infirm in the city, she was a familiar figure. Spry and active, she often walked out on those visits.

For seven years after her return to Ireland, she worked under a matron, Miss Alphonsie Curtin. Ms Curtin, who was retired, had fallen ill in early November and had been confined to bed for more than a week. On the evening of 18 November, Catherine Cooper finished her rounds and returned to the hospital. Before going home for the evening, she had one last visit: she was going to call out to see her former boss.

A fashion-conscious woman, she dressed up for the visit. She liked to dress tastefully and always cut a respectable figure. That evening she put on sensible but stylish black shoes, a brown tweed skirt and a fawn camel-hair coat. But she added a dash of colour with a yellow polo-neck, a yellow beret and a yellow scarf. In the dark evening, that flash of colour made her stand out.

At six o'clock, the Angelus bells were ringing out over the city as Sister Cooper left through a side door of Barrington's Hospital and walked the short distance across the bridge and onto the main road to catch a bus to Castletroy, where the retired matron lived. She arrived around 6.30 p.m.

The two women spent about three hours chatting, then Catherine stood up to leave. Ms Curtin was confined to bed, so the maid, Margaret Egan, saw her to the door. Ms Egan had worked in Barrington's Hospital before going into service with Ms Curtin, so she knew Sister Cooper well. They chatted briefly at the gate, then the nurse turned and walked into the night.

It was dark and chilly, but the moon was out and the sky was relatively clear. It was a fine night for a brisk walk, so Sister Cooper decided not to bother getting the bus from Castletroy back into the city. It was only a few miles and the air would do her good. It was a decision that put her in the same area as

Manning, who was now on the prowl for something other than drink.

*

There is evidence that when Manning left his horse and cart in the field and began heading back to the city his thoughts were not focused on his pregnant wife. Three women were walking out of the city as Manning was wending his way in. They were teenage sisters Eileen and Maureen Kelly and a mature woman, Mary Walsh. All three worked as servants in well-off Castletroy. The sisters had gone to see a film that afternoon, then had tea. They met with Ms Walsh on the walk home. It was after nine and they were approaching Newcastle, the ruins of a medieval fortress on the edge of Castletroy.

Maureen Kelly later told gardaí:

> I got a nudge from my sister Eileen and as I looked across the road I saw a man on the left-hand side. He was slouching along. He looked at us and he passed. But then the man turned about and followed us. I used to look around and every time I did the man was slouching up after us on the same side of the road as we saw him first.

The man who was following them had a dark hat.

A little further on they came across a grey horse in a field, with a cart nearby. She recognised the horse.

'I saw that horse several times driven by a man with a peculiar-shaped brown hat.' Manning's Mountie headgear was giving him away.

> The man on the road was wearing a peculiar hat, like a clown's all stuck up on his head. I am positive that the man I saw driving the grey horse and the man I saw on the road wore the same type of hat. I was afraid of that man because of the way he turned and followed us.

Perhaps it was because there was safety in numbers, or perhaps it was because the girls arrived at the house where Eileen was in service and went in for a few minutes, but Manning changed his mind and turned back towards the city. The evidence of Maureen Kelly makes it clear, however, that he was actively hunting a victim.

Perhaps it was because his wife was pregnant and he was experiencing sexual frustration. Maybe it was just the drink. In any case, as he made his way back towards the city, he spotted a distinctive flash of yellow in front of him and saw the diminutive figure of Sister Catherine Cooper. Dainty, well dressed, in the dark she probably passed for a much younger woman than her 64 years. And she was alone. Manning began to follow her.

'At Newcastle, near the ruins, I saw a lady walking in front of me towards Limerick on the left-hand side coming in. I walked along behind her for a few minutes,' Manning told gardaí. 'I suddenly lost control of myself and jumped on her because I saw she was alone.'

The attack was brutal and savage. Manning, a big, strong young man used to physical labour, grabbed the frail nurse and pulled her from the road into the field beyond. As he dragged her off the road, his hat fell off and so did her distinctive beret. Not noticing, Manning threw her onto the grass and punched her in the face as she fought against him. She struggled and tried to scream as he lay on top of her. Manning pinned her to the ground, his weight crushing the breath out of her. But she still cried and moaned, and he knew that the noise could be fatal to his plans. So he pulled out great wads of grass and stuffed them into the nurse's mouth. He then pulled up her skirt and roughly ripped off her knickers, attempting to rape her as she continued to moan.

Manning told gardaí:

She struggled. She let out a few screams. I knocked her down on the grass and stuffed grass into her mouth to keep or to stop her from roaring. I pulled off her knickers and tried to get at her, but I could not. I had one hand in her mouth, the other under her back. I changed my hands a couple of times, having a different hand in her mouth on occasion.

It was a sustained attack. Sister Cooper's ordeal probably lasted at least a quarter of an hour. Manning said:

She got quiet after about five minutes, but she began to struggle again and asked me to stop. She just said: 'Stop. Stop.' The next thing I knew a motor car with lights on stopped beside me. I got up and jumped over the ditch. At the time I left the lady she was quiet. She was like that for a couple of minutes before the motor car pulled up.

The car was on a rescue mission, but it had arrived too late.

*

A while earlier, John and Anne McCormack had been out for a walk in the clear night air. John was the manager of coal importers Tedcastle McCormack in the city and lived on the Golf Links Road in Castletroy. As the couple walked up Newcastle Hill, Anne spotted the two hats discarded on the road. They could hear muffled sounds coming from the grass beyond, about 20 yards away. There was no street lighting so far from town, but in the pale moonlight they could barely make out a bulky figure in the grassy area set in from the road. It looked like a woman lying face-upwards on the grass, with a man straddling her. Thinking they might have disturbed a courting couple, the McCormacks hurried on.

But as they drew away, Anne McCormack became concerned. The sounds she could faintly hear did not sound like tender sweet nothings. They sounded like a woman in distress.

'It was a low moaning of a person in agony,' she told gardaí later.

She had a foreboding that something terrible was happening, and that the woman might be in need of help. Not knowing what to do, the couple decided to hurry home and come back in their car. It took a few minutes to make the journey back to their house – precious minutes in which the life was being choked and squeezed out of Sister Cooper. Finally, they arrived back at the grassy area and slowed their car down to ten miles an hour. They were startled when a man leapt up and ran through the headlights onto the road. Then he shot back to the grass margin, jumped over a fence and ran off. They angled the car so that the headlights shone into the grass. They were horrified by what they saw: the half-naked body of a woman, ghastly white in the harsh light. Her skirt had been pushed up to her waist and she wasn't moving. Her legs were bare and her stockings had been pulled down to her ankles.

Instead of getting out to check if the woman was alive, they turned and drove to nearby Milford House, a convent of the Sisters of Charity. They wanted to phone the emergency services and get a priest.

Father John O'Regan accompanied them back to the site. He confirmed that the woman was dead and performed the last rites. An onlooker was the local curate, Father Eamon Casey. Both priests then drove Mrs McCormack back to the city to report the body to the Gardaí. They picked up a doctor from Barrington's Hospital, dropped him off at the scene, then dropped Mrs McCormack home. With the Gardaí finally alerted, a full-scale murder investigation was under way. It was now close to eleven o'clock.

Progress was remarkably quick. A scrap of paper in the victim's handbag revealed her identity. Then a crucial piece of the puzzle was unearthed. Two teenagers had come upon the Mountie hat and the yellow beret on the ground and had taken them away, not knowing that a woman lay dying or dead nearby. They had found the distinctive pieces of headgear while the McCormacks were off fetching the priest; they had put them on and had been spotted by a number of people.

Once gardaí recovered the two hats, they knew who they were looking for. Only one man in the city wore such a distinctive hat, and that man had been seen by several witnesses in the vicinity of the murder at the right time of the evening.

At half past two on the morning of 19 November, they pounced. They did it in force: two inspectors, two sergeants, a plain-clothes detective and a uniformed garda arrived at Manning's home on Moore's Lane. They knocked on the door, then banged at the windows until Joan Manning let them in. They entered Manning's bedroom and he sat up in bed groggily.

They examined Manning and found that he had blood on his hands, as well as small scratches. Manning claimed the scratches were caused when he was putting his horse away that evening in the darkness. But the gardaí were having none of it. He brazened it out for a while, but finally came clean.

'I'll tell you all,' he said. 'Drink was the cause of it.'

Over the next hour, he dictated a statement to the gardaí in the small bedroom; it was a full confession to the murder of the nurse. He told of dragging her into the grass, stuffing grass into her mouth to quieten her, then running away when the headlamps of the car picked him out.

> I ran down the fields and then got on the road again at Groody Bridge. I went up then to my brother Paddy's house, where I got my bicycle in an outhouse. I then rode the bicycle home, where I arrived about half past eleven or twenty to twelve. I believe the lady was alive when I left her and I was not aware that she was dead until the Guards told me. The blood on both of my hands must have come from the lady's mouth and the scratch on the back of my left hand was received in the struggle.

This statement was crucial to the prosecution case when the murder came to trial.

After signing the statement, Manning got dressed, had a glass of water and was taken into custody to William Street Garda Station. Manning had two visitors while in custody; the conversations they had with him were also crucial pieces of evidence.

The first visitor was his wife. It was the following morning, a little before midday. She came straight to the point, according to the garda who supervised the visit.

'Did you do it?' she asked. Manning nodded, saying, 'I confessed to it. I done it.'

The visit lasted just five minutes; Joan kissed her husband before leaving.

The next visitor was Manning's father, John Manning. He found the encounter difficult and uncomfortable, and resorted to euphemism, according to Garda Slattery, who sat in on the interview.

'Did you hear about the accident?' John asked.

'I done it,' his son replied.

'What did you do that for?'

'It was all drink.'

'You were not drunk at seven o'clock in the evening? Go on. Then what happened?'

'Then I went back the road and got two drinks in Quilty's pub.'

'Then what happened?'

'I saw a woman walking in front of me on the road when I left the pub and I jumped on top of her. Then there was a struggle. Then a car came. I jumped in over a ditch. I ran away. I got my bicycle and went home. I drank a mug of tea and went to bed.'

John Manning was shocked at the callous retelling of the night's events, and far less supportive than Manning's wife.

'I was never up in my life for anything except for having no light,' he said. 'I sweated for ye all for the last 50 years and now you have disgraced me.'

He stood up and left the police station.

*

The case, understandably, caused a sensation. Murder was rare in Ireland in the '50s. It was a repressed society, lashed into place by the power of the collar, so the sexual assault and murder of an elderly woman – a nurse at that – shocked the nation. Every court appearance drew massive crowds.

The first remand hearing was on Saturday, 21 November. Manning was escorted from the prison and taken to the City Court, a distance of, maybe, two miles. The City Court is on the banks of the river, a two-minute walk from Moore's Lane. But it was as close as he would ever get again to his home.

Up to 300 people thronged the steps of the courthouse – and they weren't there to support him. It was not like a modern Limerick gangland trial, where the whole gang attends in a show of strength. These were the ordinary citizens expressing their outrage. A week later, at the next remand hearing, the judge had to make an announcement from the bench asking for order. Several hundred people, mostly women, were gathered outside the courthouse an hour before Manning's appearance.

Judge Dermot Gleeson said the behaviour of the crowd was 'a disgrace' and condemned parents who had allowed their children to gather.

'There are numerous children out there who should be in school. The parents are worse to allow this crowd of gapers,' he said.

A huge crowd also followed the removal of the remains of Sister Cooper from Barrington's Hospital. Colleagues formed a guard of honour and escorted the coffin to the edge of the city. Hundreds joined the slow, mournful procession.

The funeral mass was celebrated in Killimer Church, with burial in Burrane cemetery. It was one of the largest funerals ever seen in the parish. The whole family were there – Catherine's brothers, Percy, William and John, and her sisters, Florrie and Clara. The little graveyard nestles in the ruins of a sixth-century chapel, dedicated to St Imy, the sister of St Senan.

By grotesque coincidence, Catherine Cooper was not the only famous murder victim to be laid to rest there. The Colleen Bawn (blonde girl), Eileen Hanly, is also buried overlooking the estuary at that spot. Eileen was a 15-year-old beauty who caught the attention of a minor member of the gentry, John Scanlan from

Ballykehan House, Bruff. He married the young girl in the summer of 1819 but kept the marriage hidden from his well-heeled parents.

After a few weeks, however, he grew tired of his child bride and he knew that his parents would not approve of the marriage. So he divorced Eileen, Irish style. He got his servant, Stephen Sullivan, to take Eileen out on the estuary in a boat. Once on the water, Sullivan opened fire with a musket, then threw the body overboard, weighted down with a stone.

Six weeks later, the body washed ashore at Moneypoint, near Killimer, on the opposite side of the estuary. Both Sullivan and his master Scanlan had absconded, but the crime horrified the populace and a big effort was made to find both men. Scanlan was arrested and put on trial in March 1820. Owing to the social status of his family, the trial was a sensation. Dannial O'Connell himself was recruited to lead the defence. It was all to no avail; Scanlan was found guilty and sentenced to hang.

The servant, Sullivan, was found shortly afterwards and went on trial in April of the following year. He also hanged. On the gallows he confessed his guilt and admitted that his master had put him up to the murder.

The case generated such widespread interest that one of the court reporters, Gerald Griffin, fictionalised it in a novel, *The Collegians*. Playwright and theatre impresario Dion Boucicault then turned the novel into a popular melodrama, *The Colleen Bawn*. This is still performed regularly, keeping the story (however altered!) of Eileen Hanly alive.

*

The inquest into the death of Sister Cooper, held on Friday, 20 November, at Barrington's Hospital, put the full extent of her injuries into the public domain. The state pathologist Dr Maurice Hickey said she had suffered considerable violence. Three of her ribs had been fractured, some teeth had been knocked out and there was extensive bruising on her body.

'Blood was oozing from the dead woman's vagina,' he noted,

saying that there was a quarter of an inch-long tear in the back of the opening to the vagina that had been caused very shortly before her death. There were superficial scrapes in the genital area and bruising on the tops of both her thighs.

There was dried blood under her fingernails, showing that she had struggled for her life, and extensive bruising on her right elbow. Both arms were bruised. There was blood oozing from her mouth, where the lower lip had been badly lacerated. There was also bruising on the chin stretching up towards the cheek bone and her right eye was bruised.

Sister Cooper had had her upper teeth replaced by dentures some years previously and these dentures had been knocked out during the struggle, as had five of her seven lower teeth. During the post-mortem one of these missing teeth was found in her stomach; she must have swallowed it during the struggle.

Her fourth, fifth and sixth ribs on the right side were fractured, probably from the weight of her assailant on her chest. Dr Hickey said that she had died as a result of shock and asphyxia from suffocation.

'The various injuries which I have described would all have contributed to the production of shock,' he concluded.

Justice moved swiftly back then. There were no two-year waits for a trial date. Manning was held in Limerick prison, and the investigating team swiftly built their case. Depositions were taken just after Christmas. These are no longer a part of the legal system, but in those days detailed statements of the evidence in major trials were put on record at the District Court and could be reported on by the media. The whole case was exposed in minute detail during Christmas week, both in the local papers, such as the *Limerick Leader* and *Limerick Weekly Echo*, and in the national papers, though in less detail.

On the second day of depositions, the court was cleared of women and of those not directly concerned in the case, as the intimate nature of Sister Cooper's injuries were detailed by the pathologist. But, despite the large crowds, not everyone was against Manning, as the *Limerick Weekly Echo* reported. As the accused was being led from the court at lunchtime, his wife rushed forward and kissed him, then gave him a cigarette. A nearby man shook hands with Manning and wished him a happy new year!

The trial opened in Dublin on Monday, 16 February 1954 – not quite three months from the date of the murder. Fifty witnesses were taken by bus from Limerick up to Dublin and put up in local hotels. The prosecution were taking no chances; they had built an extensive case.

The defence, on the other hand, did not need a bus. They had only one witness, a medical expert. They were pinning their hopes on the charge being reduced to manslaughter. Mr Justice George Murnaghan was presiding and the jury was all-male. The trial would take three days.

At the start of proceedings, Manning was asked how he pleaded. Despite his bedside confession, he replied in a loud, clear voice, 'Not guilty, sir.'

The defence attempted to play their trump card on the opening day. Manning's barrister was Sir John Esmonde. While fighting in the First World War on the British side (including being involved in putting down the Easter Rising), Esmonde had been elected to the British Parliament at the age of 22. The fighting MP had given up his seat in 1918, but in 1937 had been elected a Fine Gael TD for Wexford, becoming one of the few men to have sat in both parliaments. He was a formidable operator.

The prosecution, in opening the case, mentioned that a statement had been taken from Manning in his bedroom after his arrest. Esmonde was on his feet immediately, objecting to the use of that statement. The judge dismissed the jury, and both sides engaged in legal argument on the admissibility of the evidence. Esmonde said that anything Manning might have said that night – under pressure from a room full of senior gardaí – should not be subsequently used against him. But the judge disagreed and ruled that Manning's statement could be put before the jury. From that point on, the best the defence could hope for was leniency.

In his opening to the jury, Esmonde said that the defence was a 'double-barrelled one'. He did not deny that the killing was unlawful, but said it should be manslaughter, not murder. He claimed that the prosecution could not show any specific intent on the part of Manning to kill Sister Cooper and that his mind was clouded on the night by drink.

Over the course of the next few days, the prosecution called all their witnesses and built up a compelling case that pointed in only one direction. Then Esmonde called the only witness for the defence, a doctor.

Dr John G. Kirker was the director of the electro-encephalography department at St Laurence's Hospital, Grangegorman, Dublin. Electro-encephalography is the study of electrical signals from the brain; the subject was in its infancy in the 1950s. Dr Kirker said that he had monitored the brain activity of Michael Manning on two occasions in February, both times for forty-five minutes, while the prisoner relaxed on a couch.

'Some abnormalities were present on both days,' he revealed.

He said that those abnormalities were present in about 10 per cent of the regular population, but were three or four times more common among epileptics or people of unstable temperament. However, this evidence was somewhat undermined when the judge tried to clarify it for the jury.

'Are you an expert in mental disease?' he asked the doctor, who replied that he was not, saying that he operated the machine but was not a psychiatrist.

'Do you contend that what you did find is found with 10 per cent of otherwise healthy people?' asked Judge Murnaghan.

'That is so,' replied Dr Kirker.

'Any of us here might have the same abnormalities?'

'That is so.'

The only other significant move on the part of the defence was to cross-examine Michael Manning's father John on the history of mental instability in the family. He revealed that an uncle of Manning had died in an asylum two years previously, after being there for eight years. An uncle of his late wife had also died in a mental home, and a niece of his wife was currently in a mental home in Dublin.

Summing up before dismissing the jury, the judge clarified the issue of intent that the defence were relying on to have the charge reduced to manslaughter.

'It is not necessary that the accused should have had the intention [to murder Sister Cooper],' he said. 'It is sufficient if he used violence as a result of which the woman died. Drink is no defence in a case of this kind.'

Drink could only be a mitigating factor if Manning was so drunk that he did not realise that stuffing Sister Cooper's mouth full of grass could have the effect of choking her. The judge added:

But the accused did know what he was doing, because in his own statement he said that in stuffing her mouth with grass he had the purpose of keeping her from screaming.

The jury cannot reduce the charge to manslaughter due to drink. Drink is no defence if the effect of drink was to really allow a man to lose control of his passions. The effect of drink had to go much further than that to render a man incapable of knowing what he was doing at all.

The jury retired for nearly two hours, then returned for some legal clarification on the issue of drink and intent. The judge told them:

If the accused knew what he was doing when he put grass into the mouth of Miss Cooper, it could be presumed that death may follow. On the question of drink, the jury will have to be satisfied that the accused was so drunk that he was incapable of knowing the consequences of his actions.

The jury was not satisfied that Manning was so drunk. It retired for another hour, then returned with a unanimous verdict of guilty of murder.

Manning stood impassive and erect in the dock as the jury filed back, but he gripped the railing in front of him tightly as the guilty verdict was read out. Asked by the court register if he had anything to say, Manning replied, 'Nothing to say, sir.'

Mr Justice Murnaghan turned to the jury and said, 'If it is any consolation, I agree with your verdict, gentlemen.'

Then he took out the small black cap, as dictated by tradition, and put it on top of his white wig before pronouncing sentence:

> You, Michael Manning, will be taken from the bar of the court where you now stand to the prison from whence you came, and on Wednesday the tenth of March you will be taken to the common place of execution in the prison, and then and there be hanged by the neck until you be dead.

There would be no ten years on death row, like in American prisons. Manning had less than a month to make his final goodbyes.

There was still the question of an appeal; Sir John Esmonde immediately applied for leave to appeal the decision.

'On what ground do you apply?' asked the judge.

'I apply on the ground that you wrongfully admitted the accused's statement.' This was the statement taken in Manning's bedroom when he was initially confronted by the Gardaí.

Judge Murnaghan refused to allow the appeal.

But the fight was not over. A man's life was at stake, and his supporters would exhaust all channels before giving up. There were just two possibilities: get the judge's decision not to allow an appeal overturned, or petition for clemency. Both approaches were tried.

It was a little over a week before the designated execution day when the court of criminal appeal sat to consider whether to allow an appeal. Sir John Esmonde put the same objections as before: the statement taken in the bedroom in the small hours of the morning, while his client was still only sobering up, should not have been admitted. He claimed that a statement should not have been taken until Manning had received legal advice.

Also, there had been a heavy bias against Manning in the original trial, due to the savage nature of the killing. The defence had never wavered from their original position 'that the circumstances of the killing had been manslaughter and that if it had not been, that Manning was inflamed at the time he committed the act'. He alleged that the original judge had not put the defence side to the jury in his summing up.

In all, Esmonde presented seven grounds for appealing the original trial, but the three-strong panel of judges rejected all seven. There would be no appeal. However, the legal process had led to one positive outcome: the execution was postponed to 20 April. Manning would live for another month. All hope now lay in the petitions for clemency, one organised by his legal team and one by his wife. No one had been hanged in Ireland since 1948; there was a hope that the government would not have the stomach for another execution and would commute his sentence to life imprisonment.

The petition organised by Manning's wife received widespread support in Limerick, and some of the signatories were surprising. Several members of the Cooper family had signed, including Catherine's brothers Percy and Willie, who still lived at the Cooper farmhouse where she had grown up. Her sister Florrie had also put her name to the petition.

The appeal was considered by the government, advised by the Attorney General. Justice Minister Gerry Boland had prepared a two-page memorandum on the petition, which concluded damningly: 'The petitions do not add anything to the evidence given in court on behalf of the accused.'

The memorandum also considered the question of insanity, but concluded it was not an issue. This was partly based on Manning's behaviour in prison. A prison medical officer had noted that Manning

has shown no evidence of mental disorder. There is no impairment of memory and he is able to give a good account of his previous history. His behaviour has been normal during his imprisonment and he has taken part in any social activities during his stay here. He is quite rational in speech and behaviour. He shows no evidence of depression or anxiety since his trial and he appears to be taking his sentence in a calm spirit.

At a cabinet meeting on 3 March the decision was taken not to recommend a decision for clemency to the President.

In a last desperate throw of the dice, Manning wrote personally to the Justice Minister. The letter, written from his cell in Mountjoy, read:

I am almost seven weeks under the death sentence and it is a hard sentence to be under for such a long time. It seems no matter what I do the punishment will have to be carried out, so this is my last chance and I ask you to show mercy. As I was passing out the woman that night I suddenly lost my head and jumped on the woman and remember no more until the lights of the car shone on me. I was never in trouble in my life before that day.

I am married eighteen months and my wife is expecting a baby within the next fortnight and it is a hard strain worrying how I am going to get on. We were always happy until this trouble happened. My wife says she will never hold anything against me no matter how long we will be apart. I am truly and heartily sorry for having committed such an offence against God and the law of man.

The cabinet met once more to discuss the matter. It was a two-hour meeting, at the end of which they reaffirmed their decision not to advise President Sean T. O'Kelly to commute the sentence.

The last obstacle removed, Albert Pierrepoint took the train to Liverpool and the ferry across to Dublin. Although he did not know it, it would be his last job in the Republic. He made his preparations meticulously; the event would run with his usual precision.

On the morning of Tuesday, 20 April, a small crowd gathered

outside the main gate into Mountjoy. A little before 8 a.m. they began to chant the rosary. Inside, Pierrepoint was going about his gruesome preparations, safe from their prying eyes. The execution went perfectly. A few minutes after eight a prison warder walked out and pinned the notice to the door; the ultimate sanction had been carried out.

The execution of Michael Manning, unlike his trial, did not garner huge headlines. The Irish have always had an uneasy relationship with capital punishment. The *Irish Times* reported the hanging in three short paragraphs:

> Michael Manning (25), carter, 7 Moore's Lane, Limerick, who had been sentenced to death in the Central Criminal Court, Dublin, on February 17th last for the murder of Catherine Cooper (65 [*sic*]), nurse, of Barrington's Hospital, Limerick, was executed in Mountjoy prison yesterday.
>
> A few minutes after 8 a.m. a warder pinned up a notice which said: 'The sentence of death passed upon Michael Manning, found guilty of murder, was carried into execution at 8 a.m. today.'
>
> The last execution in Mountjoy prison took place in 1948.

Though the death sentence remained on the statute books, in one form or another, for more than 35 years, it was never carried out again. Every other death sentence was commuted to life in prison.

In his letter to the Justice Minister appealing for clemency, Michael Manning had said that his wife was within a fortnight of giving birth. This was an exaggeration, but, in a poignant footnote to the story, seven weeks after her husband was hanged Joan Manning had a healthy baby. She had lost a husband, but she was no longer on her own.

2

DIVORCE, IRISH STYLE

Majella Boland and Declan Malone

IN 1989, WHILE I was still a junior reporter and very wet behind the ears, I bumped into a photographer from a Limerick newspaper. He had returned from a grisly assignment. He had been out to Southill, one of the rougher estates in a rough city. His job was to take a photograph of a grieving young widow. Her husband had been blasted to death in a shotgun attack the previous day and she was appealing for any information about his attacker.

It was a routine appeal. We see them all the time in the papers after families have been robbed of their loved ones. But something wasn't right.

'I think she had something to do with it,' the photographer told a disbelieving bunch of newsmen. We laughed at him.

'That's why you take the pictures and we write the stories,' someone joked. We all knew that women didn't kill people. That was men's work.

But a few days later Majella Boland, 23, was charged with conspiracy to commit murder. She had paid a local thug, Declan Malone, the princely sum of £200 to blow away her husband. Women do kill and can be surprisingly vicious about it.

A couple of things make the case stand out. Limerick is a city that has produced more than its fair share of gunmen and quite

43

a few professional hit men (some of their stories will be told elsewhere in this book). But the killing of Patrick Boland had nothing to do with the city's gangland. Despite the presence of a hit man, it was an entirely domestic murder. It also marked the first time in Ireland that a woman had hired a man to kill her husband.

The other thing that made the case stand out was that Majella Boland had managed to hire a killer at a quarter of the going rate. But she forgot one thing: you get what you pay for. And quality costs. Majella went cheap and she got caught.

Time and place are important factors in any history, and to understand why a wife was willing to take the ultimate step to rid herself of a husband, we have to look at the conditions in Limerick at the time. Limerick has had a bad name for decades. Partly this is justified. In the '30s, it was a tenement city, teeming with misery. Frank McCourt, in his book *Angela's Ashes*, sums up the dreary atmosphere in that era:

> When I look back on my childhood I wonder how I survived at all. It was, of course, a miserable childhood: the happy childhood is hardly worth your while. Worse than the ordinary miserable childhood is the miserable Irish childhood, and worse yet is the miserable Irish Catholic childhood.

New estates were built in the '30s to facilitate slum clearances in the city centre. They did not so much alleviate the problem as move it to the outskirts of the city. St Mary's Park on the Island Field was isolated and without proper amenities. All those without a job, without income, without hope, were bundled into this and other impoverished estates and ignored by a succession of administrations. Then, in the '60s, a new estate was created for a new generation of the abandoned: Southill.

Michael Kelly's family were moved by the Corporation into the new estate in the early '60s (see Chapter 8). He was just 12, but he remembered it as the worst day of his life; he felt totally desolate when he arrived at the bleak estate on the southern side of the city. It was a big sprawling mess of a place, with no facilities except the school and church, both ringed by a high fence with security cameras. He ended up becoming a career criminal, and he blamed the move to Southill for that.

Southill also became a breeding ground for republicanism. Poverty often breeds activism.

This was the estate Majella Keane and Declan Malone lived in. This was not the city of the Lawn Tennis Club on the Ennis Road, the large mansions of Monaleen, the Edwardian rowing clubs on the majestic Shannon. This was a Limerick of grinding poverty and lack of opportunity. The estate was terrorised by young hoodlums, selling hash and harder drugs for their vicious masters. There was one small shop on the way into the huge and sprawling O'Malley Park, and a very limited bus service into the city centre. There was one rough pub, and local legend had it that patrons were requested to stick their knives in the wooden door on their way in, so that there would be no trouble once they were inside.

Apart from the unemployment, there was one other factor keeping the people of Southill down: lack of educational opportunity. For many, many years, there was a lack of secondary school places in the city. Despite a government guarantee of an education until the age of sixteen, right up to the mid-'90s one in twelve Limerick children failed to find a secondary school place. There were simply too many children and not enough places to go around – and this problem was ignored by government after government.

But in the poorer estates – Southill, Moyross and St Mary's Park – the statistics were even more frightening. One in four children was not offered a secondary place. For a quarter of the population in those estates, education ceased at 12. A blind fool could have read the warning signs.

Declan was born in 1969. He dropped out of school early and ended up working as a labourer. He was easy prey for the many republican factions operating in the estate. He joined the INLA (Irish National Liberation Army) initially, then moved across to a splinter group when he was 18.

With the explosion of the troubles in Northern Ireland throughout the '70s, a number of paramilitary organisations had sprung up. The Official IRA spawned the Provisional IRA. Splits at various points led to the formation of the INLA and the Irish People's Liberation Organisation (IPLO). Although the Provos had the bad name, some of the splinter groups were far more savage than them. All the organisations carried out assassinations. The INLA, established in 1974, was responsible for the assassination of Shadow Northern Ireland Secretary Airey Neave and the murder – inside the high-security Maze prison – of loyalist leader Billy Wright. They had the experience.

The INLA, like the IRA, used armed robberies of banks and other institutions as fundraisers. They carried out these robberies throughout the Republic, as well as in Northern Ireland. All over the country they were organised and ready for action. They were particularly strong in the mid-west. For historic reasons, Clare and West Limerick were hotbeds of the old IRA, from the Civil War era. But in the modern era another factor fostered the growth of republicanism. Shannon Airport thrived throughout the economic depression of the '70s and '80s. The mid-west was one of the only regions to sustain growth during the hard times. So many people escaping the troubles of the North settled near the airport. Shannon town became known as Little Belfast. Violent republicanism thrived. It also thrived in the working-class estates of Limerick.

In 1987, the INLA, already depleted by internal fighting, was riven by another split and the IPLO was formed. The organisation was responsible for twenty-two deaths in its brief, five-year life. Ironically, twelve of its victims were civilians, six were former INLA colleagues and only four were either loyalist paramilitaries or members of the security forces.

The INLA had been very strong in Shannon and Limerick, so naturally the new IPLO had its followers in both places. Southill was an INLA stronghold. When the split came, Declan Malone defected to the new organisation. The new organisation had a new source of funds: they were the first paramilitary organisation to go into drug dealing in a big way. Southill was already awash with drugs, so it was a natural fit. Malone, a labourer, was based in nearby Aster Court, Southill. He was in the centre of where drugs first got a grip on Limerick. There is no suggestion that he was involved in distribution. In fact, no member of the IPLO was ever convicted of a drugs offence, despite the fact that this, rather than armed robbery, was their chief source of income.

*

Majella Keane had been born three years earlier than Malone, in 1966. She had grown up in Southill, where her parents had a corporation house, but she was one of the lucky ones. She managed to get a secondary school place. She remained in school until her Inter Cert, and got good results – a fair sprinkling of honours. But that was as far as it would go. After her Inter Cert, it was time to quit education and get a job. She was just 16 when she went to work at Lyons Aluminium. Leaving school to take up employment at such a young age was quite common back then. She was one of the fortunate residents of Southill who had a job.

At 16 she was earning her own money. She was free from the tyranny of school – no more homework, no teachers wielding authority over her. Majella saw herself as a woman. But she was still young and innocent. She was easy prey for a domineering man, looking for a submissive woman to bolster his ego. Unfortunately, just such a man was working alongside her. Patrick Boland was just a year older than Majella. Like her, he had left school early and was working in the company as a fitter and electrician. He was from Garryowen, a better part of the city than Southill. He had five sisters and one brother.

Majella's family did not like the young man; perhaps this sweetened his appeal. The more her mother Patricia urged her to break off the relationship, the more she became besotted with him. After a courtship of just 11 months, they marched down the aisle. That was in September 1984. They were lucky: at the time there was no long housing list in Limerick and they managed to get a corporation house in the same estate that Majella had grown up in. Better than that, the house was next door to her parents on a terrace of small two-up, two-downs. There would be support there for the young couple.

At first everything was rosy, but the cracks quickly began to appear. Within months, Majella knew she had made the worst mistake of her life. Patrick was a violent and abusive bully who wanted to control his young wife. If he didn't get his own way fast enough, he would impose his will in the only way he knew how: with his fists and his boots. The beatings began within a few months of the marriage.

And the support of her parents proved an illusion. Majella's father Paul was of the old-fashioned school. He knew that his daughter was being regularly beaten, but he felt that no one should interfere between a man and wife. The wall between his house and his daughter's was thin enough for him to hear every punch and every cry of pain and agony. But he did nothing. As he told the court later, 'I preferred not to interfere.'

On one occasion, he recalled being downstairs in his daughter's house. From upstairs he heard a commotion, then his daughter's voice rose in fear, shouting: 'You're hurting me. You're tearing the hair out of my head.'

But he preferred not to interfere.

The neighbours had a similar 'hear no evil, see no evil' attitude. Their slumber was often disturbed by the shouts and screams coming from the Boland home, but no one stepped in. Majella had only one real friend in the estate. A local widow, Jean Foran, understood what she was going through and showed her support. She felt powerless to intervene, but she could at least be there for her friend.

The first year of the marriage was a nightmare. But Majella was hopeful that things would change. Perhaps being a father was what Patrick needed to settle down. In 1985, Majella discovered she was pregnant. She was delighted. A little baby would bring happiness to her home. She was so overjoyed she couldn't wait to share the news. She managed to contain herself all day, working alongside her husband. But that evening, after supper, she broke the happy news.

Patrick Boland's reaction horrified his young wife. His face went white with fury. Slowly, menacingly, he rose from his place at the table. Majella stood up and began to back away from him, knowing from experience what was going to come next. But nothing in a year of abuse could have prepared her for the fury of his onslaught.

Screaming at her that he wasn't ready to become a father, the callous man backed her into the wall and kneed her in the stomach. As she doubled up in agony, he brought his knee up again and again, smashing it into her stomach. As she fell to the ground, he turned and walked out of the house without a backward glance.

After a few minutes, Majella managed to haul herself upright and she made her way to the phone. An ambulance was on hand quickly, but it was no use. Seven weeks pregnant, she had suffered a miscarriage. She had lost the baby.

But it wasn't enough to get her to give up on her marriage. She stayed with Patrick, and seven months later she became pregnant again. But the result was predictable: when he found out, there was another beating and she lost the second baby.

It was a year before she got pregnant again; this time she kept it from her abusive husband as long as possible. She brought the pregnancy to term and had a little daughter. She named her Leonie. Majella was a devoted mum. She had dreamt of this moment for so long, endured so many disappointments, that she was determined to enjoy it to the full.

Unfortunately, Patrick was not of the same view. Babies are not particularly entertaining. They eat and cry and foul up the house, and they take the attention of the woman away from her husband. That was Patrick's perspective. The baby was a nuisance he could do without. Many couples experience that strain. The wife's affections naturally focus on the baby and the husband can feel ignored. Sometimes jealousy creeps in. But, when a man is a domineering bully with a need to be the centre of his universe, the jealousy can reach epic proportions.

The beatings continued. Now the screams of the mother were mingled with the screams of her baby daughter. But in the beginning Patrick reserved his anger for Majella. He confined his beatings to her. Because of this Majella stayed in the marriage. A break-up back in the conservative '80s carried enormous social stigma. It was almost unheard of. The only divorce recognised in Ireland was the wooden-box divorce; you stayed together until death allowed you to part.

But it was not long before Patrick turned his attentions on his little daughter. This was the final straw for Majella. She could take the beatings, but he was not going to do the same to Leonie. Yet he seemed determined to repeat the pattern. On one occasion, he held the baby at the top of the stairs and threatened to throw her down to the bottom. On another occasion, he did something even more horrific: he dangled the baby out of the second-storey bedroom window and threatened to let her go.

That was it; Majella finally found the courage to leave her husband. She walked out on him, taking the baby with her. She returned to her parents.

Patrick Boland was shocked. No one walked out of marriages in Ireland. That was the one constant he could build his life upon. No matter how often he kicked and beat his wife, no matter how many babies she miscarried, she would always be there with him. There was no escape. And yet, she was gone. She had left him.

He saw it as a reflection on his manhood. He had been weighed and found wanting. He couldn't hold on to his woman. How could he face the guys in the factory? His neighbours and family? His in-laws lived right next door. Every day he would see the wife that had defied him.

Attitudes have changed a great deal since that time, the view then being that you should control your own wife. You should be able to sort her out. Patrick Boland couldn't control Majella. He couldn't sort her out. So he did the only thing he could think of to get himself out of a difficult situation. He ran away from it. He packed his bags and moved to England.

Majella was delighted. She moved back into her home and devoted herself to her toddler. Life was good for the first time in years. She could come and go as she pleased and her body did not bear the cuts and bruises of domestic violence. Her idyll lasted a year. Her daughter was nearly two, laughing and beginning to talk. Life was good. Then Patrick returned.

He couldn't hack it in England. He was lonely. He missed his friends and the craic in Limerick. He missed his family. He even missed his little girl. After a year, he suddenly appeared on the doorstep of the small house in Southill, ready to resume where he had left off. But this time Majella had the strength to say no. She did not want to resume her married life.

The couple finally came to a compromise. Majella would continue to live in the house, on her own. But every day Patrick would come down at breakfast time and would stay in the house, looking after Leonie, until Majella returned from her job in the aluminium factory. He would then return to his parents' house to spend the night. It seemed to be the perfect arrangement, and initially it worked out very well. Patrick proved a better father than he was a husband. He minded his daughter well, and often when Majella returned in the evening the fire would be lit and a dinner ready. Sometimes Patrick stayed for the dinner and chatted. But Majella was not ready to let go of the pains of the past. She was not going to allow the marriage to be rekindled.

Perhaps this message got through to her former husband. Perhaps he was searching for a new way to hurt his estranged wife. Sometime before Christmas 1988, he came up with a new threat, one that sent shivers up her spine. He threatened to return to England – and to take little Leonie with him.

No court in the world would have given him custody. But he wasn't going to go through the courts. He was going to snatch the baby and disappear. He could do it. She had no doubt about that. Whether he would was a moot point; the threat had been made, and the threat sealed his fate. Majella thought long and hard, and finally decided that the only solution was a permanent solution. She would have to hire someone to kill her husband.

At that time there would have been no shortage of takers in troubled Southill. Top dogs in the estate were the Kelly brothers, Michael and Anthony. Michael, known as the 'Hard Man', had been accused of murder a few years previously, but had slid from under the charge. Anthony had killed two men in a knife fight in a city centre pub, but had walked because it was self-defence. There were rumours, never substantiated, of other bodies. But the Kellys were forbidding people. Though they were crooks, they saw themselves as people of importance within the community. Majella knew that they were not the ones to turn to.

Southill had a number of juvenile delinquents graduating to more serious crime: car robbers, burglars and even a sprinkling of armed robbers. But she didn't go for these either. There was another category of hard man on the estate, and they had the discipline and the experience to carry out the job. She turned to the republicans.

Majella thought that Declan Malone would be the ideal man to help her in her difficulties. He was only a few years younger than her and she had known him growing up in the estate. He was a hard man, with strong republican credentials. He could get a gun and use a gun. She approached him with her proposal. He accepted the contract readily. It seemed to be easy money to him. Patrick Boland was a nobody. There would be no consequences if he was eliminated. The only real matter up for discussion was Malone's fee for the hit. He asked for £500. This proved to be a problem. Perhaps Majella couldn't raise it fast enough, or perhaps he was just broke and in need of some readies. But Malone decided to reduce his price. He would carry out the hit for just £200. Majella immediately agreed. In December, she secured the hit by handing over a deposit of £120. The remainder would be paid upon completion.

Malone made it clear to Majella that one reason he was able to do the hit at a reduced price was because it was unofficial.

The IPLO did not know about it and would not know about it. Freelance killings were against the ethics of the organisation that sanctioned the killing of civilians and the distribution of drugs. He did not want to bring trouble down on himself.

One of these early meetings between Malone and Majella Boland was overheard by Majella's friend Joan Foran. She heard enough to know that the local thug was being hired to have a go at Patrick Boland. But she believed she had overheard a plot to scare the man, not to do him greater harm. She told the two conspirators that she was willing to help them if she could. But Malone said he could handle the job alone.

The first thing he did was pick up a weapon. Back then automatic handguns had not made their way to Limerick. The weapon of choice was still the shotgun. The shotgun has two advantages over the handgun. The spread of pellets means that aiming is not critical. And there is no rifling in a shotgun. Rifling creates distinctive marks on bullets – making identification of which gun fired a shot an easy task for forensic examiners. Malone picked up a double-barrelled sawn-off shotgun. Towards the end of February 1989, he met with Majella and they discussed their plans. When he left, he asked her to look after the gun until it was needed. She told him she would leave it in the hot press in the kitchen. As all the houses were roughly the same, Malone would know where to look when he arrived to carry out the kill.

Chance threw them an early opportunity to put their plan into operation. On 1 March, Majella had to go out to a funeral. It was the perfect alibi. While she was out Malone was to slip into her home, shoot her husband and disappear. The perfect crime.

It didn't work out like that. Majella went to the funeral, but she took Leonie with her. So there was no need for Patrick to babysit. When his assassin arrived, he found the door open (as arranged), but the house empty. In frustration, he had to leave it and go home. The hit was off.

But Majella had come so close to solving her problem. She

wasn't willing to give up now. They decided to go ahead with the murder the following evening, despite the fact that Majella would lack a strong alibi. They came up with a new plan.

The following day, 2 March, Majella arrived home from work at 5.30 p.m., as usual. Patrick was waiting there, his smiling daughter on his knee. The kettle was on, and Patrick and Majella enjoyed a cup of tea. Patrick stood up to go, but Majella stopped him. She explained that she wanted to take Leonie out to the shops for some things. Could Patrick mind the house while she was out? He sat down again.

Majella strapped her child into a buggy and left the house, pulling the door behind her. She had left the back door open. She did not go to the shops straight away. Instead, she went around to Aster Court and knocked on Malone's door.

'He's there,' she let the hit man know.

He didn't need any urging. As Majella headed towards the shops, he walked briskly to her house. He sneaked around to the back of the house and let himself in through the open kitchen door. The kitchen was empty. He could hear the sound of a television coming from the living room. That sound gave him cover while he opened the hot press and took out the shotgun. He put in two cartridges and he was ready. He pulled a balaclava over his face. Slowly, quietly, he sidled to the door of the living room. When he was quite ready, he opened the door and stepped into the small room.

Patrick, caught unawares, immediately leapt to his feet. He found himself staring into the eyes of a masked man carrying a shotgun. The gunman raised the weapon, waiting for wails of protest, pleadings, tears. But Boland was not that sort of a man. Seeing the danger, he immediately launched himself at Malone, grabbing for the gun. In his rush, he drove both of them back into the kitchen. But as he rushed the masked man, Malone got one shot off. At close range the pellets were in a tight cluster. Boland stopped dead, blood streaming from a wide wound in his chest. He had been hit on the left side, with pellets striking the left lung and lodging between the lungs and the heart. Slowly, he sank to his knees, then keeled over onto the ground. Consciousness was fading and he was in a world of pain.

Next door, Paul Keane heard the shot and thought a door had been slammed. He ignored it. He was busy painting.

Malone stood over the fallen man and cocked the shotgun. He was about to administer the *coup de grâce*. He raised the gun and placed his hand on the trigger. Normally, shotguns have a heavy trigger, and he had to pull hard. Just as he began to draw back the trigger, the man under him thrashed wildly in his death throes. He kicked Malone, the gun jerked and the shot missed. Unbelievably, at point-blank range, he had missed his target.

Frustrated, he turned the shotgun around, holding it firmly by the barrel with both hands. Then he brought the wooden stock of the gun down heavily on the skull of the dying man. He smashed the stock into his head about four times, until Boland stopped thrashing around. He thought that should be sufficient. He quietly walked back to the kitchen, opened the back door and slipped away.

Paul Keane heard the second shot and thought that his son-in-law must be in a foul mood again. He ignored it and went on with the painting.

Malone quickly made his way to a waiting car and drove out of the estate. He took his time; no point drawing attention to himself. He drove a number of miles out into the countryside and ditched the gun. It was never recovered.

Around 7.20 p.m., Majella strolled back from the shops, pushing the buggy. Her feet dragged as she neared her home. Suddenly, realising the enormity of what she had set in train and the horror of what she was going to find inside her home, she got cold feet. She couldn't face it. She could see the back door swinging open, which was their pre-arranged signal that the job was done. She panicked. So she decided to let someone else make the find. Perhaps there was also an element of shoring up her alibi.

She called next door, where her father was still painting. She told him that she had just come back from the shops and had seen her back door open. She was worried her home was being burgled and the burglars might still be in there. Burglary was a daily occurrence in Southill. Her father had heard what he thought was his loutish son-in-law slamming doors a few minutes earlier and he was sure there were no burglars. But he agreed to go next door to check. Perhaps, after years of minding his own business, he had decided the time had come to be a father to his daughter. In any case, he left his painting and went next door.

He walked in the back door and into the kitchen. He could hear a television coming from the living room. The kitchen reeked of cordite and on the floor sprawled the body of his son-in-law. There was blood everywhere, and the face was almost unrecognisable. Paul Keane ran back to his own house and phoned the Gardaí.

He later told a reporter from the *Limerick Leader*:

It was the [most] callous thing I ever saw.

I was painting in the kitchen next door and I heard the back door banging, but took no notice as sometimes fellows play football against the doors.

Majella and Leonie were gone to the shop and Patrick was to get the ten past seven bus into town, where he was going to play a game of pool.

Majella arrived in from the shop a short time afterwards and said that the back door was opened. I went next door and found Patrick lying in a pool of blood.

There was just so much blood. I ran out immediately and called the ambulance. We just don't know why someone would have done this.

Majella's mother, Patricia, added, 'You wouldn't give a dog a death like that.'

Majella played her part to a tee, acting the grieving widow for neighbours, friends and reporters. She said, 'I noticed the back door opened when I came back. I was only gone for a short while.'

One neighbour, who obviously was not close enough to hear the sounds through the thin wall, commented, 'Patrick was a very quiet young man. The whole area is shocked by the news.'

A few days after the killing, Patrick Boland was laid to rest in Mount St Oliver cemetery. Gardaí continued their door to door enquiries. They also received a number of tips on their confidential phone line. One tip let them know that Declan Malone had been spotted running from the scene at around the time of Patrick Boland's shooting.

A week after the murder, supposedly frustrated at the slow progress of the investigation, Majella did what was expected and went to the papers, appealing for information. She told the *Limerick Leader* that the unbearable strain of not knowing what had happened was taking its toll on all the family. She had moved back in with her parents.

> I just wouldn't be able to live in the house again. Everyone is under so much strain at the moment. We would all be able to relax more if the killer could be found. The strain of not knowing is just terrible. Everyone is just so upset. And there just seems to be no light on it at all.

She added that Leonie was too young to understand what had happened but she would be asking for her father when she visited her grandparents.

But, all the time, she knew the Garda investigation was proceeding and the net was closing in on her. She was questioned a few times. On one occasion, Detective Sergeant Mick Browne, a tough old-school cop from Kerry, asked her if she was aware that a contract had been put on her husband's life. Did she know Declan Malone? She could see the game was up. She finally confessed to having paid Malone to eliminate an abusive husband.

> I pressurised him into doing it. I didn't think he'd be caught

because of who he was. He was in the IPLO or the INLA. I'm very sorry. Will my child be taken off me? Oh my God, will Leonie be taken from me?

She went on to admit haggling over the price of the hit and getting Malone to do it for £200. She knew the plan was to kill her husband. This was crucial – she had intent to murder.

Confession in the bag, the Gardaí were ready to draw their investigation to a conclusion and hand over to the prosecutors. Declan Malone was taken into custody. Majella Boland was arrested shortly after.

The case came to trial the same year, before Christmas. On day one, Declan Malone pleaded guilty and was sentenced to life imprisonment. He refused to testify against Majella Boland, preferring to maintain his silence. He might have blown the hit, but he was playing the professional now.

Majella's trial began on 5 December. She had offered to plead guilty to manslaughter but the state would not accept this. They wanted her for murder. The state's barrister, Anthony Kennedy, said:

Declan Malone was a contract killer hired by Mrs Boland to murder her husband. He was the hit man but she was every bit as guilty. This was not a crime committed on the spur of the moment. There was careful planning in all the details. She hired and conspired and advised Malone when to do the job. She is as guilty of murder as if she fired the shot herself.

Majella was defended by the experienced Patrick MacEntee. He argued that the domestic abuse Majella suffered created a case of severe provocation. She changed her story about hiring Malone. She admitted she had hired him, but not to murder her husband. She wanted him scared so badly he would return to England. She told the jury she was 'shattered' when she discovered he had been killed.

The jury didn't buy the new story. They took just an hour to arrive at their verdict. She was convicted of murder and sentenced to life imprisonment. However, life does not always mean life. Majella Boland broke the mould when she became the first Irish woman to hire a killer to provide her with a uniquely Irish divorce. She broke the mould again with the length of her life sentence: just a few months above four years.

On 17 January 1994, a spokesperson for the Department of Justice revealed that Majella had been given 'conditional temporary release'. In layman's terms, she was out free, as long as she kept her nose clean. Still in her mid-20s, she was able to rebuild her life.

It would be another decade before her co-conspirator would see freedom.

3

A FALLING-OUT AMONG FRIENDS

Deborah Hannon and Suzanne Reddan

IT WAS A warm summer night and plenty of people were still milling around the streets. The walk from Moyross had taken the bubbly teen a little over 20 minutes. She was walking on her own, after leaving her friends at their home. But now she was on familiar streets, just minutes away from home. It was rapidly approaching 11.30 p.m. and she was crossing a green area very close to her mother's house.

She nodded a greeting at one of the neighbours, then spotted two figures slipping out of the shadows onto the green. Though they were both dressed in black from head to toe, she knew them well. There was no mistaking the swagger of one of them, a swagger that prison and grief had not diminished. The teen's lips curled into a smile. But then she saw the hard look on the faces of the two women and the smile froze. They were moving fast; she didn't have time to turn. She could see that one was holding a Stanley blade, while the other held a vicious-looking kitchen knife.

As the two launched their attack, she tried to run, but the force of the attack knocked her to the ground. She staggered to her feet, but they continued stabbing at her, and as she tried to flee to safety they pursued her, bringing her to the ground once more. It was all over in seconds. As she lay on the grass, trying to wheeze through punctured lungs, she could hear their footsteps as they ran into the darkness.

*

Some faces you will always remember. Some women stand out. They might be extraordinarily beautiful, extraordinarily ugly, or just carry themselves with a certain *je ne sais quoi*. Deborah Hannon stood out. Tall and willowy, with golden curls cascading down her back and pouty lips, she could have passed for a younger Daryl Hannah – if Daryl Hannah ever played a violent thief with a taste for cheap tracksuits.

More than 20 years later, I still remember the first time I saw her. She was standing with another girl and they were giggling together, obviously close friends. As they stood at their ease, they could have been any two teenagers lounging around outside a shop, or waiting for a bus. The second girl was short and pretty, with dark hair and sparkling eyes.

But Deborah Hannon and her dark-haired friend, Tracey Butler, weren't lounging outside a shop, or waiting for a bus. They were grinning at each other as they stood in the dock of the modern District Court building in Limerick. They had been caught shoplifting and now they were facing the consequences. But the odds were stacked in their favour: as women, with relatively clean rap sheets and a good free legal aid solicitor, they would escape with probation, or at worst a community service order.

The reasons I remember them are that they were grinning all the time and women defendants were not common 20 years ago. To see two of them together was as rare as an honest politician. I don't remember the outcome of that court case, but over the coming year both Deborah Hannon and Tracey Butler would become familiar figures in the court.

No one could have guessed that a year later the pretty brunette would be dead, hacked and slashed by the pretty blonde, her best friend, and another woman in a killing so gruesome it horrified experienced cops in a city that has a reputation for violence. Such was the viciousness of the attack, the Gardaí wasted time looking for men; they did not believe women were capable of such violence.

The savage murder of Tracey Butler by Deborah Hannon and Suzanne Reddan is a story of friendship, love and family gone tragically wrong. To tell the story we have to look at the lives of the three women – and the man who linked them together.

Tracey Butler was born on 14 December 1975; she grew up during the rough years of the '80s recession. Limerick is the third-largest city in Ireland. It has busy docks, a depressed centre and soulless industrial estates on the outskirts. Back then, unemployment was high and the city was architecturally and culturally uninspiring. It was a depressing and dreary place, but the people had an intense pride, especially in their sports teams.

Limerick always had a reputation as a tough town, and during Tracey's childhood years it earnt the nickname Stab City – thanks in part to a series of assaults and murders involving the Kelly brothers and the McCarthy family. What was to happen between the two teenage friends only added to that reputation.

Tracey grew up on Creagh Avenue, Kileely, a short distance from where that stabbing took place. Kileely is an old part of the city, an area of small corporation houses and narrow streets. It is a few minutes' walk south of the city centre and is one of the less gentrified neighbourhoods. Five minutes' walk in one direction brings you to the Island Field, while fifteen minutes away in the other direction lies Moyross. The Island Field is a corporation estate from the 1930s, with some of the worst poverty in Ireland. Moyross is a corporation estate from the '70s that makes the Island Field look affluent. Both estates spawned drug gangs that tore the city apart in a series of turf wars during the '90s.

Kileely, between the problem estates, is a different world. Here the people hold down jobs, the houses and gardens are well maintained and crime is something you read about in the local paper, not something you experience every night.

Tracey was one of four children born to Christina and Terence Butler. She had an older sister Sharon (21) and brother Mark

(20), while young brother Terence (11) was the baby of the family. Everyone described Tracey as bubbly, personable and outgoing. Her parents were separated at the time of her death, and Tracey was living with her mother. Separation was rare in Ireland back then. Divorce was still illegal and most couples remained in destructive relationships rather than face the shame of breaking up.

But Deborah Hannon's background was far more dysfunctional. Deborah's early years highlight the breakdown in family life in Ireland in the '70s and '80s. Her mother Teresa was just 15 when she became pregnant. Her family did not approve of either the pregnancy, or of her boyfriend, Willie Hannon. He was also just 15, but had a reputation as a hard man and a trouble-maker. The teenagers ran away together and set up home in London. Deborah was born on her mother's 16th birthday. It was a recipe for disaster, and the British authorities could see that. Social Services tried to take baby Deborah into care. But when they arrived at the house, Willie Hannon refused to open the door and threatened to blow their heads off if they returned. He didn't have a gun, but they didn't know that. He was an intimidating man, and they took no chances. They did not go back.

Deborah was left with her teen parents. Eventually, they tired of London and returned to Limerick. They got council housing in the rough estate of Cosgrave Park, Moyross, and they had two more daughters and a son. They got married. But their relationship had its ups and downs. Teresa wasn't happy in Moyross, with its constant violence, joyriding and burglaries. Neighbours were being burnt out and drugs gangs ruled the streets. On top of that, Willie, who worked as a pub and nightclub bouncer, fancied himself as a Casanova. Ignoring his marriage vows, he had a string of girlfriends and affairs, but his blonde daughter adored him and his wife always took him back.

It was a far less stable family background than Tracey Butler had, but the two girls became firm friends when they met at a local playschool, while still just toddlers. The two children became inseparable. They began primary school together, played in the yard and fought each other's fights. Both girls made their first Communion together, in pretty white dresses, and were still close friends when they left primary school and entered their teen years.

'From the time they were in playschool until the death of my husband, those two girls were inseparable. They both left school after primary together, and they looked after each other. They were always fighting on each other's behalf,' said Deborah's mother, shortly after Tracey's killing.

*

But throughout her formative years Deborah's father kept straying. Her mother, Teresa, didn't seem too bothered by his philandering, telling a journalist:

> The first affair was around 1990, with a neighbour. She was married. My husband started having an affair with her. He was doing that eventually four nights a week for the next few years. I found out about it after two weeks.
>
> Her husband came home with him from the pub one night. My husband climbed into the bed beside me and said: 'Your man is down there wanting to talk to you.'
>
> I said I had no man, but I got up and went downstairs, and there was this woman's husband. He said: 'Do you know your husband is having sex with my wife?'
>
> I said: 'What do you want me to do about it? I can't control him. You can control your wife. If you can't control her you're obviously not pleasing her. I don't know why you have to come to me. You should be able to sort her out.' That was that and he left.

It was an unusual reaction to the situation. Teresa was equally unconcerned when Willie met his next mistress at a disco. For a while, Willie managed to juggle both women, and still came home to his wife and children. And his little girl Deborah still adored him.

She became immune to her father's affairs and her mother's acceptance of them. As Deborah reached her teen years, the dysfunctional state of her family and the constant violence that surrounded her in the troubled Moyross estate left her with a warped sense of right and wrong. A moral compass was a luxury for the better parts of town. In her world, it was all about survival.

Deborah and Tracey remained firm friends, and together they also began to drift towards the wrong side of the law. Both unemployed, they began to shoplift and were caught. Tracey ended up with two convictions and did some time in a juvenile centre, as well as being ordered to do community service. At the time of her death, she was doing voluntary work at St Martin's Youth Centre on New Road in the city. Deborah was not so lucky. She was sentenced to 14 months in Limerick prison for larceny. In July 1993, she was halfway through her sentence.

Around that time the friendship between the two girls had begun to cool off; they were not talking to each other because of an incident that had happened about six months previously. But the events that led up to the murder began even earlier than that, the previous December, with Willie Hannon meeting yet another woman, Suzanne Reddan, and starting a torrid affair. It was to lead to his death. Pretty brunette Suzanne, born Meaney, had married at 17 and was a mother of three when she first met Willie. The 25 year old had started to run a small shop in Moyross; Willie used to call there every morning for his paper.

The shop was one of the gathering points of the neighbourhood, and often groups of youths would congregate outside. Sometimes the teens would turn nasty, abusing and harassing customers. Suzanne herself was often the brunt of the abuse. A few times, she called the Gardaí, but that wasn't always a good idea. By the time a squad car arrived, windows could be broken, goods stolen and the culprits long gone; and the sight of the flashing blue lights only inflamed the louts more.

There was an instant attraction between Willie Hannon and the new shopkeeper. She fell for him quick and hard. He loved the attentions of a pretty woman and began to fight her corner against the youths gathered outside her shop. As the infatuation grew, Suzanne began to believe the couple had a future.

One evening, Suzanne called at Teresa Hannon's house with her mother. After the trial, Teresa told a reporter:

> She called in for a chat and I didn't know what was happening. Willie was there that evening. I think she just fancied him.
>
> Then she asked me to go swimming with her the following night. I said I couldn't swim, but Willie said he could, so they arranged to go swimming the following evening. I didn't think anything of it, as her mother was there with her.
>
> The next thing was they were going swimming three nights a week. Then they were swimming every night for hours. Then they were swimming overnight, and he wasn't coming home at all. I realised that it was happening again, and Willie owned up to it. He said it was just another thing he was doing, and he needed to do it. It wouldn't last.

Suzanne thought it was the real deal. She left her husband to be with Willie Hannon, and she told Teresa that she loved Willie and wanted him to move in with her. By then, she was living in a council house in Cosgrave Park, just a few houses away from the Hannons. It was too close for comfort.

'You're dreaming. He says that to all the girls. You want to wise up,' Teresa advised her young rival. Remarkably the wife and the mistress remained on cordial terms. It was an unusual love triangle, with Suzanne a regular visitor to the Hannon house. She got to know Deborah, Willie's daughter, quite well.

In February 1993, an incident happened which set in motion a chain of events which led to two murders. It started at the Savoy Disco. This was a popular nightspot just off O'Connell Street, the main street in the centre of Limerick. Willie Hannon was a bouncer at the club. One night a row broke out in the disco between a number of rival families. There are conflicting accounts of how it started. Some people thought it was over the division of the spoils of an alleged crime. Others said that Willie was being teased about his relationship with Suzanne. Teresa Hannon says the cause was a lot simpler: Willie spilt a drink and it landed on the wrong person.

The girl's boyfriend sprang up and attacked Willie. Suddenly the place erupted, as Teresa told a reporter later:

It was like the Wild West. I never saw anything like it in my life. Suddenly the whole place was fighting, with bottles flying and fists being thrown. The whole house went haywire. I locked myself in the ladies' toilet. I could hear the shouts, screams and noises outside.

Though the spilt drink triggered the fight, there is no doubt that there was some teasing going on – some of it good-natured but some of it more pointed. It stung Willie, who knew he was doing wrong by his family. So he was not in a good mood when the fight began. And he was the security man, so it was his job to throw himself into the fray. He launched himself into the mob with enthusiasm. A number of people were injured as the melee descended into a near riot. Even the gardaí were scared. Teresa remembered:

Three guards burst in to the toilet where I was, and then braced themselves against the closed door, keeping people out. They were terrified. I said my husband is out there. Get him or he'll die.

They said: 'We will in our arses go out there again.'

I learnt afterwards that some people had hopped over the bar and were helping themselves to free drink while all this fighting was going on. It lasted for over an hour. Then lorry-loads of cops came, some of them in riot gear. There was also a fleet of ambulances. It all calmed down then and we went down to the hospital.

She embellished the tale in the telling, but Willie did need nine stitches that night. He had bruising on his face, neck and body

– and he was a long way short of being the worst casualty, as Teresa recalled: 'He was swollen and puffy. He had been hit in the face from blows of stools. His friend lost the sight in one of his eyes from a broken bottle.'

Tracey Butler sustained minor injuries on the night. She suffered cuts and bruises when Willie lashed out at her. This was the incident that led to a rapid cooling off between Tracey and her friend Deborah. She blamed the daughter for the father's actions.

Given time, the relationship would have been restored. They had been friends for as long as they could remember. But they did not have time to get the friendship back on track, because shortly after the riot Deborah's past caught up with her. She was convicted of larceny and jailed for 14 months. She was more brazen than her partner in crime and had a number of previous convictions, including one for assault. She had struck a security guard in one store after getting caught shoplifting. For this reason, she was jailed.

Tracey began a sentence of her own, but not a custodial one. It was a community service order, also for larceny. She was ordered to help out in St Martin's Youth Centre on the New Road.

Tracey Butler's bruises healed quickly, but she was not the only one who fell out with Willie Hannon following the row in the Savoy. Gardaí were well aware that a number of people had vowed to get Willie, but the burly weightlifter was a hard man and not too worried.

'Bullets won't kill me,' he joked.

He failed to consider what would happen if his enemies chose not to use bullets. That's just what happened a few months later.

In the small hours of 2 July, the world of the Hannons came crashing down. The previous evening, Teresa and Willie had gone out for a drink. They bumped into Suzanne Reddan, who joined them. Later in the evening Willie told Teresa that he would be staying with Suzanne that night.

'I said: "You're not doing that – you've stayed with her twice already this week." He said: "Well, I'll walk her home then."'

So that is what he did; he walked the two women back to Moyross. It was now past 1 a.m. on 2 July and Willie Hannon's enemies were out and about, eager for any opportunity to get at him. They were on the footpath of the main road, close to home, when a gang, including a number of youths, surrounded and attacked him.

Moyross is as much a ghetto as an estate. One wide road runs through it, which contains the church and community centre. Off this main road run smaller roads into the parks, such as Cosgrave Park. These parks, composed entirely of corporation houses, were generally poorly maintained. The houses were small, often shabby, and were piled on top of each other. Graffiti was everywhere and many of the houses had been boarded up after arson attacks. Nightly, large groups of youths would gather on the small green areas, drinking and causing havoc. Anyone who didn't fit in ran the risk of the group turning on their house, breaking the windows, or even firebombing it.

As Willie, Teresa and Suzanne walked home, a number of people were out around Cosgrave Park and the surrounding estates. Willie Hannon chose the wrong time to appear with his two women.

No one knows what started the attack. Some reports suggest that Willie might have had words with a group of people he passed and then struck one of the women, before walking on. A number of people left the group and began to chase him. Some had impromptu weapons. Among them were Alan Duggan (22) with a length of wood, Eric Ryan (19) with a sewer rod and John McGrath (18) with a sheet of plywood. According to what Teresa told a reporter,

There were at least eight people who jumped us, all with batons, iron bars and planks. I was held down by the hair by another woman and Suzanne Reddan was grabbed as well, but we weren't touched. It was well planned. It was Willie they were after. He was a weightlifter, 13 stone and tough, but now they were all battering him.

Willie found himself in the midst of an angry mob, some of whom were armed. A group of onlookers stood by as the men began to beat him with their weapons, but no one intervened on Willie's behalf. He was not liked. As he tried to fight his way through to the safety of his own home, only yards away, the blows rained down on him. He was beaten to the footpath and the attack continued.

Teresa told gardaí:

> I was let go and I got up and saw Willie lying on one side of the street with his eyes closed. Blood was coming out of his mouth and out of his ear. I panicked then and ran away. I didn't know it was serious.

Willie's other woman didn't run. Suzanne rushed over to her fallen lover. As she bent over his bloody and battered face, she heard laughter coming from the onlookers. She looked up and was convinced that it was Sharon Butler, talking to her younger sister Tracey. She could see no sympathy on either of their faces.

In her statement to the Gardaí, Suzanne recalled:

> I saw them walking away. They were smirking and laughing as they walked away. I saw Willie's gold watch on the ground and blood coming from his head, and he was lifeless. I heard Sharon Butler say to Tracey to get the fucking gold watch from the ground. They were laughing at me, and Tracey said to let Willie fucking die.

The Butler family deny this version completely. They admit that Tracey and others in the family were out that night but say they were not part of the mob that attacked Willie. They say that Tracey, who was a friendly and good-natured teen, would not have spoken in that way had she been there. They are adamant that the family took no part in the attack and said nothing to provoke Suzanne Reddan's murderous rage.

Willie Hannon was rushed to Limerick Regional Hospital,

suffering from serious head injuries. Later that morning the hospital released a statement describing his condition as 'critical'. In fact, he had suffered a massive brain haemorrhage and was already brain dead.

Under the circumstances Deborah Hannon was granted temporary release, on compassionate grounds, to be with her family. As they gathered around the bedside of the dying man, Deborah brooded on the loss of the father she worshipped, while Suzanne Reddan was consumed with hatred for the two girls who had joked about his watch as he lay bleeding on the ground. On 4 July he died.

No one was charged with his murder. Eventually, three men were charged with assault causing actual bodily harm in connection with Willie Hannon's death. Alan Duggan and Eric Ryan were jailed for a year and a half, while John McGrath got 11 months.

'Debbie was very upset when her da was killed. She said she was going to kill them all, every one of them. But I never thought it would come to this,' Teresa told the Gardaí after events reached their tragic conclusion.

The grief-stricken Hannons prepared for Willie's funeral. Deborah and Suzanne were inconsolable. Both women seemed close and Willie's death seemed to strengthen the bond between them.

Deborah's temporary release from prison was extended to allow her to remain at home for a few days after the funeral, to help with the grieving process. But she had other things in mind. Suzanne was torn with grief. She had walked out on her husband for Willie and now he was dead. She wanted to hit back at the world. Both women decided that the solution to their problems was biblical – a life for a life. In the days following Willie's funeral, they plotted their revenge. In a statement to the Gardaí made a few days later, Deborah said:

We planned it all the time, Suzanne and myself. We planned to kill Mark or Sharon or Tracey. I blamed them for killing my father. I kept thinking about my father. We planned it after the funeral. I had a Stanley blade and Suzanne had a knife.

Suzanne said: 'Willie's face kept flashing in front of me and I was in a fit of temper.'

On the evening of 11 July, the two women tried to put their plan into action. Copying TV shows, they dressed head to toe in black and armed themselves with knives. They set out looking for one of the Butlers. It didn't matter to them which one. Any of the three would do. They prowled up and down roads, laneways and paths in Ballynanty and Kileely, but to no avail. Although they passed several people, they saw no sign of the three siblings they were looking for. Reluctantly they came home and called it off for the night.

The following evening, 12 July, was warm and balmy. It was an evening for lounging in the summer heat. Tracey Butler hadn't a care in the world as she sat on the wall outside her house. She chatted with her mother, then went off to a neighbour's house for tea. Her mother told her not to be out late. Tracey said she'd be back early, then crossed the road to the neighbour's.

She returned early and spent the evening at home with two friends, Paula and Margaret Woodland from Moyross. The friends chatted away until about 10.30 p.m., when they decided it was getting late and they should head home. It being such a nice evening, Tracey decided to walk with them. As darkness fell, she left her home on Creagh Avenue.

She didn't know someone else had crept out around the same time. Suzanne Reddan and Deborah Hannon had met for the second night running. This would be their night. Any one of the Butlers would do. Dressed in black, they were seen leaving the Hannon house at 10.30 p.m. by Deborah's younger sister Julie. They were gone an hour and a half, stalking the shadows.

Oblivious, Tracey walked with her friends. The journey took half an hour. When she left her friends in Moyross, she turned and headed for home.

With no friends to while away the time, she decided to take

a short cut. She cut through Ballynanty Beg via the Monabroher Road, coming out close to Thomond Park. Thomond Park is the spiritual home of Limerick rugby. Now it is a magnificent structure that can hold the largest crowds. Back then it was just another playing field, though, with stands able to accommodate quite a large attendance. It faces a busy and well-lit road, the main artery through the city from Galway to Dublin. Tracey was safe under the street lights. From there, she went to the bottom of Ballynanty Road, where it curves past a green open space to enter the main Kileely Road, beside St Lelia's Church. This brought her onto quieter roads, with sparse passing traffic. But Tracey knew these roads well, having spent all her life in the neighbourhood.

After St Lelia's Church, she took a sharp left down a footpath running past some bungalows; she was nearly home. All she had to do was reach the end of the path, a distance of some 50 yards. The path ended at the Kileely Road. There was a wide pedestrian opening in the concrete wall at the end of the pathway, guarded by a safety rail. Once through the opening she would cross the main road and walk the last few yards to her home. She was within a few minutes of safety. But this would not have occurred to her, as she didn't know she was in any danger.

She nodded a greeting at a local man, Paul Sheehan, as she passed him. It was now around 11.30 p.m., and the path she was on was not well lit. But there were a few people milling around, despite the late hour. Suddenly, two dark figures detached themselves from the shadows. Both were dressed head to toe in black and were hooded. But she recognised them instantly. The distinctive swagger of one was unmistakable. It was Deborah Hannon. She also knew Suzanne Reddan.

According to Suzanne, when Tracey recognised the two women she began pulling faces at Deborah. Then she started taunting her, saying they had got Willie, and Teresa would be next. It was too much for the grieving women. They attacked Tracey in a frenzy.

'You are going down like my father did,' shouted Deborah.

It was a savage attack. Both women were armed with knives. Suzanne had a kitchen knife, while Deborah had a sharp-bladed Stanley knife. They tried to drag Tracey to the ground, so that they could carry out their butchery unhindered. They slashed and stabbed at the teenager as they tried to knock her down. Even in the darkness they could see the gouts of blood and feel the wetness.

But Tracey would not go down without a fight. Screaming for help, she pushed Suzanne away and tried to break free of Deborah. But Suzanne came back at her with the kitchen knife, plunging it into her body. At one point, Suzanne dropped the knife, but she bent to pick it up and continued to stab at her victim. Squirming and ducking to avoid some of the blows, Tracey managed to stagger to her feet. Her attackers, intent on hacking and slashing, had not been holding her down properly and she took her chance to flee.

She tried to run across the green area towards the bungalows, only yards away. If only she could reach one, she might get help. But Deborah and Suzanne were on her heels, and they were fuelled by hate and rage; they weren't hampered by gaping wounds and searing pain.

Tracey did not make it to the bungalow. Her pursuers dragged her to the ground. Ignoring the horrified witnesses, they continued their vicious work. With Tracey lying prone before them, they began to kick her savagely. Then Deborah slashed at her face with the Stanley knife. Suzanne drove the carving knife into her chest time after time. One lung was punctured three times. In all, Tracey received 49 wounds. Whole chunks of her flesh were hacked off.

The attack was as swift as it was savage. Suddenly, both assailants straightened up, turned away and began to jog off into the darkness. Their work was done.

There were a number of witnesses to the assault, but none had the time to react and save Tracey. It had all happened so fast.

Paul Sheehan, whom Tracey had passed moments before, was

convinced he had seen two men carry out the attack. He said he had heard screams and turned to see what he took to be two men attacking the girl. The men were dressed in black from head to toe, and they seemed to be dragging Tracey by the arms. He saw only one of the assailants stabbing her. This was Suzanne, as she had the carving knife. You don't stab with a Stanley blade, you slash; in the darkness, from a distance, this could have looked like a slap or a punch.

He thought they were trying to drag Tracey towards a house. She pushed one of the attackers aside. But the person she pushed came back and started sticking a knife into her.

She shouted, 'Help! Help!' and then, 'Stop!', he recalled.

Edward McCarthy was another witness. He told the court he heard someone shouting for help, and saw two people attacking that person. The two were dressed in black and he could not make them out. One of the two had Tracey by the hair and the other was coming behind her.

The one behind her dropped something, then picked it up again. I saw that it was a knife. The person started stabbing the girl, and stabbed her about five or six times.

I could not say if they were men or women, but when they ran away they jogged like girls.

He saw Tracey fall to the ground and her two attackers run off.

Tracey managed to stand and staggered towards one of the cottages. Phyllis Dumas related to the court that she was in bed in the cottage when she heard someone knocking on her window. Her brother, who shared the house on Ballynanty Road with her, went to the door. A girl fell in.

'She was covered in blood and asked for an ambulance to be called. She said: "I can't breathe,"' said Mrs Dumas.

Her brother, John Brommell, said that he had also heard the knocking on the window, and a voice calling: 'Somebody help me.'

'I opened the front door and she stumbled into the hallway

and fell on the floor. Her face was cut and covered with blood,' he remembered. He phoned for an ambulance immediately, while doing his best to make the girl comfortable. She was complaining that she couldn't breathe and asked for water.

An ambulance was at the bungalow by 11.34 p.m. At 11.40 p.m., Tracey's mother, living only 150 yards away, was given the news that the siren was for her daughter, who lay bleeding in a nearby house. Tracey was taken to Limerick Regional Hospital. She was still conscious and able to talk a little, despite the punctured lung. But by 1 a.m. the following morning, less than two hours after the attack, Tracey was dead.

The autopsy showed her right lung had been punctured once and her left three times. There were 14 stab wounds to her neck, back, chest and arms, and 35 other injuries, including many cuts to her face and arms. Death was due to a combination of shock, haemorrhage and collapsed lungs.

Gardaí had spoken to her briefly before she slipped away, but her account was to prove a major red herring in the early hours of the investigation. She said that she had been attacked by two men. Clearly she recognised both of her attackers. So why did she conceal their identity? Perhaps she was confused and delirious with pain and blood loss. Perhaps she kept their identity secret as a last act of friendship to Deborah. Or perhaps she did not know she was about to die. She was in the safety of a hospital with expert care on hand. Did she keep silent because she wanted to deal with this situation herself, as soon as she was out of hospital?

Whatever her reasons, the Gardaí focused on two male attackers for a while. They toyed with the idea that Tracey's death was tied up with one of several ongoing feuds. Feuding between families is a peculiar feature of crime in Limerick, resulting in several deaths and several hundred shootings in the past three decades.

*

Deborah and Suzanne had fled from the scene. It was quite a distance back to Deborah's house in Cosgrave Park, and they jogged most of the way. Deborah's sister Julie told the court she remembered them arriving home. 'They just ran past me. I followed them into the kitchen and asked them what had happened. They said they had stabbed Tracey Butler,' she said.

The first thing they did was to get rid of their bloodstained clothing, putting their black garments into a plastic bag for disposal. Then they cleaned themselves off. Several members of the household spotted them.

Teresa Hannon remembered seeing her daughter and Suzanne leaving the house a few hours earlier, both dressed in dark clothes. It was around midnight when she heard a knock on the door, then went into the kitchen. She saw both women taking off their clothes. Their hands were stained scarlet with blood. She saw them put the clothes into the plastic bag, then one of them produced a bloody knife, which also went into a bag. Overcome with the horror of what she instantly knew must have happened, Teresa became weak and fainted.

Others in the house at the time took a more pragmatic approach. Cooler heads began to help with the clean-up. Suzanne's young brother, Christoper Meaney, was one of those. He was in the house by accident, babysitting for his sister. Now he had other work to do for her. He removed the bloody clothes from the plastic bag, tore them up and then burnt them. He then took the knife, snapped it in half and burnt that, obviously in an attempt to burn away the forensic evidence. He then disposed of the broken knife and the Stanley knife.

But he had never been involved in anything like this before and he botched the disposal. Instead of going to a river and losing them forever, he dropped the murder weapons on waste ground nearby. The Garda investigation was thorough and Detective Con Daly would recover the broken knife on the green at Moyross about six days later. The day after that, he recovered the Stanley knife in Kinsella's Field, Moyross.

The day following the killing, Limerick woke up to the shocking news that a teenager had been savagely butchered within walking distance of the city centre. Initial reports suggested the Gardaí were looking for two men dressed in black and were appealing for witnesses to come forward.

Deborah Hannon was one of the first to come forward. Brazen to the last, she thought the best way to throw the Gardaí off the scent was to come forward openly. She knew that they were looking to talk to anyone who knew Tracey. So she went to the Garda station and told them that she was a very close friend of the murdered girl, but had no idea who would want her dead. She did not wait long to make her statement – she was up to the station first thing in the morning after the killing.

She was putting on a brave front, and so was Suzanne. But Suzanne was not handling the pressure well. Right from the start the strain was telling on the older woman. Deborah had a history with the law. But Suzanne had never been in trouble before. She began taking Valium to bring her emotions under control.

It wasn't just the girls who needed to remain calm if they were to get away with it. Those around them who knew what had happened were also feeling the strain. Deborah's mother was reeling from the shock of what her daughter had done. Teresa Hannon needed to talk to someone. The day after the killing she approached Detective P.J. Barry, a cheerful veteran of the force whom she knew slightly. She told P.J. what she had seen the previous evening. The shocked detective knew this changed the investigation completely. The girls didn't realise it, but the shadow of the prison had already fallen on them.

Within 24 hours, investigators were solidly building up a case against the two women. They eventually recovered the murder weapons and interviewed every potential witness.

Tracey's funeral mass was held on 17 July, four days after her death. The church was thronged. But one person was missing. Deborah, despite telling the Gardaí they were great friends, didn't have the neck to show up at the church, or at the burial afterwards at Mount St Lawrence cemetery.

After the service, Tracey's devastated mother Christina appealed to the general public for help.

'Please, I am begging with you, to come to get these that did that,' she said to reporters, including myself, who were at the funeral.

The Gardaí were still playing it safe. They had issued a description of the killers, saying they were aged between 19 and 25, and dressed in black. They were around 5 ft 4 in. and 5 ft 6 in. in height, and the police were keeping an open mind as to whether they were men or women. We reporters knew they were looking for two women. So, it seems, did the rest of the city.

Within a few days, everyone knew the identities of the two women behind the savage murder. And the two knew that everyone knew. Deborah and Suzanne abruptly left Limerick and went into hiding. Deborah had nine uncles in County Tipperary, and both women went to stay with one of them, in Tipperary town. This is a small market town about 20 miles from Limerick. In retrospect, it was not the best option, as the net was closing fast.

On the morning of 17 July, there was a knock on the door of the house in Tipperary. There was a squad car parked outside. The two women were arrested by Detective Sergeant Daniel Haugh and taken to Henry Street Garda Station, where they were questioned for several hours before making statements. Then, at a special evening sitting of the District Court before Judge Michael Reilly, they were charged with murder. The judge knew Deborah well. He was the one who had sentenced her for larceny. Now he saw her charged with murder. He remanded both women in custody to await trial.

Suzanne, from the first, was not suited for prison life. She became deeply depressed and was suicidal. She made at least one attempt on her life, following which she was moved to the Central Mental Hospital in Dublin for treatment. She was also concerned about the future of her children – and their safety. Threats had been made against her young daughter – and she knew the violence of the community she lived in.

Deborah fared better, settling into prison life. She was no stranger to it, as she was already serving a larceny sentence. So it was life as normal for her. The months before the trial passed easily. She was even given temporary release for Christmas – despite what had happened on her last temporary release. But it was made a condition that she stayed in Tipperary with one of her uncles. If she was seen in Limerick, she could be killed as a reprisal for Tracey's murder. Deborah blithely ignored this and spent Christmas in Moyross.

The trial lasted a month. Several days of it were taken up in legal argument in the absence of the jury, as the defence fought to have some statements made by both women in interviews with the Gardaí excluded from the trial. They lost this application.

Both women pleaded not guilty to murder. Several witnesses gave evidence, but the two defendants chose not to. However, the statements they made to the Gardaí were read out. These were frighteningly graphic, as these extracts show.

After meeting Tracey on the night, Deborah said,

I told her: 'You are going down like my father did.' We were holding on to her and I was thinking about my father. She said something about getting my mother next. We grabbed her and were stabbing her. I think I used the Stanley knife on her face.

Suzanne Reddan and I decided to kill one of the Butlers. I got a Stanley knife from my father's tool box. We were dressed in black, because that is what we see them wearing on television. I was not nervous as I was thinking of my father. We were looking for any one of them to kill them. I didn't care if they died because they did not care if my father died.

At 11.30 p.m., we met Tracey Butler coming out onto the road. We grabbed her by the arms and pushed her into a wall. She managed to get halfway across the road towards the houses. I kept thinking about my father. I was hitting her with the knife. She kept saying to fuck away, that Mark and Sharon would get my mother. She was crouching. I didn't care if she was dead because we had gone out to kill her.

Suzanne's statement was also read out. Her account of the night Willie Hannon was killed threw some light on motive.

They were laughing at me, and Tracey said to let Willie fucking die. I took this very hard. I have been missing Willie and have very bitter feelings towards those involved in killing him.

Before we left the house I put a knife up my sleeve in case we met anyone. We met Tracey Butler. As we were coming close to one another Tracey began making faces at Deborah. We grabbed her on each side and started fighting with her. She fell on the grass, and I fell too. Then she got up and started running towards the bungalows. She fell and we both started kicking her. I got the knife out of my sleeve and stabbed her in the chest at least once.

When I stabbed Tracey I kept thinking about Willie and the night he was attacked, and his face kept flashing before me.

It was explosive stuff, and it had a profound effect on the jury. At the end of the prosecution case, Suzanne's barrister had a tough case to answer. Limerick solicitor Shaun Elder had hired a heavyweight: Patrick MacEntee was one of the most experienced and wily criminal defenders in the state.

He informed the court that he had just three witnesses, including consultant psychologist Dr Art O'Connor. They were all medical experts who were there to testify as to the psychological condition of Mrs Reddan at the time of the killing. But the state objected to these witnesses. The jury was sent out yet again and both sides got down to two hours of intensive legal argument. Mr MacEntee argued that grief had thrown Suzanne into a psychological state which mitigated the murder. As evidence of this, he pointed out that, after her arrest, she suffered from depression and attempted suicide, needing treatment at the Central Mental Hospital. But this was not considered a defence. Mr Justice Richard Johnson ruled that the medical evidence was inadmissible. The defence case had fallen at the first hurdle.

The jury was called back and the trial resumed. Mr MacEntee announced that he had no witnesses to call and the defence rested. Deborah Hannon was represented by barrister Michael Feeham, instructed by Limerick solicitor Ted McCarthy. He stood and announced that he too had no witnesses. Neither girl offered a defence. With no defence on offer, the guilty verdict was a certainty.

But the formalities had to be observed. The judge gave the jury its final instructions, telling the jurors they had three options: guilty of murder; not guilty of murder; or not guilty of murder, but guilty of manslaughter.

'A verdict of not guilty is unlikely in view of the statements we have heard, but it is still open. There is no concept of diminished responsibility in Irish law,' said Judge Johnson.

The jury of six men and six women took six hours to deliberate. It returned at 9 p.m.; the court was still packed, despite the late hour. The judge read out the result. Both women had been found guilty of murder, by a majority verdict.

Suzanne, now 26, broke down and fell from her chair in the dock to the floor. Deeply distressed, she had to be assisted from the court. Friends and family were there for her, but there was nothing they could do.

The judge said he was aware that she had been ill and he would like to ensure that she was looked after and received proper treatment. She should remain in the Central Mental Hospital until she was deemed fit to return to prison.

Deborah, in contrast, had no family in the court. Her mother Teresa had attended some of the earlier days of the trial (she was a witness against her daughter), but by the end she was no longer there. Under the intense strain of the whole experience she had decided she had to leave Limerick. So she moved her entire family to England, where she remained for several years. She told reporters, 'Limerick will always be Stab City to me. I can never go back there.'

Clutching three packs of Benson & Hedges cigarettes, Deborah was led from the court to begin her life sentence.

But it didn't end there. As Suzanne was being led from the court, she heard vicious whisperings. Then someone screamed at her and his words chilled her to the core.

'I'm going to get Nicole and I'm going to cut her up.' It was

Mark Butler, Tracey's brother. Nicole was Suzanne's daughter and not yet ten years old.

Then another voice shouted: 'You whore! You whore! Nicole's next.' It was Sharon Butler. Clearly Tracey's family were not satisfied that justice had been served.

The judge, when he was told, was furious. He immediately issued an arrest warrant. Sharon and Mark Butler spent the night in Dublin, then boarded an early morning train to Limerick with their aunt, Deirdre Mulqueen. As soon as they stepped onto the platform in Limerick, detectives pounced on them. They were arrested and taken back up to Dublin, where they faced the irate judge.

Suzanne Reddan told him what they had shouted at her. Other witnesses corroborated her story. Superintendent Liam Quinn, in charge of the Limerick division, confirmed that there had been threats made since the murder and said there had been a very difficult atmosphere for the past five or six months.

All three were bound over to keep the peace for three years, or face contempt of court and jail. They agreed to sign the bond, which ordered them to stay away from the Meaney and Reddan families.

Suzanne Reddan spent a number of months at the Central Mental Hospital. When she returned to the prison, she got on well, taking part in drama activities and getting good reviews for a play she acted in. Deborah also tried her hand at prison drama and developed an interest in martial arts.

But back in Limerick the bitterness lived on. In the immediate aftermath of the murder, there was remorse, as well as recriminations.

Christine Butler, Tracey's mother, said she wished she had kept her daughter away from the girl she called a devil. She told the *Limerick Leader*: 'She's a devil from hell, and my Tracey is an angel. The two will only serve eight years. Is that justice? Pigs in the slaughterhouse don't get a death like they gave my daughter.'

A few miles away, in a quiet neighbourhood, Suzanne Reddan's parents were asking themselves how their lovely daughter had strayed so badly. And, like Christine Butler, they blamed Deborah Hannon.

'We still can't understand what happened,' her mother, Rose Meaney, told the *Leader*. 'All we know for sure is that our daughter is not a murderer. That's a gut feeling we both have. We believe she was set up, probably as revenge for her affair with Willie Hannon.'

Her father, Christy, an electronics engineer on disability following an accident, told the *Leader*:

> I said to her: 'Suzanne, tell me if you did it, because we'd rather know.' She said: 'I was there, but I didn't put a knife into that girl. I swear.' We think she's holding something back, there's something she's not telling us. She's obviously terrified of Deborah Hannon. You could see her shaking every time she had to pass her in the court.

In letters to her mother and her mother-in-law, Suzanne expressed her regret at what she had done. In contrast, Deborah Hannon seemed unconcerned about it all and showed no remorse.

Both women lodged unsuccessful appeals against their convictions. They served out their time and are now quietly trying to rebuild their lives. Neither lives in Limerick.

Christine Butler's prediction as to how long they would serve for killing her daughter proved very accurate. Eight years after their sentence began both women were released on licence and were living in luxury apartments in Dublin – paid for by the state – as they worked as hairdressers. They had been trained while in the prison.

Suzanne settled back into society quickly, meeting a new man and planning on moving in with him. Deborah, however, was spotted drinking with a Dublin criminal and lost some of her privileges. The apartment was taken from her and she had to report back to the prison every evening at ten. But this didn't last long and soon she too was out on full licence. She quickly moved to Manchester, to join her family.

BLOOD ON THE STREETS

Christine Butler was devastated. She told the *Limerick Leader*:

I am heartbroken to the depths of my soul to hear my daughter's killers are out. My little girl lies in a cold grave and her murderers are free to live their lives. I am tormented by the death of my daughter. I am dead for the last nine years, and now I hear that justice has not been done.

They stabbed Tracey's little body countless times. I would put them in the same category as Myra Hindley.

4

DEATH IN ADARE

The Murder of Detective Garda Jerry McCabe

IT WAS A quiet, peaceful summer's morning in the beautiful little village south of Limerick. Adare is considered one of the prettiest villages in the country, full of quaint cottages and elaborate thatched roofs. There is an old abbey and a great manor house converted to a luxury hotel, as well as a beautiful church on the main street that seems to be constantly celebrating weddings. People travel from all over the country to get married in Adare, and have their wedding photos taken in the splendid surroundings of the little town.

That morning it was too early for weddings; it wasn't quite 7 a.m. Two friends sat in a squad car outside the post office, idling the time away and waiting for the convoy to move on. Detectives Jerry McCabe and Ben O'Sullivan were veterans in the force and they had done this run dozens of times. It was a simple job; all they had to do was guard the An Post van as it delivered the social security money to rural post offices in south Limerick.

The run took them that morning from Henry Street in Limerick, out through Adare and on south towards Kerry. Jerry was from north Kerry, so they were driving towards his home place. Ben O'Sullivan was behind the wheel, while Jerry McCabe was in the passenger seat. McCabe was colour blind, so his partner did all the driving. It was Garda regulations.

Traffic was light and they reached Adare quickly. During the day, especially in the summer, Adare can be a bottleneck, with a constant stream of traffic heading towards Killarney or Dingle. But now they had the village to themselves. It would be an easy morning.

Then the two men noticed something strange in their rearview mirror; a Pajero jeep was driving towards them faster than it should have been. Before either man had a chance to react the jeep struck the back of their car, throwing them forward. Then three men in balaclavas jumped from the jeep and ran forward.

The quiet of the summer's morning was shattered by a burst of automatic gunfire. Fifteen shots rang out in an instant and McCabe slumped forward, dead. His partner, Ben O'Sullivan, was critically injured.

Death had come to Adare.

*

Two things changed the landscape of Irish crime more than anything else, and they happened within weeks of each other. Detective Garda Jerry McCabe was gunned down in a botched IRA raid on the post office van in Adare on 7 June 1996. Less than three weeks later, in Dublin, journalist Veronica Guerin was assassinated. One was a serving garda, killed while on duty. The other was a campaigning journalist who had devoted the previous few years to her own personal battle against the drugs gangs and organised crime syndicates that had come to dominate the Irish underworld.

Their killings showed us that something had gone fundamentally wrong with our country, and they highlighted two enemies. Detective McCabe was gunned down by the IRA, whose campaign of terror in the North was financed in part by armed robberies in the Republic. Republican groups of various sorts had been operating south of the border for two decades, robbing banks and post offices, carrying out punishment beatings, distributing drugs and acting as vigilantes.

Ms Guerin was killed by the other enemy: the new breed of

organised criminals. The chief crime reporter with the *Sunday Independent*, she had broken several stories about the 'Mr Bigs' who controlled the underworld. She had become a thorn in their side, and one of them, John Gilligan, had had enough. So he ordered a hit on her. She was gunned down as she stopped her car in traffic near the Red Cow roundabout in Dublin on 26 June 1996.

That morning she had been in court in Naas on minor traffic matters and she was making her way back to the city, unaware that a motorcyclist with a gun was following her. The death of Ms Guerin showed us that the gangs thought they were invincible. It was a wake-up call for the country.

When Jerry McCabe was laid to rest, 50,000 people lined the streets in the centre of Limerick to pay their final respects. They were not just saying goodbye to a cop who had given his life in their service. They were also sending out a message to the gunmen that enough was enough. The IRA had begun a ceasefire in 1994, bringing to a temporary end 25 years of bloodshed in Northern Ireland. The ceasefire ended in February 1996, but people still had high hopes of a peaceful resolution. When Jerry McCabe was callously murdered, we all knew the ceasefire was well and truly over. Veronica Guerin's death so shortly afterwards indicated that law and order – the safety and stability of the state – were under threat from subversives and from the criminal underworld. The public demanded action; the government responded.

Within months, draconian new measures were introduced. The most significant was the formation of the Criminal Assets Bureau (CAB), a first anywhere in Europe. Justice Minister Nora Owen established the CAB in August, just two months after the two killings that had galvanised the country. Legislation was rushed through the Dáil and in October the CAB went to work. Their task was to go after the proceeds of organised crime. They would hit the criminals in their pockets. If they could not put the gang leaders behind bars, at least they could make sure that crime did not pay.

They were spectacularly successful; in their first decade alone they recovered £89 million. Other countries saw the success of the CAB and copied the idea. All that came from the murders of Jerry McCabe and Veronica Guerin.

*

I remember the day of the botched post van raid. It was a Friday. At the time I was working for the *Limerick Leader*, the largest of the city's papers. The *Leader* came out daily, but on Fridays the city edition was published. Early in the week the paper is a small tabloid, but the Friday edition is the flagship, a bumper broadsheet with several sections. Friday mornings are busy, as the latest news is squeezed onto the front page.

When I got in at nine, the newsroom was a hive of hectic activity – far busier than usual. As I crossed to my desk, about three voices told me in shocked tones that Jerry McCabe had been shot and killed. I knew the name and could immediately put a face to it. He was a detective who dressed neatly and always had a smile on his face. Beyond that I didn't really know the man. Most reporters have a cherished list of contacts, the people who they can call upon for the inside track on things. There were a few gardaí that I could give a quiet call to, or who would give me a quiet call. Jerry was not one of my contacts.

The news editor, on the other hand, was a native of north Kerry and knew Detective McCabe well. He was genuinely upset, as were many of the others. For the next four or five days, the paper was full of nothing but the shooting in Adare, and that was all anyone was talking about. For the removal, people lined the streets six deep. The death of Jerry McCabe hit the city hard.

*

The drama had begun quietly enough, in the wee hours of that Friday morning. Jerry McCabe left his wife Anne and his family as usual, sneaking quietly out of the house in Greystones, off the Ennis Road, so as not to wake everyone. Aged 53, he was coming within a few years of being able to retire. From Ballylongford in Kerry, he had been educated in Rockford

College, Tipperary, and was transferred to Limerick within a few years of joining the Gardaí. He had married the daughter of a local garda, Anne Cuniffe, and they had raised five children. Two followed him into the force.

In younger days, he had been a keen rugby and Gaelic Athletic Association (GAA) player, but in later years had switched to the more sedate golf. Most people would have described him as a sociable family man who enjoyed tinkering with engines and doing odd jobs in his time off.

He left his home at 5.45 a.m. and drove the short distance to Henry Street, the biggest Garda station in the city. This morning would be a routine run, providing security for An Post as the van delivered cash to rural stations around Limerick. Jerry was looking forward to a few easy days, then he was off on his holidays, chasing the sun with his family.

At the station he was joined by friend and colleague Ben O'Sullivan. Detective O'Sullivan was another country boy, who grew up near Newmarket, County Cork. A veteran of 32 years on the force, he had been a keen athlete in his youth. He had met Jerry when they were both new to the city, and they became firm friends. Ben was involved in tug of war and rowing, among other sports. In fact, he represented the Gardaí at rowing events. Their friendship grew over the years and they socialised together all the time outside of work hours.

On the same day in 1972, both men were promoted to detective. They were part of a four-man unit, but often paired as partners. They investigated serious crime, gathered intelligence from their sources in the city and acted as security for money transfers, such as the regular An Post run. Both men were qualified to carry firearms, and on the morning of 7 June they both checked out .38 Smith & Wesson revolvers, which they wore in shoulder holsters, and an Uzi machine gun.

Both men got to Henry Street Garda Station for 6 a.m., the start of their shift. At 6.30 a.m. they got into their unmarked blue Ford Mondeo car and drove the short distance – barely 100 metres – to the main post office in Limerick, further down

Henry Street. They had stowed the Uzi in a case on the back seat of the car. It was unloaded, though the clip of bullets was packed in the case with it.

At the post office they were joined by the An Post van, with regular driver Willie Jackson behind the wheel. They had done this run so often it was purely routine. The van contained IR£80,000, but none of the three was worried. They had never had any incidents on these runs.

They pulled onto O'Connell Street, then headed out through Dooradoyle and out of the city. Once they cleared Patrickswell they were on open road all the way to Adare. They got there around 6.50 a.m. It was a clear, bright morning and the town was asleep. They had no difficulty pulling up outside the main entrance to the post office for their first drop-off of the day.

But, unknown to the two detectives, plans had been afoot for more than two weeks. The IRA ceasefire was over. The Canary Wharf bombing in the UK, which caused £100 million in damage but mercifully killed just two innocent civilians, had shown that the armed struggle was back on with a vengeance. And the struggle needed to be funded. Armed robberies were a popular way for the subversives to raise funds. Both detectives knew this, but they still felt safe. One planned robbery had been foiled a few months previously, but they had no intelligence of an operation in north Munster.

However, on 31 May, a Mitsubishi Pajero jeep had been stolen from a house in Rathfarnham in Dublin. And on 4 June a Mitsubishi Lancer was stolen, again in Dublin. The Pajero is a big strong jeep, a workhorse, while the Lancer is a fast and comfortable family car. Both cars were fitted with false number plates, then taken down to Limerick from Dublin. They were left in the car park of a bar, Finnegans, on the Dublin Road, just outside Limerick, on the night before the raid and were picked up from there by the raiders.

The IRA unit gathered in Patrickswell. Associates had fuelled the stolen vehicles and had collected the Kalashnikov AK-47s and their ammunition. It was all good to go. The men involved were Kevin Walsh, Pearse McAuley, Jeremiah (Jerry) Sheehy, Michael O'Neill and Gerry Roche. They spent the night in the house of Walsh's father and sister, on a farm near Patrickswell. When they set out the following morning, they were armed to the teeth. In addition to the AK-47s, they had a sawn-off double-barrelled shotgun and a number of handguns.

By 5.30 a.m. the following day, the team were in place at Adare. They watched the van with its Garda escort arriving in Adare, then the Pajero pulled out and began to drive up the main street of the village. In the unmarked car, the two detectives were initially unconcerned. Then they noticed that the Pajero was picking up speed.

'Oh Jesus, Jerry,' shouted Ben O'Sullivan. He knew this was a well-known paramilitary tactic. Two years previously a post van had been rammed during a raid in Kilmallock, disabling it. But this time there was clearly a change of tactics – the jeep was coming straight for the two gardaí. They barely had time to brace themselves before the impact. The heavy jeep slammed into the back of the Mondeo, and both men were flung violently forward. The impact of the crash was so bad that Ben's arm was broken when he was thrown against the steering wheel.

Both men were dazed but fully aware of what was happening. They could see Willie Jackson, the van driver, frozen in shock in front of them. He had just opened the rear door of the van when he heard the bang, and watched in horror as armed men poured out of the jeep. They were wearing battle greens and black balaclavas, and there was not an Irish man at the time who would not have recognised the uniform. He thought he was about to die.

The two detectives had an even surer idea of what was happening. They recognised the distinctive AK-47 automatic weapons that the raiders were carrying.

Designed by Russian army sergeant Mikhail Kalashnikov in 1947, the AK-47 is the most popular assault rifle in the world to this day. Approximately 75 million of them have been made and they are the favourite weapons of paramilitary groups, revolutionaries and drugs runners worldwide. One reason for their popularity is that the guns are virtually maintenance-free and ultra-reliable. Light, sturdy and almost indestructible, the AK-47 fires 600 rounds a minute when on automatic and is accurate up to 400 metres.

In the mid-'80s, the IRA were given more than a thousand of the assault rifles by Libyan leader Colonel Gaddafi, in a misguided retaliation against the Americans, who had bombed Tripoli. The guns fired copper-plated bullets and the magazines held 30 rounds – which took less than a second to exhaust on full automatic.

Ben O'Sullivan could see that the men running towards the Garda car knew what they were doing. They fanned out, one approaching the car from each side. Ben had a gun in his shoulder holster, but did not have time to reach for it. The Uzi in the rear seat could have been on the moon for all the use it was.

The armed and masked men arrived at the car and positioned themselves on either side, their guns covering the terrified detectives. It was not the first time Ben O'Sullivan had faced a gun in the line of duty, but it was by far the most terrifying. Back in 1992, he had encountered a genuinely dangerous situation on a public road in the centre of Limerick. It was the middle of the day and a man was brandishing a shotgun at him. Without hesitating Ben flung himself at the man, wrestling him to the ground. He got a Scott Medal for bravery on that occasion.

But this time there was nothing they could do. It was all in the hands of the gunmen who flanked the helpless men. Suddenly, the morning quiet was shattered as the man on the driver's side of the car opened fire. Within less than a second, 15 shots had slammed into the Garda car.

When on automatic, a gun tends to spray. Ten of the bullets shattered the driver's side window, passing into the vehicle. Travelling at unbelievable velocity, as the bullets struck things they began breaking up – and breaking up bits of the car, which caused a firestorm of shrapnel and vastly increased the damage that was done.

In the driver's seat, Ben O'Sullivan took the first shots. A bullet caught him in the right shoulder and passed straight through. Another hit him in the torso, exiting just half an inch from his spinal column. The impact threw him from the steering wheel and he ended up slumped over the central well of the car. Both hands suffered damage and there was a bullet wound beneath his right eye. He had wounds on both sides of his head and a bullet grazed his leg.

On the passenger side, Jerry McCabe had suffered even more massive injuries. Two of the bullets had pierced his back. One shattered his right shoulder blade and another caused massive damage to his right upper arm. But one shot had done more damage than all the others. It entered from his back, shattering a rib and a spinal vertebra, severing his spine. This alone would have left him paralysed for life and could have been fatal. But the bullet continued on, ripping through his lungs and tearing his pulmonary vein and aorta, the main vessels carrying blood to and from the heart. The bullet exited through his left side. It was a fatal shot; the veteran cop was killed instantly.

It was over in seconds. The shots and their echoes died out, and an eerie silence descended on the village. Ben O'Sullivan was slumped over the handbrake, immobile but conscious. Time had seemed to slow down during the crucial few seconds. As he told the Special Criminal Court: 'It was automatic fire and there was silence between each blast.' He did his best to speak, calling out: 'Jerry . . . Jerry.' But he got no response. As he later told the court, he knew his partner was 'in great difficulty'.

He could see that Jerry's arm was turning blue. Although his own hands had been injured by the firestorm of bullets and shrapnel, he managed to put a finger on Jerry's wrist. He couldn't feel a pulse and feared the worst.

'Death would have been very rapid,' confirmed assistant state pathologist Dr Margaret Bolster. The detective would have been dead within two seconds of the fusillade of gun fire.

Willie Jackson, the driver of the An Post van, thought he was going to be killed when he saw three men in paramilitary gear pouring out of the Pajero. He remembered opening the rear of the security van, when he heard a bang. He turned and saw that a jeep had smashed into the rear of the Garda car. He saw three men in battle fatigues and balaclavas surrounding the Garda car. The men were armed with AK-47s and they were firing on the Garda car. He jumped down from the back of the van and ran for the cover of a nearby doorway.

'I thought I was going to die,' he said at the subsequent trial.

Then a silver car – the Lancer – pulled up beside the three armed men and a voice shouted: 'Go!' The gunmen got into the car, which sped off.

Jackson took out his mobile phone and tried to call for help, but he had no reception. He ran to the Garda car, and his first glance convinced him both detectives were dead. Garda McCabe was slumped over, immobile. Unfamiliar with the layout of the inside of a squad car, he picked up what he thought was the microphone for the radio and tried to call for help. It was only when the badly injured Garda O'Sullivan told him that he was using the wrong microphone that he realised one man had survived the shooting.

Despite the early hour, there were a number of witnesses to the carnage.

The Adare postmistress, Elizabeth Twomey, was dressing in her bedroom when the raid began. She heard the bang of the car crash, followed immediately by rapid gunshots. She ran to the window and saw a man in a balaclava at the driver's door. She also saw a second man. As the raiders made off, she got to the phone and rang for help. Then she ran out to the street to try to assist the stricken gardaí.

Gerry Hanrahan, an Adare native, was dropping a neighbour off at the nearby Dunraven Arms Hotel when they heard the bang of the Garda car being rammed. He said that he saw a number of gunmen in dark clothing and one of them appeared to be firing into the Garda car. When he turned and drove down towards the scene, there was a car pulled across the road. Someone threw him a phone, shouting at him to ring the emergency services.

Oliver Noone worked for the Dunraven Arms and lived in a house in the village. He was woken by the commotion and heard a voice say 'Oh Jesus', as if in great distress. When he got to the window, he saw a man holding a rifle with a large magazine, which was aimed at the Garda car. Behind the Garda car was the black Pajero, its doors open and its wipers dancing furiously.

Terry Hogan lived directly across the road from the post office; she too was woken by the bang. She saw a man with what she described as a 'short, stubby gun'. Her husband shouted at her to get away from the window, as the shots rang out. She heard a lot of shouting and someone moaning very loudly.

The armed raiders took off from Adare in the stolen silver Lancer. They left one man dead and another in critical condition. Ben O'Sullivan would spend four days in intensive care, needing medical treatment for eighteen months. He attended a hospital in Belfast, which had expertise in gunshots from 25 years of IRA violence in the Northern troubles, but he eventually made a full recovery.

The raiders had not taken a penny. The fundraising effort had been a complete failure.

Quick-thinking postmistress Elizabeth Twomey had phoned a local doctor as the shots died away. Dr Nicholas van Kuyk was a GP from the Netherlands who lived just 300 metres up the road. Despite the early hour he was there within ten minutes. He told the court:

> I could see that the car had been badly shot up. The person in the passenger seat was slumped over and wasn't moving. I had been told by the postmistress that she thought he was dead. The other man was obviously in very bad pain but his vital functions were stable and he was not in immediate danger.

He straightened up Jerry McCabe and listened to his chest, confirming his worst fears. He pronounced the detective dead at 7.10 a.m.

It did not take long before a full-scale murder investigation was under way. The village was swarming with gardaí and the road was blocked off. A forensics team led by Sergeant Brendan McArdle of the ballistics section combed the area for clues. One of the first things he noted was that his late colleague had never stood a chance. His handgun was still in its holster and the Uzi was still in its case, unloaded. It had been a cold-blooded execution.

But it had not been a careful execution. There were plenty of spent cartridges scattered around; the Pajero was a mini-armoury. In a bag in the back, they found 66 9mm parabellum rounds, 27 rounds of .22 ammunition and 18 shotgun cartridges. The raiders could have started a small war. Between the two front seats of the jeep was a radio scanner tuned in to the Garda frequency. The only thing that the raiders did not leave was fingerprints. Despite exhaustive examination of the Pajero, no prints were lifted. The Lancer, which was later recovered, was less clean; two prints were lifted, but they did not belong to the four men who were eventually charged with the murder of Jerry McCabe and the attempted murder of his partner.

The IRA team involved knew what they were doing and were careful not to leave too many clues. But they probably planned on torching the Lancer, which is why two of the occupants had not bothered with gloves. The getaway car was recovered in a forested area near Kilmallock.

Almost from the start, the Gardaí knew that they were looking for the IRA active service unit operating from Patrickswell. Gardaí knew the main players and their associates. They kept close tabs on subversives. If they were looking for ordinary criminals, there could have been several dozen suspects in the city, and many times that number when the net was cast further. But when it came to subversives, they were fishing in a small pond. Although the IRA and Sinn Fein, the group's political wing, denied involvement in the Adare raid, the Gardaí had a clear idea who they were looking for within hours of beginning the investigation.

They found petrol in the abandoned jeep and also in the

Lancer, indicating that the raiders intended to burn out their vehicles. A balaclava was recovered which had hairs on it, identifying one of the raiders. Another could be traced through the shotgun cartridges that were found in the Pajero.

Forensic examination of the cartridges found in Adare confirmed that the gun which shot Jerry McCabe had been used two years previously when gardaí had come under fire in Kilmallock during another post office raid.

*

As the Garda investigation got into full swing, Limerick prepared to mourn a fallen hero. And doctors worked furiously to save Ben O'Sullivan. He had been rushed to Limerick Regional Hospital, but his condition was stable.

A colleague told the *Limerick Leader*:

He could see Jerry had changed colour. He checked his pulse with one hand and knew then he was dead. It was terrible for him, sitting there helpless. All he wants to do is get out of bed and catch them. Everyone in the force is determined that justice will be done.

Inspector John Kerin had the unenviable task of knocking on the door in Greystones to deliver the bad news to Anne McCabe. Inspector Kerin was a new appointment, just promoted to the rank and transferred to Henry Street. That Friday was his first day on the job. Delivering the worst possible news was his first duty.

Anne McCabe was up and getting her two youngest children ready for school. One was doing the Inter Cert, while the other was facing the Leaving Cert. A friend had phoned to tell Anne there were news reports on the radio about an incident in Adare. Worried, she had tried to phone Henry Street Garda Station, but all the lines were engaged. Then came the knock. When she was told what had happened to her husband, she collapsed in the hallway. One of the children ran screaming up the stairs.

As the IRA phoned RTÉ to deny any involvement in the shooting, the city and county were struggling to come to terms with the tragedy. Huge crowds turned out to pay their respects and to sign the books of condolences at the reception of the *Limerick Leader* and at City Hall.

All through Friday a large, solemn crowd gathered outside the family home at 47 Avondale Drive, Greystones, while inside a garda was on constant duty, giving what support she could to the family. Detective McCabe was a popular man, and his neighbours spoke very highly of him, especially of his helpfulness and his ability as a DIY fanatic.

Everyone wanted to share their memories and their grief. Jim Guerin told the *Limerick Leader*:

He was a very good man. I remember once being set upon late one night by a group of drunken thugs, and Jerry saved me. He didn't look that big a man, but he scattered them. I always remember after that, any time we met he had a great greeting for me. He was the sort of man who, if you were feeling down, would cheer you up.

Mary Harty, a close neighbour and friend of the family, told the *Leader*:

He was an absolutely incredible fellow. He was the best neighbour anyone could wish for – a genius with his hands. A very gifted man who would always be there if you needed a hand with anything in the house. He was at everyone's beck and call. If anyone was in trouble, then Jerry was always there.

He was the grandest fellow that ever stood in shoe leather, and what happened to him was positively horrific. Such a waste. I got a bad feeling when I heard the first bulletin on the radio, because we all knew Jerry and his schedule. When he left early on a Friday, he was on some sort of escort duty.

There's been people in and out of the house all day, and there's a bangarda there all the time. My own house is full. We've been making sandwiches. Himself and his partner Ben O'Sullivan were inseparable friends. They were always together. It wasn't only when they were on duty. Jerry was the sort of guy who initiated everything, and whenever anything was happening Jerry was in the thick of it. He was a very popular man.

Declan Deegan lived beside the McCabes for nine years, only moving a few weeks before the shooting. He was devastated.

Jerry was an extremely helpful neighbour. He always looked after our house if we were away on holidays. He fixed our car a number of times when it broke down. I would get the parts and he fitted them in for me. Golf was his thing, and his car. It was a BMW and he converted it to gas. I remember he was a great family man, and a great man to chat to in the driveway.

Colleagues in the force were also quick to pay tribute. Garda Ronan Connell said: 'He was one of nature's gentlemen.' Garda Paul Brown, GRA executive member for Limerick, said:

Jerry was one of God's gentlemen, always willing to help other members and the public, at any time, on or off duty. He was very active in the Garda Golfing Society, and was also interested in angling. But his main interest was his family. He was a great family man. He had five children, and two are sitting exams at the moment.

Ben O'Sullivan and himself were great friends, both on and off duty, and their families were very close.

Over 20,000 attended the removal on Sunday night. Mourners, six deep, queued down Thomas Street and Catherine Street and back along Wickham Street for up to six hours to shake hands with or hug the grieving family. It lasted until after midnight – almost unheard of for a removal. Four hundred gardaí in uniform marched behind the cortège, which arrived at the Holy Rosary Church at 1 a.m.

Among those who attended were Tánaiste Dick Spring, Justice Minister Nora Owen, Health Minister Michael Noonan and members of Ben O'Sullivan's family. Anne McCabe and her five children – John, 27, Mark, 25, Ian, 24, Stacy, 17, and Ross, 16, took what comfort they could.

The following morning the funeral mass saw a thronged church, with several hundred people outside, unable to squeeze in. President Mary Robinson and Taoiseach John Bruton were there, along with American ambassador Jean Kennedy Smith.

Celebrant Father John Daly, a personal friend of the dead man, said:

The parish community is shocked, saddened and angered at the senseless killing of Jerry in the course of his duty as an officer of the peace. Jerry was very well respected in the community for his dedication as a police officer; for his impartiality and humanity in implementing the law, which was appreciated by young and old alike. An excellent family man, his home was always most hospitable and welcoming. An ever obliging neighbour, his was always a ready hand to help, and his wisdom was freely available to those who sought it.

John McCabe, also a garda, spoke to the congregation about his father.

Jerry will always be remembered as a friend, a colleague, a member of the Garda Síochána, but for us, his family, he will always be remembered as the most wonderful husband and father. Dad's deep and abiding love for his children was obvious to everybody. Each one of us always felt very special to him and, as we grew, our relationships with him developed into ones of friendship as well as family. I know that I speak for my sister and brothers when I say that we have a tremendous pride in everything Dad did, from career to golf to conservatory construction!

Over the last few days our home has been filled with friends and neighbours, some of whom we hardly knew, each of whom had their own story of how Dad helped them, supported them, or simply shared a joke when they needed to. On behalf of my mother, sister and brothers, I wish to express our deep appreciation to all who have supported us in the last few days.

Ben O'Sullivan was not able to attend. He was still in intensive care. After four days, he was removed from intensive care and, on the following Wednesday, five days after the shooting, he was transferred to Croom Orthopaedic Hospital. He had suffered massive injuries to his arms and shoulders, and would require months of specialist care before making a full recovery.

But the Gardaí were making progress with their investigation. Within hours of the shooting, a number of people had been hauled in for questioning; some were still being held under Section 30 of the Offences Against the State Act on Monday morning. Four, including two being held in Monaghan, had been released, but the Gardaí were homing in on those they were after.

On Tuesday, there was a major breakthrough. Jeremiah Sheehy, of Abbey Park, Rathkeale, was brought before the Special Criminal Court in Dublin and charged with IRA membership and with having a gun with intent to endanger life in Adare the day of the shooting. Security was tight for the hearing.

There were also reports of sightings of suspects from around the county. One man was seen outside the Woodlands Hotel in Adare before the shooting and was being sought in connection with the murder. Senior detectives believed he or one of the other raiders might have been injured during the shooting by a stray bullet.

'There were a lot of ricochets and it is possible that one of the raiders at the far side of the car was hit,' a senior member of the investigating team told the press. The stocky, sandy-haired man was said to be a leading member of the IRA and had not been seen at his home in Patrickswell since the murder. A man fitting his description had been seen near the Woodlands Hotel half an hour before the murder. He was one of two men on the run that the Gardaí were anxious to speak to.

Investigators believed that eight people had been involved in the Adare incident – four raiders and four in support. Just one of the raiders had opened fire. It was thought that the shooting was a mistake. There were plastic ties (similar to those used for bailing briquettes) recovered from the scene, which should have been used to tie up the gardaí and the post office staff while the van was being robbed.

As the *Limerick Leader* reported: 'One gunman lost control; when they looked into the SDS van all they could see were big cages with parcels. There was no sign of any money.' An An Post worker confirmed that the contents of the van were deceptive:

> It would have taken them anything between ten and twenty minutes to get all the money, because of the new cage security system. The only feasible way they could have carried out the robbery was to take the truck, and it was too big to hide away somewhere.

The raid had been a complete hash. The raiders got nothing because one panicked and opened fire, and because the money was not on open display in the van. Not only was it a failure as a fundraising effort for the IRA, it was also a publicity disaster. The public outcry was so strong and so immediate that the IRA was forced to distance itself from its own active service unit, trying to claim that the men were acting independently of orders. It damaged Sinn Fein badly. On top of that, the raiders left a plethora of physical evidence. Despite this, it proved a frustrating thing for investigating gardaí.

In the end, four men came to trial for the murder of Jerry McCabe, and one man was charged with offences in connection with the raid. Two others were identified but never apprehended.

It took two and a half years to bring the case to trial. The case opened on Monday, 11 January 1999, and was expected to last between three and six months. Four men faced forty years' imprisonment without parole, so the stakes were high. They would fight the charges tooth and nail.

Pearse McAuley (34) from Strabane, County Tyrone, but with

no fixed address, and three Limerick men, Jeremiah Sheehy (36) of Abbey Park, Rathkeale, Michael O'Neill (46) and Kevin Walsh (42), both of Lisheen Park, Patrickswell, all pleaded not guilty to the murder of Detective Garda Jerry McCabe at Adare and not guilty to the attempted murder of Detective Garda Ben O'Sullivan. In addition, they denied possession of firearms with intent to endanger life, conspiracy to commit a robbery and possession of a quantity of ammunition with intent to endanger life. They also pleaded not guilty to charges of unlawful possession of two rifles, a handgun and a shotgun at Toomevara, County Tipperary, on 7 June 1996, and possession of three shotgun cartridges on the same date. That was the day of the Adare murder.

A fifth man, John Quinn (30) of Faha, Patrickswell, denied the unlawful possession of ammunition at Patrickswell on 6 June 1996 and conspiring with others to commit a robbery at Adare. Quinn had not been in Adare, but he had bought the plastic ties the raiders hoped to use, as well as petrol that was found in both of the raiders' cars.

On the second day of the trial, the evidence was harrowing. Ben O'Sullivan told of the events leading up to his friend's death. The An Post SDS van pulled into Adare and the driver opened the rear doors. It was then Detective O'Sullivan saw the Pajero; there were two people in the front wearing balaclavas.

'I shouted to Jerry, "Oh Jesus, Jerry."'

Then the jeep struck them from behind.

I was driven forward. I regained my composure and looked out the driver's window. I saw two men armed with guns. At this stage they were about four yards from the driver's door. They were wearing dark balaclavas, dressed in black and green camouflage battle-dress. They carried what appeared to be Kalashnikov rifles. I have seen them, but I have never used them. I know that subversive groups use them. They had the guns pointed at us. They trained them on our car but they were still moving, moving very energetically.

In an instant without any warning, without any opportunity

for us to protect the SDS van, one of them opened fire. It was automatic fire. The first blast struck me on the right shoulder. The second blast blew my hands off the steering wheel and I was forced onto the handbrake. The driver's window blew in around me.

I saw Jerry's hands going into a spasm. I was conscious. I was conscious that Jerry was in great difficulty. His hand was contorting, his arm was blue and white. When the shooting ceased I heard shouting but I had no idea what was being said. I called Jerry three or four times. I said, 'Jerry, Jerry, Jerry.' There was no response. I then put my small finger on my left hand into his wrist. There was no pulse. The pulse was absent.

Chillingly, Detective O'Sullivan told the court that he knew three of his assailants personally – O'Neill, Walsh and Sheehy – and knew the other two by sight. They also knew the two gardaí. They were not firing on strangers.

Indeed, one of the raiders knew Jerry McCabe rather well and owed him a debt of gratitude. Michael O'Neill's sister had been murdered by her husband three years before the Adare raid; Detective McCabe was one of the main investigators who brought him to justice.

Over the next few days, witnesses such as the postmistress and the security truck driver told the court what they had seen. Garda forensic experts also testified and the court heard from assistant state pathologist Dr Margaret Bolster. Three hundred witnesses were scheduled to testify; the prosecution case was going well. But on the sixth day the case for the prosecution derailed dramatically.

On that day, two witnesses – who had voluntarily given statements to the Gardaí – were suddenly struck with amnesia. One of them was jailed for contempt for refusing to testify. It was a dramatic collapse of the prosecution case.

The drama began when Patrick Harty, a farmer from Toomevara, County Tipperary, was called to testify. After the raid at Adare, the gunmen had fled to Toomevara. Mr Harty had given four statements to the Gardaí about the movements of the IRA team in the hours after the murder. But now he refused to take the oath. He told the panel of three judges that he could not take part in the trial.

This was a blow. Laying out the prosecution case at the start of the trial, barrister Edward Comyn had indicated that Mr Harty would provide evidence of how the IRA men had arrived at his farm and stayed there on the night of the shooting. There would be evidence about weapons which were left for collection at the farmhouse and instructions given for the burning of potentially incriminating clothing. Now this valuable evidence was in jeopardy.

Mr Justice Richard Johnson, presiding judge, told Harty that he had been summoned to appear as a state witness and had a duty to give evidence. He would be in contempt of court if he failed to do so. There was a short adjournment to allow Harty to consult with his solicitor. Then he was called back to the witness box.

In a low voice, he whispered: 'I am very sorry. I can't.'

Rather than admit defeat, prosecuting counsel Edward Comyn asked the court to postpone a decision on the matter until the following day. Patrick Harty was remanded in custody at Mountjoy prison for the night.

Then came the second blow. Patrick Walsh and Sally Walsh, father and sister of the accused Kieran Walsh, both developed selective amnesia. They repeatedly told the court that they could not recall the events of 6 June, the night that the IRA active service unit had stayed in their home and prepared for the Adare raid.

Sally Walsh said she could not recall making a statement to the Gardaí identifying the four defendants as having stayed at her house the night before the murders, and could not recall the rifles and other weapons that were there. Mr Comyn applied to have the court declare her a hostile witness and commenced a cross-examination. He produced Garda statements she had made and asked a Garda witness to recall these.

Inspector James Browne then told the court he interviewed

Ms Walsh in her house on 22 May 1997. He said she made a statement which she did not sign. In the statement, Ms Walsh said a number of men arrived at her house at different times on the night of 6 June 1996. These included Gerry Roche, Jeremiah Sheehy, her brother Kevin and Michael O'Neill, as well as a man with a Northern accent whom they called Pearse.

She had also seen a bag with four rifles and magazines, as well as handguns and a sawn-off shotgun. Michael O'Neill had cleaned the guns.

The inspector said that Ms Walsh told him: 'I had a very bad feeling that something bad was going to happen.'

Then Ms Walsh was recalled to the witness box. She said that she could not remember making any statement to Inspector Browne.

Her father Patrick Walsh was also declared a hostile witness after he told the court he could not recall making a written statement to the Gardaí. When he was presented with the signed statement, he denied that the signature was his.

'My memory is not great,' he explained.

The following day Patrick Harty was brought from Mountjoy back to the court. Mr Justice Johnson told him: 'Mr Harty, from the book of evidence, you have evidence to give of an extremely important nature.' He warned him that it was a grave matter not to do so. Harty refused to take the stand, and refused to say why he would not. He was jailed for 18 months for contempt.

Worse was to come. John Quinn, the one defendant not charged with murder, alleged that he had been assaulted while in Garda custody. Inspector John Courtney denied the charge, but clearly the prosecution was struggling. The trial limped on for a few days, then, on Tuesday, 2 February, John Quinn's solicitor asked for an adjournment because there had been a 'development'.

The following morning that development became clear; the four men accused of murder had changed their plea. They agreed to plead guilty to the lesser charge of manslaughter. Manslaughter can carry a life sentence, but not a mandatory 40-year sentence. They could potentially be out in a few years, if the state accepted the plea. Given the way the trial was going, the state opted for the lesser of two evils. Manslaughter was a better result than allowing any of the four to walk free.

Edward Comyn said the new pleas (manslaughter of Jerry McCabe and malicious wounding of Ben O'Sullivan) were acceptable to the Director of Public Prosecutions and he dropped the other outstanding charges against the men, including IRA membership, firearms and ammunition possession and conspiracy. The court was packed with gardaí and detectives shocked at the new twist.

Each of the four men accused of murder in turn stood up and said, 'Not guilty to murder, guilty to manslaughter,' when the capital murder charge was put to them. John Quinn also changed his plea to guilty of the conspiracy charge. It was the 15th and final day of a trial expected to last a number of months, and an unsatisfactory conclusion for everyone but the accused.

The decision to accept the new pleas was a controversial one. Taoiseach Bertie Ahern immediately made a statement saying that the government had put no pressure on the prosecution to accept the manslaughter plea. He knew it was political dynamite and could blow up on him. There was mounting frustration in the Dáil about the decision, with the opposition calling for an explanation.

The Taoiseach told journalists at Government Buildings that he could understand that the public would have liked to have seen the murder charge 'dealt with'. He had thought that was the way it was going to go.

'I had no knowledge that anything else was going to happen, but the Director of Public Prosecutions obviously made a decision based on what he thought was the best thing to do,' Mr Ahern said.

The big fear was that the four men would qualify for early release under the provisions of the Good Friday Agreement. They would literally have got away with murder, a fact the opposition jumped on.

Limerick TD and Labour Party justice spokeswoman Jan

O'Sullivan said the public would find it difficult to reconcile the acceptance by the state of the change to charges of manslaughter with the graphic account given by Ben O'Sullivan of the details of Jerry McCabe's violent death.

'What took place at Adare was murder, not manslaughter,' she said.

The former leader of the Progressive Democrats, Des O'Malley, said the implications of the decision were huge: 'I think the Gardaí should be supported and protected fully in these kinds of circumstances. To describe what happened in Adare as anything less than murder is a travesty of the truth.'

Garda Commissioner Pat Byrne was more pragmatic, saying that it was a rational decision based on the 'reality' of the case, to ensure a successful prosecution. He told journalists:

> I would have been aware of developments in the case as it progressed in court, and also aware of the strengths and weaknesses of cases, and at the end of the day decisions in relation to accepting a plea are a matter for the DPP [Director of Public Prosecutions], both legal teams and also my officers.
>
> We're all professional and we understand what's involved in prosecuting a case. Our job is to gather evidence and make it available to the DPP. We must face reality and understand, as I said, that in all cases there are strengths and weaknesses.

Mr Byrne's comments echoed the sentiments of investigating officers, who believed the plea was the best possible outcome. The right men were behind bars.

A hearing was held for sentencing and the court heard details about the five accused. Jeremiah Sheehy was married with two children and worked as a casual farm labourer. He had a number of convictions, including one for a post office robbery in Rathkeale. He got ten years for that, the final five suspended. Michael O'Neill was married with nine children and was a forklift driver who had long periods of unemployment. His family were in poor circumstances. He had no previous convictions and was remorseful. Pearse McAuley was single and worked in the construction business. He had a previous conviction for having a pistol and ammunition, for which he got a seven-year sentence, of which he served only two because of the early release programme for republican prisoners. The state accepted he had not fired the fatal shots.

Kevin Walsh was a married father of two and a bricklayer by trade. He had convictions for the robbery of a post office van, for having firearms and for IRA membership – for which he had got an eight-year sentence. Finally, John Quinn was a carpenter who worked for his father's construction company and had no previous convictions. The state accepted he was a 'messenger boy or gopher' with limited involvement and he deeply regretted what had happened in Adare.

It was accepted that Kevin Walsh, a local man, was the shooter. He was the commander of the Limerick unit and a senior figure in the Southern Command of the IRA. He was close to the brigade staff and army council, and had the consent of the IRA hierarchy when he planned the Adare raid, despite their attempts to distance themselves from the incident afterwards. They needed to distance themselves because he had broken one cardinal rule: General Order No. 8 of the Provisional IRA's handbook of rules, known as the 'Green Book'. This stated that IRA members were 'strictly forbidden to take any military action against 26 County forces under any circumstances whatsoever'. This was not for ideological reasons. It was because those sorts of actions brought too much heat down on the organisation.

No one knows why Walsh opened fire. The gunmen had the situation under control. They had the plastic ties. They had caught the two detectives unawares and could have tied them up, then taken the money from the van. When he opened fire, he endangered his own men, one of whom narrowly dodged one of the bullets. It is speculation, but Walsh had been involved in an armed robbery in 1998 and had come under fire from gardaí. Walsh managed to escape, but his fellow IRA man, Hugh Hehir, was killed in the exchange of fire. Perhaps he saw helpless armed gardaí and acted instinctively to avenge his fallen comrade.

Pearse McAuley and Kevin Walsh were each jailed for 14 years, Jeremiah Sheehy for 12 years and Michael O'Neill for 11 years. John Quinn was jailed for six years. The judge noted that all the defendants except Walsh had expressed regret about the death of Jerry McCabe. The man who pulled the trigger was the only one who showed no remorse.

Patrick Harty, jailed for contempt when he refused to testify, was released following the sentencing of the five raiders. Government sources were still insistent that the men would serve their full time, but Sinn Fein thought differently. Martin McGuinness expressed confidence that the five men would qualify for early release under the Good Friday Agreement and could be out in two years.

'I believe that they will qualify,' McGuinness told RTÉ radio. 'I know there's a difficulty at the moment because there's a wide-ranging debate in the South about the events of this week. We should approach this in a very cool, calm and collected fashion.'

Taoiseach Bertie Ahern countered by saying he was glad the 'murderers' had been brought to justice. He said he had legal advice that the five did not come under the terms of the agreement and would serve their sentences.

'Jerry McCabe was murdered, as far as I'm concerned,' he said, adding that any attempt to get them released would be 'vigorously opposed'.

The actual agreement said that any paramilitary prisoners convicted of offences committed before 9 April 1998, when the agreement was signed, were due for release within two years. But, under the terms of the amnesty, the Minister for Justice had to recommend prisoners for release to a three-member commission. And the government made it clear they would not do this.

Justice Minister John O'Donoghue was quick to reassure the public that the government would not consider an early release for the Adare five. Sinn Fein took the opposite view, and the matter remained a source of controversy over the coming years. In the end, the government, for a change, did not do a U-turn.

The men never qualified for early release. The memory of Jerry McCabe was at least done that honour.

And as the prisoners languished in jail, Jerry's widow Anne proved a very effective thorn in the side of Sinn Fein. As the party tried to distance itself from the gunmen and go legitimate, she was a constant reminder of the blood on their hands. Gerry Adams came to know and dread the familiar figure who would show up at public events and ask him when he would be prepared to apologise for the death of her husband.

Sinn Fein became increasingly involved in politics south of the border and was a key part of the Northern peace process. But its leaders consistently tried to deny their links with the IRA. Party President Gerry Adams claimed never to have been a member of the organisation, a claim doubted by journalists and gardaí. Martin McGuinness claimed to have left the organisation in the '70s; again many found this difficult to believe.

In front of fawning politicians, they might get away with that, but not with Anne McCabe in the crowd. Perhaps the sweetest moment for her was when she confronted Mr Adams in New York, at a St Patrick's Day celebration in 2006. His transformation to constitutional politician was nearing completion when he travelled to America to attend the New York parade. Two days before, on 15 March, he was a guest speaker at a popular Irish venue in Yonkers, New York. After the speech at Rory Dolan's pub, Mr Adams got a standing ovation from the mainly Irish American audience. The crowd were on their feet, shouting and clapping. But, in the front row, one woman sat resolutely on her seat, refusing to join in the adulation: Anne McCabe.

When the ovation died down, Mr Adams threw the event open to questions from the floor. Now Anne McCabe got to her feet. Mrs McCabe told the *Limerick Leader*:

> I knew where he would be talking and I said I would go for it.
> I wanted answers. After he was finished speaking I stayed rooted

to the spot and did not get up off my seat. I was in the front row and people were clapping all around me.

She decided to question something he had said in an interview on *The Late Late Show* some months earlier, when confronted about the Adare raid.

'Could I ask you, some time ago on *The Late Late Show*, you said my husband's murder was not authorised by the army council but at a lower level. Can you tell me who this lower level is and why?' Mrs McCabe asked an unprepared Adams.

He tried to fudge, replying that many people had suffered in the troubles and that he himself had lost family members and friends. He repeated the current party line:

> I have outlined clearly my revulsion at the killing of your husband, but the people who killed your husband should be released under the Good Friday Agreement. I know that is hard for you. That is what the Irish government have signed up to do.

But Anne McCabe would not let it go at that. She told him that he had not answered her question, and then she left the meeting. She said later:

> I didn't envisage myself being in the same room as the president of Sinn Fein/IRA. I never thought of it in my wildest dreams. I felt that a weight had been lifted from my shoulders. I felt good after confronting him. Sinn Fein/IRA tried to talk themselves out of it, but could not give an answer. I didn't get an answer and walked out.

The mother of five continued: 'After ten years, it does not get any easier. I can't describe the feeling. Every day is the same and every one of us misses him.'

The men convicted of shooting Jerry McCabe served their full sentences. There was no Good Friday early release for them. They did get moved to the low-security surroundings of Castlerea prison in 1999 and did their time in relative comfort. But they did do the time.

In 2004, the government almost wobbled and conceded to Sinn Fein that the killers would be released early as part of the peace process. But they knew that would not fly with the McCabe family, or many of the public. They held firm in the end.

Michael O'Neill was the first to be released, on 15 May 2007. He had served a decade behind bars. Jeremiah Sheehy was the next to be released, on 4 February 2008. Finally, Kevin Walsh and Pearse McAuley were released on 5 August 2009, after completing their full sentence.

Jerry McCabe's family said that the completion of the sentences brought closure. Declining to become involved in further controversy, the family released a statement saying:

> The life of Anne McCabe is now and will continue to be focused on her five children and the six grandchildren who have been denied a loving and gentle father and grandfather because of a treacherous deed for which there is yet no healing word of apology or expression of sorrow.
>
> The entire McCabe family rejoices in the recovery to full health of the retired Detective Garda Ben O'Sullivan, who will always have an honoured place in the hearts of the family.
>
> Although there are outstanding matters from the events in Adare, for the McCabe family the completion of the sentences brings closure and consolation that the rule of law at least has been served.

For everyone else, the matter is over. The prisoners have done their time and the peace has been won. But there were more than five people involved in the planning and execution of the post office van robbery in Adare. At least two IRA men are still wanted in connection with the killing and are still on the run.

Anne McCabe said she will never give up fighting for justice for her husband. And she will continue to remind people that he died for Ireland. But, unlike many other patriots, he did not have the luxury of a choice in the matter.

5

SHOT IN THE FACE

Mark Cronin and the Murder of Georgina O'Donnell

LIMERICK IS A city of connections. On the surface things appear unrelated, but when you begin to pull at a thread everything unravels to reveal unexpected networks, a tapestry linking people in different areas and from different backgrounds in surprising ways.

Georgina O'Donnell was a young woman with the world at her feet. From a close family, she and her sisters were lively, vivacious and bubbly. They were also – in a city which values such things – respectable. They came from Corbally, a middle-class suburb a short drive from the city centre. Her father worked for Limerick Corporation.

Corbally is the area along the banks of the Shannon as you drive out along the river towards Ardnacrusha – site of the massive hydroelectric plant – and on towards picturesque Killaloe. It is a collection of leafy estates with quiet roads, lots of trees and laughing children. It could be a million miles from the ghettos of Moyross and Southill. In Corbally, people have jobs. The children go to school every day – with full stomachs. Gangs of hoodied youths do not haunt the corners. It is suburbia, with all the safety and security that implies.

Corbally was where Georgina O'Donnell grew up. She played by the tree-lined banks of the river, went to the local school and grew up with expectations of a happy and normal life. She had a young baby and was living in St Mary's Park. It was downmarket from where she grew up, but she was just starting out in life and all the possibilities were stretched out before her.

All that ended on what should have been a happy night out with her friends. The bubbly 21 year old was happily dancing when a crazed and jealous husband ran across the dance floor and pulled a gun on his wife. He shot Georgina by mistake.

*

Georgina was an innocent woman. In May 1998, she was in the wrong place at the wrong time. Her death was as simple as that.

Yet, when you begin to pick, threads come loose revealing surprising connections. Georgina was a niece of Ray Collopy and his brothers, the crime lords from the Keane-Collopy drugs gang. Her young brother Jason, just ten when his older sister was gunned down, eventually became a minor player in the gang. Pick at another thread, more surprising facts unravel. The Henry Cecil, the pub where Georgina was shot, was owned by Jim O'Brien, a major player in the growing Limerick drugs business. It is unlikely any of the players in that night's tragedy were even aware that the pub they chose for their innocent night out was a cover for a major drugs gang.

Limerick is a small place and such coincidences are common.

*

Georgina, who was described by those who knew her as a 'very innocent and quiet' girl, had decided to go out for the night with friends. Having a nine-month-old baby, such opportunities were less frequent than they had been. But she found someone to mind her precious daughter Courtney and headed from her little corporation home on St Brigid's Street, St Mary's Park, into town. It was the evening of Saturday, 2 May.

It was a clear night, but cool. It was not typical May weather; the temperatures were down and there were strong breezes and occasional drizzle. The country had been experiencing downpours of biblical proportions only a few days before. The races in Punchestown had been mired in muck, with long traffic delays caused by the car park being turned into 'the Somme', according to the *Irish Times*. Around the rest of the country flooding was widespread, especially in country areas. Now the weather was beginning to turn for the Bank Holiday weekend.

It is less than ten minutes by car from St Mary's Park into the centre of Limerick, but a long walk along the main central street, O'Connell Street. Once in town, Georgina ended up in the Henry Cecil, a popular pub and nightclub on Cecil Street. The venue was about 50 yards from O'Connell Street, on a side road down towards the river. Originally warehouses, the pub had an impressive limestone facade, which was subject to a preservation order. It was owned by Jim O'Brien, a very interesting character.

A country man, he was raised on a small farm in the heart of the Golden Vale. The farm was at Raleighstown, Lough Gur. This is about ten miles from Limerick and is one of the most historic sites in Ireland, having been continuously inhabited for several thousand years. There is a stone circle in Lough Gur that is older than Stonehenge.

There were five children in the family – four boys and a girl. All did well at school and went on to respectable careers such as accountancy and the law. But Jim – known as Chaser since his childhood – had a taste for the high-life. As he matured, this grew into a love of fast cars and even faster women.

'He wanted it all and he wanted it fast,' said one friend of the family.

The pub trade seemed a natural fit for a man who liked to party. After finishing his Leaving Cert at the De La Salle Christian Brothers secondary school in nearby Hospital, County Limerick, Jim entered the business. He worked in several well-known pubs around the county and city, and he was a quick learner. After a few years, he was ready to take the plunge. He bought a bar in Pallasgreen, which he named Chaser O'Brien's.

Pallasgreen is a sleepy village on the main road between Limerick and Tipperary town. Cars whizz by on urgent business, but in the village life moves at a slow, rural pace. The pub was large and modern, and prospects looked good.

None of his neighbours thought to ask where the young man had got the money to invest in a pub. But the Gardaí were beginning to take an interest. O'Brien's name had begun to pop up in investigations into the growing drugs trade in Limerick city. Sources were indicating that Chaser had followed up some leads and acquainted himself with the city's underworld. He soon moved into the city, acquiring the Henry Cecil.

Jim was a hard worker and would have made it eventually, just like his siblings. He was busy at the Henry Cecil and the bar was often four-deep with customers. It was a cash cow, right in the heart of the city. But he had the criminal mentality; he wanted the short cut. So his links to the underworld grew.

All this was irrelevant to Georgina O'Donnell, who was just looking for a fun pub to spend the evening in. The Henry Cecil was not only busy, it also drew a young crowd. As the pub closed, action moved upstairs to the nightclub. When last orders were called, Georgina followed the crowd into the disco. It was now around midnight. But, unknown to the young mother, the lives of other people were beginning to unravel that night and she would be caught up in the chaos. She partied on, oblivious to the forces that would destroy her life.

*

Mark Cronin was a small-time crook. He was 30 and was well known to the Gardaí. He had a long record, which included assault, possession of a weapon and causing criminal damage. He had served a number of prison sentences, the most recent being ten months for possession of a weapon. He had also done a year for assault and ten months for causing criminal damage. The fair-haired man with the moustache also had links to the INLA. He was a rough, violent man, whose record was described later in court rather euphemistically as 'not very good'.

Cronin lived on Hyde Road, Ballinacurra. This is a tough old part of the city, an area of run-down corporation housing dating from the 1930s. It spawned some of the worst criminals the city had ever seen, including the Kelly brothers. It later became the heartland of the notorious McCarthy-Dundon gang, dubbed 'Murder Inc.' by the press.

Cronin had been married for nine years to Angela 'Biddy' Collins and they had three young children. But the relationship was a bit of a roller coaster. Just a few months previously, in November 1997, Cronin had badly assaulted his wife; those charges were still hanging over him.

The relationship was going through another lurch in April of 1998. Cronin had not been to the home he shared with Ms Collins for a number of days. But, on 2 May, he contacted his wife and asked to meet her at the Henry Cecil that evening. They arranged to meet at 9.30 p.m.

Perhaps to fortify himself, or perhaps just out of habit, Cronin turned up at the pub early. He began drinking at 6.30 p.m. By the time his wife arrived, three hours later, he was drunk and aggressive. The meeting did not go well; after a stormy encounter Cronin got up and left the pub.

Angela Collins remained in the pub, chatting with friends. Although they knew each other slightly, Georgina O'Donnell was not part of the group. When the pub closed, she moved into the disco with the rest of the crowd.

At that point, Mark Cronin returned to the Henry Cecil. He found his wife in the crowd and rushed up to her, grabbing her by the shoulders. Before she could react or escape he lurched forward and head-butted her, the old Ballinacurra Weston handshake. She pulled her head back and lessened the impact of the blow, but he tried to head-butt her a second time. People rushed forward and grabbed him by the shoulders, preventing him.

Claire Phelan was one of the witnesses who saw the assault on Angela Collins by her irate husband. She said that the two had a row in the disco, then he grabbed her by the throat and shoulders and head-butted her in the forehead. He tried to do it again, but was pulled away from her.

Cronin stormed off, but shouted that he would be back. It was now after 1 a.m.

The disco continued until 2 a.m., then the music stopped, the bar closed and people began milling around, saying their goodbyes, getting their coats. It was time to head out onto the street. This was the time Cronin chose to return.

A security camera from the venue picked up the man in the light sweatshirt entering the club against the flow of people beginning to exit. He seemed to be hurrying. The camera picked him up reaching the dance floor, but then lost him. What happened next took only seconds.

Willie Clancy, a doorman at the venue, spotted Cronin walking purposefully across the dance floor.

'He approached his wife and he raised a gun to her chest. She pushed the gun away from her and the gun went off,' he told the court later.

Mr Clancy added that Cronin had his arm fully extended when he pointed the gun at his wife, explaining,

As he raised his hand his wife hit his hand. His hand went out to the right-hand side and the gun went off. Mark turned and walked out the door. I heard someone say there was a girl shot. I went up to where the crowd was gathering and there was a girl on the floor.

Another witness, John Grant, said that he saw Cronin point his hand at his wife. As Mr Grant was turning away, he heard a loud bang. He told the court, 'Someone jumped off her chair screaming, and there were people around Georgina, who was lying on the floor.'

There was a lot of confusion and chaos, but the Gardaí and an ambulance were called immediately. It was obvious that Georgina O'Donnell was seriously injured; she had been shot in the face at point-blank range. She lay on the floor of the nightclub bleeding profusely, surrounded by her friends and concerned onlookers.

Not everyone was sure what had happened. Some people initially thought that Georgina was with Angela Collins at the time of the shooting and had stepped forward to protect the other woman. Not many had seen that the gun had been brushed aside by Ms Collins and that Georgina had been an innocent bystander in the wrong place as the firearm went off.

Georgina was rushed to the regional hospital in Dooradoyle, just a few minutes away. Her condition was described as 'critical' as she was admitted. Doctors worked through the night to save her life and placed her on a life-support machine. She remained in a critical condition for several hours, but lost her battle for life at 6.30 p.m. on Sunday, 3 May. As her close family surrounded her in the hospital, other family members were minding her daughter Courtney. Meanwhile, the Gardaí had swung into action with a full murder hunt.

Initially, they reported that Georgina had stepped into the path of the bullet to save Ms Collins, but after interviewing witnesses it became clear she was hit by mistake. Gardaí issued a description of the killer: a man in his late 20s, 5 ft 11 in., with fair hair and a moustache. He was wearing light-coloured clothing. They were sure of the description because they knew who they were looking for. Cronin had even been filmed leaving the disco floor, although he had his hood up to try to prevent identification.

Deputy state pathologist Dr Marie Cassidy arrived in Limerick to carry out a post-mortem on Ms O'Donnell (and one other victim of holiday weekend violence in the city). Her report found that a bullet had entered Georgina's eye-socket, piercing the brain beyond. She never stood a chance.

Garda Inspector John O'Reilly, based at Henry Street, only a minute from the crime scene, appealed for public cooperation in finding the fugitive Cronin in a statement to the press: 'We would be anxious to talk to everybody who was at the disco at the time of the shooting in and around 2 a.m.'

*

It was a busy weekend for the Gardaí – Georgina O'Donnell's death brought the death toll up to four for the two-day period. Two were in Limerick.

The second was a drowning, which the Gardaí were treating as suspicious. Early on Sunday morning, the body of a man in his late 20s was taken from the River Shannon in the city. A search had been going on for the body, after an incident at the Treaty Stone. The Treaty Stone is a well-known Limerick landmark. It is supposedly the stone on which the Treaty of Limerick was signed to end the siege of the city by the forces of William of Orange in 1691. It is located on the north side of Thomond Bridge, a few minutes' walk from the city centre.

Two men were spotted fighting near the monument at around 10.45 p.m. on Saturday evening. A few hours later, at 1.40 a.m., a body was spotted in the river near the bridge and the emergency services were alerted. The man was identified as Thomas Murphy, of Cross Roads, Thomondgate. Gardaí interviewed a number of witnesses and were questioning a man in connection with the incident.

In Dublin, there had also been two suspicious deaths. A man was charged with murder following the stabbing of a young man at Firhouse, Tallaght, late on Saturday. Stephen Morris, 17, of Killakee Walk, was stabbed near his home shortly before 10.30 p.m. and died of the injuries. Vincent Flynn, 18, of Kiltipper Close, Tallaght, was charged and remanded in custody.

And gardaí in Clondalkin were investigating the fatal stabbing of a security guard at George Cooke's wholesalers in Camac Park, Bluebell Industrial Estate, at 1.15 a.m. on Saturday. The premises stored quantities of cigarettes and alcohol. The security man was a German national, Herman Clausen, 44, who was living in the Coolock area. Working alone, he had been confronted by a number of men and stabbed.

It had been a bad weekend – four young people met their deaths by violence.

*

As the O'Donnell family prepared for the funeral, the Gardaí were intensifying their efforts to locate Cronin. He was considered armed and dangerous, and the public were urged not to approach him if they spotted him.

On Wednesday, 6 May, the remains of Ms O'Donnell were taken to St Mary's Church for burial after a funeral mass the following morning. Hundreds of sympathisers gathered for the removal and for the funeral mass.

Two white lilies adorned her coffin and a framed photograph of the young mother was placed on the altar for the ceremony. The mourners were led by Georgina's mother Vera and father Anthony. Her six sisters – Sandra, Tracey, Audrey, Breda, Pamela and Olivia – and her two brothers, Anthony and Jason, were there, alongside her baby daughter Courtney and her boyfriend Andrew.

The offertory gifts included a tray to symbolise Georgina's work in St John's Hospital. The crowds were moved to tears by the music at the service, which included 'Hero' and 'Be Not Afraid'.

Father Tomas Grealy said that everyone in the parish had suffered shock when they heard of the tragedy that had befallen Georgina. He described her as

> a happy girl who brought sunshine into the lives of her family
> and friends. For one so young, she had a deep sense of the equality
> of people of whatever race, colour or creed. This she derived from
> her religious sense that God made us all equal.

*

Gardaí were working under the assumption that Cronin was still in the city. Superintendent Tony Kenneally said that the investigations were progressing satisfactorily and they had received good cooperation from the public. But he believed the chief suspect was being harboured by someone.

Cronin, who was still not being named as the suspect, was described as 'one of the most violent people in the city'. His wife, Angela Collins, was now under constant police protection.

But Cronin had not remained in the city. He is believed to

have fled to Ballybunion, a coastal resort in north Kerry. Limerick people traditionally go to one of two places when they head to the sea: to Kilkee in County Clare or down to Ballybunion. Kilkee tends to be for the toffs, while the rest go to Kerry.

Some days after the shooting, the Gardaí received a report that Cronin had been spotted in Ballybunion. They took the report seriously, searching the seaside town for him. But they remained open-minded about his whereabouts; they also alerted Interpol and his photo was circulated to ports and airports, as well as Garda stations throughout the country.

At the end of May, a full month after the shooting, the manhunt came to an end; Cronin was taken into custody. At the remand hearing at the local District Court, Detective Sergeant Declan Mulcahy told of having arrested and charged Cronin a little after midnight on 27 May. He told Judge William Early that Cronin had replied 'not guilty' to all charges.

Cronin was charged with the murder of Georgina O'Donnell. He was also charged with possession of a firearm and with an assault on his wife the previous November. He was remanded in custody.

It was almost two years before the case came to trial. On Monday, 27 March 2000, the trial opened in Dublin at the Central Criminal Court. Senior Counsel Michael Durack, for the prosecution, told the jury that Cronin had pointed a gun at his wife, but ended up shooting Georgina O'Donnell through the eye. She died of her injuries the following day.

Mr Durack outlined the turbulent relationship between Cronin and his wife, telling the jury that the man had not been to his home for some days prior to the shooting. When he met his wife in the Henry Cecil, the meeting was bad-tempered.

'Some class of disagreement arose between them,' he said, adding that there was another altercation some hours later at the disco, which resulted in Ms Collins being head-butted by her husband.

'Words were exchanged, and he left the disco in what appeared to be foul humour, indicating that he'd be back,' said the barrister.

Ms Collins went downstairs to see where her husband was, but when she did not find him, she returned to the disco and was chatting with her friends. Ms O'Donnell was one of the group of people present. She was standing close to Ms Collins when the lights came on around 2 a.m. and the disco ended.

He told the shocked jury that Cronin returned to the disco and walked through the crowd to where his wife was standing, surrounded by her friends. He produced a small handgun, held it out, pointed it at his wife and fired. But he shot Ms O'Donnell instead.

Cronin then left the disco; the gun was never found.

The jury was shown a video taken from the security system of the Henry Cecil. It showed Cronin walking towards the dance floor. Moments later the cameras picked him up leaving the dance floor, pulling his hood up and his sweatshirt over his face as he walked away.

The trial lasted seven days; Cronin took the stand himself on the fifth day, to deny any involvement in the shooting. He said that he had been in the nightclub on the night of the shooting, with his wife, and he had witnessed trouble at the venue, but he had nothing to do with it. He said that the trouble broke out near where he was standing. Someone threw a bottle at him, which hit him in the face.

> I fell back, grabbed my mouth and sort of crouched down to the side. The bang came a couple of seconds later. It was just a bang. I don't know where it came from. I decided to get out of there. I got hit with a bottle. I stumbled back and the first thing that came into my mind was it was a gunshot.

He told the jury that the sound caused him to have a flashback to an incident some years earlier, in which he had witnessed a shooting. He also denied trying to conceal his identity from the security cameras and bouncers as he left the club, saying that he had not tried to cover his face with his sweatshirt.

The jury did not believe his account of the night. They took their time reaching their verdict and had to be sent to a hotel for the night after failing to reach a conclusion after the first few hours of deliberation. But when they returned to the court on 3 April, they did not need much more time. After a total of four and a half hours, they found Cronin guilty of the murder of Georgina O'Donnell and guilty of possession of a firearm for an unlawful purpose on the same occasion.

Justice Patrick Smith imposed the mandatory life sentence on the murder charge. On the possession charge, he sentenced Cronin to ten years, to run concurrently with the life sentence.

'His record is not very good,' the judge remarked, after hearing the list of Cronin's previous convictions. These included ten months for possession of a weapon, one year for assault and ten months for causing criminal damage.

A successful prosecution is never the end of the matter; Cronin had to have another day in court for his appeal. It took three years, but in April 2003 the appeal was heard. He tried to wriggle out of the murder charge by muddying the waters, saying the gun had gone off accidentally. Cronin's lawyers claimed that the original trial judge, Justice Smith, had misdirected the jury in relation to the circumstances of the shooting.

The lawyers claimed that no witness actually saw a gun in Cronin's hand. But if he had a gun, it could have gone off accidentally. A three-judge panel, headed by Mr Justice Adrian Hardiman, heard the appeal.

Barrister Hugh Hartnett, for Cronin, said that nobody had seen his client with the gun. The closest any witness came was somebody who said they saw him with something in his hand as he walked away. Although a number of witnesses said he raised his hand and there was a flash and a bang, no one had seen the gun. And nobody had any intention of shooting Georgina O'Donnell, he said.

He went on to say that the trial judge had failed to address the jury on the possibility that the shot could have been caused by the actions of Angela Collins, who pushed Cronin's hand away. That action could have caused him to squeeze the trigger

Detective Garda Jerry McCabe.
(courtesy of the *Limerick Leader*)

The aftermath of the robbery in Adare.
(courtesy of the *Limerick Leader*)

The shattered windshield of the car Jerry McCabe was killed in.
(courtesy of the *Limerick Leader*)

Limerick's first hit man, Eddie Ryan.
(courtesy of the *Limerick Leader*)

John Ryan, murdered in a feud his brother Eddie helped start. (courtesy of the *Limerick Leader*)

The scene at the murder of Kieran Keane, the man who killed Eddie Ryan. (courtesy of the *Limerick Leader*)

Christy Keane, once the leader of the Keane-Collopy drugs gang. (courtesy of the *Limerick Leader*)

Brian Fitzgerald, gunned down on the orders of the drugs gangs. (courtesy of the *Limerick Leader*)

Anthony Kelly, the King of Southill.
(courtesy of the *Limerick Leader*)

Michael Kelly celebrating his victory in the city council elections
alongside his brother Anthony. (courtesy of the *Limerick Leader*)

Michael Kelly on the election trail.
(courtesy of the *Limerick Leader*)

Hitman Gary Campion entering court to face a murder charge. (courtesy of Press 22)

Paul Crawford, with his mother, cradling a picture of his murdered brother Noel. (courtesy of the author)

Shane Geoghegan, a completely innocent victim. (courtesy of the *Limerick Leader*)

The weaponry available to Limerick gangs includes AK-47s, such as this one seized by the Gardaí. (courtesy of the *Limerick Leader*)

Armed gardaí have become all too common a sight in Limerick, particularly during high-profile criminal trials. (courtesy of the *Limerick Leader*)

by accident. He maintained that the shooting was an accident rather than a mistake. It was possible that Ms Collins, in sweeping the gun aside, had caused the shooting.

Bizarrely, he told the panel of judges that the fact that Cronin did not raise this at the original trial – he claimed to have heard someone else shooting – was not relevant. Cronin had no argument with Ms O'Donnell, who was clearly never the intended target of any attack.

But Michael Durack, barrister for the DPP, stressed that the question of an accident had never been mentioned by the defence during the original trial. The jury had the option of returning a manslaughter verdict, but chose instead to convict Cronin of murder. The appeal failed and Cronin returned to his cell in Portlaoise prison to serve out his life sentence.

*

And what happened to the other players in the drama?

Cronin's marriage to Angela Collins, shaky to begin with, did not survive. In April 2007, from behind bars, he filed for divorce. He was escorted by gardaí and prison wardens to the court in Limerick to complete the divorce formalities. Joined by three children, the couple were still in contact, but neither wanted the marriage to continue. Ms Collins did not oppose the divorce.

Though he was behind bars, Cronin was moving on with his life. He had a new girlfriend. She was a regular visitor to the prison, as part of a Good Samaritan prison visit scheme. Another inmate introduced her to Cronin and there was an immediate attraction. She was in her 30s, and at the time of his divorce the new couple were described as 'very much in love'.

Some of his connections were not doing so well. In 2008, his nephew, James Cronin, was brutally murdered by the McCarthy-Dundon gang. The 20 year old was forced to dig his own grave before being shot by fellow gang members who feared he might talk to the Gardaí about a murder he had participated in a few hours earlier.

It seems that if you pull at any thread in Limerick it will lead to a grisly end.

*

As for the Henry Cecil, the shooting marked the beginning of the end for the popular premises. A week after the shooting a local solicitor, Aeneas McCarthy, appeared at the District Court and withdrew an application made some months prior for a late-night drinks licence for the nightclub. As the papers noted at the time, 'The licence was not due for renewal or review, but had been before the courts on a number of occasions in recent months.'

The ordinary bar licence was still in operation in the downstairs part of the premises, but the nightclub was closed within a week of the shooting and never reopened. With the loss of the nightclub, and a bad reputation following the shooting, business in the downstairs bar plummeted. The premises was sold, then ceased to trade.

Jim 'Chaser' O'Brien was involved, with others, in the Henry Cecil. His other pub, Chaser O'Brien's in Pallasgreen, also went into a decline and eventually ceased to trade. But by that time Chaser was working closely with one of the top drug dealers in the country, who also kept up a front of a respectable business. The Clare man, with O'Brien as his lieutenant, built up strong contacts with English criminals, as well as drug dealers on the Continent.

O'Brien continued to play the dapper swank, favouring designer labels and driving a 5 series BMW. He had a child with a steady girlfriend, but was still an unrepentant ladies' man. He was also versatile and willing to get involved in a number of different schemes of questionable legality. In 2001, he was arrested with three others from the mid-west, in connection with a scam involving computer parts. The scam was carried out in the UK, but he never faced prosecution for it.

It was his connection with the drugs trade that finally proved his undoing. In early 2003, he fled Ireland after being one of the men arrested in connection with the Kieran Keane murder investigation. Garda sources say he was fearful that Keane's associates would target him for revenge after the arrest. O'Brien and the County Clare businessman he worked with were heavily involved with the McCarthy-Dundon gang at the time. The McCarthy-Dundons were responsible for the murder of Kieran Keane.

O'Brien himself had not been directly involved in the murder or the attempted murder of Keane's nephew Owen Treacy, but one of Keane's killers, Dessie Dundon, was driving O'Brien's car when he was arrested in Roscrea. When he was stopped, he gave his name as Jim O'Brien. So Chaser had good reason to be worried. He fled to Spain initially. But he had strong connections further north from his drugs network, so he quickly relocated to Belgium.

'He has always had an ability to ingratiate himself with those on the top of the organised crime ladder,' said a Garda source. 'He did it when he went to Limerick, and he did it when he skipped to the Continent.'

But his luck would not hold forever. In November 2005, he was arrested as part of a Belgian police swoop on a Continental drugs baron, and he spent a year in a Belgian prison. It was a far cry from the leafy fields of the Golden Vale and the busy roadside pub on the Limerick to Tipperary road, which would have been enough for most ordinary people. He is now based in Cork and was most recently involved in the wine-importation business.

*

The O'Donnell family coped with their loss as best they could. But tragedy continued to dog them. Georgina's young brother, Jason – only ten when she was shot – became a troubled teen, slipping into drug use. One of his other sisters, Olivia, was a former partner of Philip Collopy. Collopy was one of the leaders of the Keane-Collopy gang, the main rivals of the McCarthy-Dundons in the city. A violent and dangerous thug, he had risen to the top in a dog-eat-dog world. He was a professional hit man and a major figure in the drugs world. He was also, for a while, within the family circle of Jason O'Donnell. Collopy eventually met an end befitting a gangster: he was shot in the head. But it was more *Carry On* than *The Wire*. He shot himself in a mishap that would have been comical if it had not been tragic.

Collopy was just 29 when he threw a party for a few mates at his home in St Mary's Park. It was the night of Friday, 20 May 2009. He was no stranger to his own merchandise – drink and drugs were consumed during the course of the evening. There were about six people in the house at the end of the night. It was now nearly 2 a.m. on Saturday morning.

As gardaí from the Armed Support Unit roved the troubled estate, keeping order, the gangsters in the small corporation house thought it would be fun to mess around with a handgun. Philip Collopy took out a Glock and began to show his henchmen the correct way to shoot a man in the head.

Stoned though he was, he still had enough wit about him to remove the magazine from the gun. But he made one fatal error. He forgot that there was one bullet in the chamber. Initial media reports suggested he might have been egged into playing a game of Russian roulette. But this was not what happened; a Glock is an automatic handgun, not a revolver, so it is impossible to play Russian roulette with one. What Collopy was actually doing was far more sinister: he was showing his mates how to execute someone.

As his young brother watched, and one of the others took out a mobile phone to take pictures, the drunken hit man held the Glock to his head and pulled the trigger. There was a deafening bang and everyone sobered up fast.

The men immediately ran out to the street to flag down the armed gardaí they knew were close by. An ambulance was called, and Collopy was rushed to hospital, where he was put on a life-support machine. After a number of hours, the family accepted the inevitable and the machine was switched off. Gardaí candidly admitted that they got an unprecedented level of cooperation from Collopy's friends; no one wanted to be suspected of ending the life of the hit man.

This was one of the circles that Jason O'Donnell moved in. He was a good friend of Philip's brother Ray and hung out with the gangsters. He also used drugs. As one person who knew him told the *Sunday World*:

> He was the baby of the family and they gave him everything any child could ever want, but he just got sucked in with the wrong crowd. Jason was a loveable character, but he just wanted to be one of the gang. Jason hung out with all the Keane-Collopys, but he was a softie really.

As a teen, he looked up to would-be gangsters such as Liam Keane, son of murdered crime boss Kieran Keane. He was involved with the periphery of the gang.

Ray Collopy, a senior member of the gang, was the older brother of the boss, Brian. Brian had taken over the gang after the death of Kieran Keane. Ray was one of his right-hand men. He spent a lot of time in Spain, where he had a base near Benidorm. In the summer of 2010, Jason travelled out to Spain for a holiday on the Costa del Crime. After living it up in the hedonistic haven, he returned to Limerick, smuggling some recreational drugs back in his luggage.

A few weeks later, he was dead.

He went out for the night with friends, then returned home and had a massive heart attack after overdosing on prescription tablets he had brought back from his holiday. They were 'downers', and he reacted badly to them.

The funeral was a sad but tense occasion. Alongside the mourning family were notorious figures from the underworld. These included Ray Collopy and Christy Keane, brother of Kieran Keane.

'It is a real tragedy. Jason comes from a lovely family – his father worked hard all his life,' one friend of the family told the local paper, the *Limerick Leader*.

John Gilligan, former mayor of Limerick, knew the family well and was shocked when the second tragedy visited them. The straight-talking politician told the *Leader*:

They are a well-respected family in Corbally. My son is very upset, as he was in the same class as Jason at primary school. They made their first Communion together when they were kids.

For someone with so much potential to die so tragically is what makes this so sad. Also, given the fact his sister died in such tragic circumstances. It's hard enough for the family to bury one of their children. To have to bury two is something which is just a tragedy, just dreadful.

6

LIMERICK'S FIRST CONTRACT KILLER

Eddie Ryan

THE SHARP CRACK of a pistol shot rang through the crowded pub not once but several times. Some screamed, some dropped to the floor, others ran for the toilets. None made for the door – that was where the gunmen stood, masked. The flash from the pistol threw ghastly light on the funeral mourners who had come to the wrong pub for their friend's wake.

The two gunmen turned and calmly walked from the pub. Carefully, heads began to look up, as people tried to assess the damage. Suddenly, the window of the pub shattered and a bullet smashed into the wall above the bar. They were still firing, from outside.

Everyone went back down.

A moment later, an engine roared and the gunmen were gone. Slowly, people stood and looked around. Two women lay on the ground, bleeding. Both were conscious and moving. One man lay huddled, blood seeping through his jacket.

'Where were you hit, Eddie?' someone asked.

'Everywhere,' whispered the fallen man.

They were the last words spoken by Limerick's first hit man for hire.

*

Throughout the 2000s, Limerick became a city under siege, on a par with any of the notorious trouble spots worldwide – places such as Bogotá, Palermo and Beirut, cities the very names of which struck fear into the heart of the traveller. Limerick was a killing ground, as a number of increasingly violent gangs battled for control of the lucrative drugs market along the western seaboard – and battled to settle old scores.

There were several hundred drive-by shootings, firebomb attacks and assassinations. Gang bosses were executed and their minions fought for control after their deaths. Knives were replaced by sawn-off shotguns, then by handguns and, finally, by highly sophisticated automatic weapons. Gang members were sent to specialised training schools in Florida and Eastern Europe to hone their firearms skills. Grenades and sophisticated bombs were found during Garda searches. At one point, one gang even brought in a rocket launcher to take out the wife and family of a jailed rival. Limerick was no longer Stab City. It was far more dangerous than that.

We are used to the images of high-profile Mafia trials in Sicily, where the court would be ringed by a cordon of heavily armed police. Those scenes were mirrored at the majestic limestone courthouse on the Shannon. Whenever a gang member faced a serious charge, the Gardaí were on full alert for trouble. Up to 50 armed detectives, cradling Uzis, surrounded the courthouse in a show of strength.

Helicopters hovered overhead. In the troubled estates, the distinctive low whoop-whoop of the rotors became a familiar background noise. Armed patrols guarded the entrances to the estates, carrying out checks on all cars entering and leaving. People with no prior involvement in crime became sucked into the feuds. Drugs became more valuable to the local economy than Dell computers – which employed 5,000 people at its peak.

The criminals were a regular sight in the city. Everyone knew who they were and where their strongholds were – and avoided those areas. But inevitably it spilt out, with killings in quiet suburban estates and a gang presence everywhere. At one point, a leading gang member who had given evidence in court against rivals was being followed by a bodyguard of armed gardaí. But he had also arranged his own security. So more than half a dozen armed men, from both sides of the law, followed this man as he did his bread run, his cover for his more sinister activities.

Even children became embroiled in the war. When one journalist asked a primary school boy what he wanted to do when he grew up, he got the shocking answer: 'I am going to get a gun and kill the Keanes.'

That was not bravado but reality on the mean streets of the Treaty City. Kids as young as 14 ended up before the courts on possession of firearms charges. Teenagers became killers. How did things ever get that bad?

It all began with bad men. And few of them were as bad as Eddie Ryan, a teenage thug and murderer who went on to become an enforcer for Limerick's first gang and a killer for hire. He was Limerick's first hit man.

Eddie was born in 1960 and grew up hard. He was raised on Hogan Avenue, Kileely, a poor area just across the river and a few minutes' walk from the notorious St Mary's Park. St Mary's Park, in the Island Field part of Limerick, is a poor working-class estate, which has become a ghetto due to the feuding. Back in the '60s, it was already 30 years old, the first of Limerick's corporation estates. It had been built to bring people out of the tenement slums of the city centre, immortalised in Frank McCourt's book *Angela's Ashes*.

Life was not easy. Unemployment was high, there were no amenities in the estate and families tended to be large, which put pressure on already strained resources. To survive, many discovered it helped to be a little crooked. Petty crime thrived and many families suffered the twin curses of drink and violence. The park, which consists of two main streets joined by several alleys, has only one entrance and exit, and is on an island in the Shannon about fifteen minutes' walk from the city centre. This island location further enhances the ghetto feel of the estate and the isolation of the inhabitants.

Kileely, though not on the island, was similarly disadvantaged.

Eddie was a wild child and was in trouble from a young age. He first came to the attention of the Gardaí at 12, and was never out of trouble again. He got the name of being a vicious, extremely dangerous hoodlum, who enjoyed inflicting pain. His brother John also grew up to be a violent man with a severe drink problem, which indicates the sort of family background they came from.

One of Eddie's school companions grew up to be 'ruthless, extremely violent and highly strung' according to gardaí who had to deal with him. That was Christy Keane, from St Mary's Park. Keane came from a large family and drifted into the family business of coal and horses – adding petty crime as well.

As the friends entered their teen years, they dropped out of school and began breaking into houses, as well as carrying out robberies at garages and shops. When he was 18, Christy Keane picked up his first conviction, for larceny. Over the following few years he added considerably to this record.

But Eddie Ryan was way ahead of him. From his teens he was hanging out with older criminals and had moved well beyond juvenile delinquency. One of the men he associated with became a close friend: Michael Kelly.

Michael Kelly was six years older than Eddie and came from Prospect, another impoverished corporation estate in the city. Prospect was on the south-west of the city, whereas Kileely was on the east. The areas are not close geographically, but are similar in every other way. Small houses, lack of amenities, large families and unemployment linked them.

Kelly's upbringing was typical, to an exaggerated extent. His father James was from Kells and was in the army. He was an orderly in charge of the officers' mess in Sarsfield Barracks and did a good job. He was well regarded. He married Rita Kenny from Prospect when she was just 20. She was from a family of 27 children – one of the neighbouring families had 26 kids.

'They had no television and I suppose they had nothing to do,' Michael Kelly jokingly told me.

While James Kelly was liked, his military career stalled. He had epilepsy and TB, and a more serious problem. He was an alcoholic – just like his wife Rita. He quit the army, just a year shy of his full pension. That left his growing family facing the breadline.

Michael turned to petty crime, stealing from local shops and neighbours to help feed his brothers and sisters. A cunning and physically strong boy, he quickly gained a reputation as a hard man. As he said himself, up to the age of 16 he lost more fights than he won because he was fighting older men. But as his body matured he began to clock up the wins. He also began getting in trouble with the law and, in 1972, a local cop, Detective Sergeant Mick Browne, offered him a choice: the army or a spell in prison.

He survived a year in the army before the discipline got too much for him and he quit. He was now 18 and about to embark on a career that would make him one of the most notorious criminals in Limerick's bloody history. That is the man Eddie Ryan chose to look up to and hang out with.

Although Ryan was a number of years younger than Kelly, their similar backgrounds and willingness to use violence linked the men. By his teens, Eddie was drinking, smoking, fighting and thieving. He was not afraid of a fight and mixed it with the hard men of the city.

Michael Kelly had the name of being the hardest man. The young thug was drawn to the older thug. Kelly was a charismatic figure and in some ways saw himself as more than a petty thief. He saw himself as a leader and a mentor. His younger brother Anthony had followed Michael into crime, often partnering him in teenage raids on local shops and filling stations. Now Eddie Ryan stepped into that role.

He and Michael became regular partners in crime, travelling through Munster indulging in the latest criminal fad: armed robbery. This was not glamorous raids on banks for millions. This was more basic bread-and-butter crime. The two would steal a car, drive to Ennis, Tipperary or Kerry and hold up a garage, shop or post office. They would be armed with knives, bats, hatchets and, occasionally, shotguns. Michael was a great man for intimidating people. Big and burly, he was energetic and violent and not afraid to throw his weight around.

Couple this with a scarred face and a fearsome scowl and it is easy to see how they succeeded in getting cashiers to open the tills. They made a good living on these low-key robberies. On 10 June 1978, the post office on Upper William Street was held up by two armed men. On 8 July, they took along an extra man; three armed men raided the Bank of Ireland at the Roxboro Shopping Centre and made off with £30,000. Two of the men had shotguns, while the third had a pistol.

This had been a particularly well-planned raid. The Roxboro Shopping Centre was only a few minutes' walk from Michael Kelly's home in Southill, but it was not chosen for convenience. German multinational electrics company Krups had a huge factory at the edge of Southill, and the gang was after the payroll.

On 25 November, a Friday, three men burst into the Allied Irish Bank in Rathkeale, about 15 miles from Limerick. This time they only got £1,400.

Kelly, who eventually went straight and ran successfully for Limerick City Council, was open about his chequered past. Before his death in 2004 (ruled a suicide), he often spoke about his criminal activities, telling reporters: 'I did take part in armed robberies. If there was money someplace, I would get it. I had one partner in crime and we did everything.'

Privately, he admitted to me that his partner at the time was the young Eddie Ryan.

Another lucrative source of income for the two was household burglaries. With the new prosperity, a consumer society had been created, and thieves and fences found an easy outlet for their takings. Michael Kelly readily admitted that video recorders were the making of him. They were popular but expensive, so he and Ryan had a good market for stolen ones.

'We got into serious crime when the videos came out. They were a colossal price. We made great money, robbing four, five, six or seven places a night for the videos.'

But the good times couldn't last. Already both partners were well known to the Gardaí.

'Eddie was a juvenile delinquent, breaking into houses and making a good living at it,' one retired detective told me.

It was only a matter of time before one or other of the partners made a mistake. As it turned out, the first mistake was made by the cocky teen. His violent temper got him into trouble.

On 29 May 1977, a Sunday, Ryan went with some friends to a cinema, the Central on Bedford Row, near the city centre. The late movie that night was *Horror Express*, starting at 11 p.m. It was a low-budget supernatural thriller starring Christopher Lee, Peter Cushing and Telly Savalas, about a fossilised man who is killing passengers on a train. Earlier in the night, the cinema had been showing *Rocky*. The violent fare foreshadowed what was to come.

As the crowd spilt out of the cinema, after midnight, they mingled with people leaving the other late-night cinema, the Carlton, where *Confessions of a Pop Star* was showing. It was a clear, warm night and people lingered on the street. Late-night gatherings of teens are always flashpoints and some scuffles broke out.

At one point, a fight broke out between Ryan and an older man, Christopher Jackson. Ryan produced a knife and plunged it into the chest of the 28-year-old Jackson, who fell to the ground and died shortly afterwards. Ryan ran, but there were witnesses. Within hours, he was in custody, charged with murder. He was only 17.

While awaiting trial, he continued to associate with Michael Kelly, breaking into houses and taking part in armed robberies. But in 1978 he was convicted of manslaughter and sentenced to five years. The light sentence was probably due to his young age.

Five years in prison was like a master's degree in criminality for the young thug. He emerged a man, ready to make his mark in the Limerick underworld. He went back to his buddy Kelly (who had also been charged with murder while Eddie had been in prison, but who had not been convicted). They went into business together, reverting to the old reliable: armed robbery and burglary.

It went well, but they were too well known for it to last. Gardaí had their eyes on the two partners, and they were regularly stopped and searched. During one search of Eddie's house, detectives found a number of items which had disappeared in a recent robbery in the plush Ennis Road area of Limerick. Eddie was caught red-handed. It was back to prison, for another five years.

When he came out this time, his association with Kelly came to a natural end. A hardened criminal with a reputation for violence, Eddie Ryan was looking for the next big thing. And a blind man could see that drugs were where the money was. Kelly was still a thief, while Ryan was moving on. He hooked up with his old schoolmate Christy Keane.

*

Limerick had been slow to catch up with the drugs epidemic that had taken Europe by storm in the '70s. While Dublin succumbed to heroin in the '80s, it was a decade later before Limerick fell. It was one family who orchestrated the downfall.

The Keanes were based in St Mary's Park, where they were well known as coal merchants; they were also into horse trading. Horses are a way of life in some parts of Limerick, and it is not uncommon to see them grazing in gardens and in public areas of Moyross, Southill and St Mary's Park. Sulky races, where the horses tow two-wheeled carts like chariots, are still common in some parts of the city and large sums of money are wagered on them. Gardaí believe that it was through trading horses with Dublin gangs that the Keanes first became aware of the possibilities of the drugs trade.

They had not been involved in crime to any real extent before (apart from Christy's burglaries throughout the '70s and '80s), but they quickly began to deal in a small way, then expanded rapidly through the '90s. Eventually, they were supplied by a millionaire who used legitimate business as a front for his smuggling activities. He imported guns, drugs and ammunition, and he called a lot of the shots in the Limerick underworld – up to and including murder.

He managed, for many years, to avoid any serious charges. Outside Dublin, crime bosses don't have colourful names, such as the Psycho, the Viper or the General, but the Gardaí believe that they are as efficient, successful and dangerous as their Dublin counterparts. This man was one of the most significant criminal figures in the country. He was on a par with men such as John Gilligan, the Dublin gangster who orchestrated the murder of journalist Veronica Guerin in 1996.

'He lives in a rural area without much policing,' said one detective. 'He has a big organisation and is able to stay at a distance from the criminal activity, but we are watching him.'

The drugs went down the chain of supply to the Keanes, who organised the distribution throughout Munster. The Keanes would get the drugs into the city, then distribute them to their network of dealers in estates, as well as sending them on to gangs in Cork, Galway, Ennis and other towns.

Councillor John Gilligan, an independent politician who served as mayor of Limerick, recalled in a 2002 interview with me:

> There were vast sums of money floating about. Some of these criminals would think nothing of blowing a couple of thousand on a night out. They are on the dole and driving around in big swanky cars and taking foreign holidays. If you asked some of them to use a shovel, they'd ask you which end you hold on to. And with that much money, corruption follows.

Detective Inspector Jim Browne, one of the key figures battling the drugs gangs, told me: 'All major cities have drug gangs. The criminal fraternity saw that the days of taking televisions and videos were no longer profitable. There is major profit in drugs. The market and the money are there.'

Running a drugs empire is essentially a business exercise. Supply, storage and distribution must be controlled, and staff (or gang members) must be kept productive and in line. But the difference is that it is a business outside the law and there is no recourse to labour courts or unions. On top of that, you are handling very valuable goods and you can't complain to the Gardaí if they are stolen. That is why drug gangs have their leg-breakers and enforcers.

When the Keanes were looking for a heavy to enforce their will and protect their operation, Ryan was looking for a way into the drug trade. Michael Kelly was keen to distance himself from his old comrade in arms.

'When he got out of prison the second time, I asked him was he into drugs, and he said, "What if I am?" I said I would have nothing to do with drugs. He said he wasn't dealing, but I said, "Good luck to you," and I stopped working with him,' Kelly told me.

Not only was Eddie Ryan getting involved in dealing, he was also using drugs, particularly cannabis, on a regular basis. The two remained friends, but Kelly disapproved strongly of drugs, preferring to stick to more traditional criminal activities.

Ryan quickly became a key member of the Keane gang and he was not afraid to get his hands dirty on their behalf. He collected debts and interrogated people suspected of breaking Limerick's strict code of *omertà*, or silence. Snitches grew to fear the hard man from Kileely, who enjoyed inflicting pain during his 'enquiries'. Ryan often boasted of his strong links with republican groups, which only reinforced the tough image.

The Keane gang did not confine themselves strictly to drugs. They controlled one of the biggest distribution networks in the state, but they were also involved in prostitution, protection rackets, and counterfeit money and documents, as well as handling stolen goods, fencing and supplying weapons to criminals. Christy Keane, like Ryan, had republican links. He had strong associations with the INLA. But he had equally strong links with the Dublin gangs, regularly doing business with Declan 'Whacker' Duffy, Troy Jordan and John Gilligan. These contacts were made through horse dealing and sulky racing. In Cork, he had close links with the O'Flynn family, and he had a network of associates in the North and Britain as well.

But on the ground in his native city, Eddie Ryan was the man he came to rely on. His trusted lieutenant was by his side, willing to get his hands dirty in any nefarious activity. He was even willing to kill for the Keanes. Rumour around Limerick had it that he was occasionally 'loaned out' to carry out hits for gangs in Dublin, though the Gardaí say they have no evidence of this.

One of the most notorious hits that Eddie Ryan was involved in came in the winter of 1993–4. And, like all good hit men, he got away with it.

It all began a number of months previously, early in 1993. Monday, 1 February was a bitterly cold night. Thirty-year-old Kathleen McCarthy, née O'Shea, was walking through St Mary's Park with her common-law husband Patrick and her brother. She was a native of Southill. Patrick, a traveller, was also from the city. Childhood sweethearts, they had been together for fourteen years and had four young children.

It was not long after midnight and they'd had a few drinks. Perhaps Kathleen was slightly unsteady on her feet. At 12.15 a.m., the three had reached the junction of St Ita's Street and St Brigit's Avenue. St Ita's Street is a long street that runs the length of St Mary's Park and is the main route through the estate. As they got to the junction, Kathleen either stepped off the path or stumbled onto the road. No one is sure. What is sure is that a van was coming down St Ita's Street and it struck her. An ambulance rushed her to Limerick Regional Hospital, but she died an hour later of her injuries. No one else was injured in the incident, which the Gardaí were satisfied was an accident.

The driver of the van was Owen Treacy, a nephew of Eddie Ryan's boss, drug lord Kieran Keane. He was Keane's sidekick and often in his company. But for once there was no stain of suspicion about his actions on the night.

Kathleen was buried and Patrick McCarthy moved out of the city. To escape his grief he took his four children to Cork. But his attempts to build a new life were hampered by grief, anger and drink. On his visits back to Limerick, he was often abusive towards Owen Treacy. More than once, he threatened the life of the young gangster, demanding money in compensation for his loss. It is believed that he was given a few pounds now and again to appease him, but his resentment grew and his threats continued.

Patrick McCarthy travelled up from Cork to spend that Christmas with his family. He took his children with him and they stayed with his mother on Clare Street, about ten minutes from St Mary's Park, on the same side of the city. It was a chance to visit Kathleen's grave – and catch up with friends and family.

His sister Angela remembered, in an interview with the *Limerick Leader*:

> I met Patrick two days before Christmas. It is supposed to be a time for happiness. He had left Limerick after Kathleen was killed. He couldn't stand being in Limerick as it had too many memories. She was a very nice person. He had been torn to pieces when she was killed. When I met him he was in good spirits but he was still very sad for his wife. He really was missing her on this first Christmas without her. He spoke to me about his sadness. He had been to her grave – he regularly went to the grave.

She said that her brother was the fourth eldest in a family of seven boys and four girls. 'He was very good to us all. Everyone who knew Patrick liked him. He was a soft person.'

Soft or not, he had stepped on the wrong toes. And the clock was ticking for him.

Patrick spent Christmas with his family. Four nights later, a little before 11 p.m., he was in a van driving through St Mary's Park with one of his brothers, Martin. He was up to his usual tricks, demanding money and threatening Treacy. Close to where his beloved Kathleen had been killed ten months previously they came across a van occupied by Treacy and one of his uncles, Christopher Keane. Keane was already known to the Gardaí.

He and his brothers were well on the way to dominating the city's drug trade – and Treacy was a trusted lieutenant.

The occupants of both vans spilt out on to the road. Words were exchanged and McCarthy began cursing Treacy over the accident. It was not long before words turned to blows. The fight was short – someone produced a knife and Patrick McCarthy was stabbed twice in the chest, falling to the ground. Within minutes, he was repeating the final journey of his departed wife: a rush to the regional hospital and death within 40 minutes.

This time it was no accident and the Gardaí immediately swung into action. It seemed to be a simple enough case. Owen Treacy and Christy Keane were brought in for questioning, then released as a file was sent to the DPP.

The McCarthy clan prepared for another funeral. Patrick (known as Pa) was to be buried on Friday, 1 January 2004. Various family members took over the care of his four orphaned children. His sister, Angela, told a local radio station: 'The people who did this must be brought to justice.'

On New Year's Eve, the whole city was in celebratory mood, ready to ring in a new year. But 12 people were not feeling the excitement. The McCarthys crowded into one caravan at the Cooperage, a halting site on the Canal Bank, Clare Street, for their brother's wake. Among them were two children. Drink flowed, stories were told and tears shed. Then some callers arrived – but not to pay their respects.

It was late and pitch black outside. The time was 10.30 p.m. and two of the people inside the caravan decided to call it a night. They opened the door and stepped out. Two figures emerged from the shadows and confronted them. The strangers checked the two who had emerged and told them to get away quickly. Then they moved back into the shadows.

Inside, the McCarthys were tired and feeling the effects of the drink. Suddenly, the door of the caravan crashed in and the two strangers burst into the cramped space. The two were armed. Kieran Keane carried a shotgun, while Eddie Ryan was armed with a .32 handgun. Both wore masks.

Eddie opened fire, indiscriminately spraying lead. He emptied all six rounds. Keane loosed off a round of the shotgun. The acrid smell of gunpowder filled the room. There was pandemonium as the armed intruders ran from the caravan. They left behind a scene of carnage. Michael McCarthy lay dead from a bullet which had ripped through his neck, while his sister Nora and his brother Joe were injured and bleeding. A 22-year-old cousin, Noreen, was also hit in the leg. By a miracle, there were no more deaths – and the two children were spared.

Pa's brother Martin (Minty) was the first to recover his senses. He ran to a drawer and took out two vicious-looking carving knives. Bravely, he plunged into the darkness after the two assassins, nearly catching one of them. But they managed to evade him.

The Garda overtime bill was about to shoot through the roof.

They didn't have to search far for a motive: the elimination of witnesses to the murder of Patrick McCarthy. Certainly the family felt this: Martin McCarthy was convinced the killers were after him. It was his caravan that the family had been in at the time. He told the *Leader*: 'My caravan stands out on its own. It was me they came for. The target was me.'

Detectives did not rule this out. Initial progress was rapid. As Patrick's burial went ahead that Friday, witnesses and suspects were being called in for interview. These included Eddie Ryan, his wife Mary and his bosses, Christy and Kieran Keane. By the following Tuesday, 4 January, one woman and two men were still being held. Gardaí confirmed that seven shots had been fired – six by Eddie. Nora and Joe McCarthy were stable in hospital.

That Tuesday, the Garda charged Christy Keane with the murder of Patrick McCarthy in St Mary's Park on Tuesday, 29 December 1993.

On the second murder, of his brother Michael, Superintendent Liam Quinn confirmed they had brought in two more people for questioning; the total number of those interviewed was now six. He added that a pistol was an unusual weapon in Limerick and that at least five people had been involved in the military-style attack. Eddie Ryan was making his mark.

'I think that the violence that existed on this occasion exceeded any possible motive,' the superintendent said to the *Leader*. But he refused to be drawn on what security arrangements had been made for the remaining McCarthy family, or whether they would have round-the-clock protection.

At the funeral mass for Michael McCarthy, Canon Willie Fitzmaurice said:

> Within four days we are back here again, this time to pay our final respects to another member of the McCarthy family, Michael, a victim of mindless and senseless violence. Violence begets violence and leads inevitably to more suffering, more grief and more loss of lives.

He urged tolerance and forgiveness.

Politicians, on the other hand, saw the opportunity for a sound bite. The local powerbrokers were up in arms about the two murders. Fine Gael's Michael Noonan was first off the mark, calling for a review of policing in Limerick to establish if there were sufficient resources to meet the needs of modern and traditional crime patterns. He called on junior justice minister Willie O'Dea to push for it.

O'Dea dismissed the suggestion out of hand. As reported in the *Limerick Leader*, he said, and later events proved him right, that it would be impossible to stamp out feuding by putting extra gardaí on every street corner:

> If people want to get others they will lie in wait, and it is dishonest to pretend that this type of crime can be prevented by extra policing. We have expanded the criminal law, and we are putting £66 million into a crime package on top of the Department of Justice estimate to tackle crime head on.

He said that policing in a democracy must take into account people's rights – no one wanted Big Brother watching them all the time.

By Wednesday, those taken in for questioning had been released without charge. In a statement, Superintendent Quinn said:

> We are following a number of lines of inquiry, but we have not yet firmed it down to one definite line. We are appealing to those who know exactly what happened to come forward and break this cycle. There are people who are covering up for those responsible. It is as simple as that.

Gardaí were particularly interested in tracing a tall, thin, clean-shaven man in his mid-20s who had been seen in the Clare Street area between six and seven on the night of the killing. He was carrying a white plastic bag and was about 5 ft 7 in. tall, with tightly cropped black hair, and had been wearing a summer-type jacket and blue jeans. This description could quite easily have applied to Christy Keane or Eddie Ryan, neither of whom were big men.

On Wednesday too, Joe McCarthy was allowed home from hospital, but his sister Nora was still being treated. Meanwhile, the search continued around the Canal Bank and surrounding countryside for the murder weapons. Ballistic experts examined the bullets recovered from the McCarthy caravan and discovered that the pistol was an illegally held one, but this was no great surprise; licences are not issued for handguns in Ireland, so they are all illegal. The shotgun pellets yielded no clues, identification of the gun that fired being impossible.

The following day Kieran Keane was arrested in Galway, but was never charged. And Christy Keane, facing the charge of murdering Patrick McCarthy, was granted bail despite the strenuous objections of the Gardaí. Within ten days of the murder, and just a week after the burial, the chief suspect was back on the streets, regardless of the fact that an attempt had been made to murder the one witness to the original killing. The ways of the law are strange indeed. Eddie Ryan was never charged in connection with the second killing.

The McCarthy family were understandably furious. James

McCarthy, who had been injured himself and who had lost two brothers in the orgy of violence, told the *Leader*, 'The family are very upset about this. There is no justice.'

In a further blow to the family, Kieran Keane was released without charge.

Gardaí kept the investigation open, and theories abounded. One rumour doing the rounds was that the handgun Eddie Ryan used in the attack had been supplied by a republican group. Several such groups were at work in the Limerick area and many active republicans were living in St Mary's Park. Eddie would have known such people well. As his friend Michael Kelly said, there were lots of them around.

But the Gardaí were sceptical about that rumour; they believed that Ryan had got the gun through regular criminal contacts. Back in 1993–4 handguns were not usual among Irish criminals, but they had made their way into the arsenal of the Dublin gangs. Ryan was an enforcer for the Keane gang, and the Keanes had extensive links with many of the Dublin gangs.

'We are quite satisfied that we know the source of the gun and it was not the IRA,' Superintendent Quinn revealed enigmatically to reporters. But the gun itself was not located.

Eventually, Christy Keane was brought to trial in Dublin for the murder of Patrick McCarthy and was acquitted. On his return to Limerick, he consolidated his control of the drugs trade and continued to rule over his ever-expanding empire. No one was ever charged in connection with the attack on the caravan, in which Michael McCarthy lost his life.

Now approaching 40, Eddie Ryan was a mature and ruthless criminal, comfortable with using violence to further the aims of his employers. In American mafioso terms, he was a 'made man'. But he was also a man on the make. As a youth, Eddie had been a burglar and a minor armed robber. It was a precarious living, but if you didn't get caught and you didn't want the flash lifestyle, it got you by. Drugs were different. Drugs were where the real money was to be made. Ryan could see the Keanes were sitting on a goldmine. He decided to do a little prospecting of his own.

He began to call on a range of contacts made over two decades of criminal activity.

Initially, he began to work with the Dillons, a local family who dealt in a minor way. The Dillons had worked closely with the Keanes in the early days of the drugs trade in the city, then they had branched out on their own. But an uneasy peace existed between the two families.

Ryan was also associating with Sean 'Cowboy' Hanley. Cowboy was a small farmer on the north side of the city, who dabbled in petty crime and associated with the criminal underworld. Although he was managing to avoid any charges, his farm had been raided and the Gardaí had recovered a large haul of drugs. One of his sons, Brian, was charged with drug-trafficking after he was caught with a massive stash of ecstasy tablets in 2001. The case never came to trial. A week after his initial arrest he got involved in a row in a pub. The row spilt onto the street and a terrified woman, Sarah Craig, drove a knife through his chest. She was subsequently convicted of manslaughter. Brian Hanley's death was not feud-related.

Those were the sorts of families Ryan was now doing business with – although he still maintained close ties with the Keanes and was still a key member of their organisation. He was treading a tightrope and the rope was beginning to sway. Eddie's problem was that he was being pulled in a number of different directions. He had a decade of loyalty to the Keanes, he was working for himself on the side – and seeing that there was big money to be made – and his family were urging him to join in their growing feud with the Keanes.

The feud between the Ryans and the Keanes had nothing to do with drugs. Initially, it did not even involve the Keanes; the feud was actually with their neighbours, the Collopys. It began in the early '90s when John Ryan, Eddie's brother, accused members of the Collopy family of slashing the tyres of his sister-in-law's car. Jack Collopy denied the accusation, saying his boys had nothing to do with the damage. But the bad feeling festered. John Ryan's in-laws, the McCarthys, were rough and tough, and he found himself sucked into a feud with the Collopys.

A few weeks after the tyre-slashing incident, some of the McCarthys were in the Moose Bar on Cathedral Place when they spotted Jack Collopy's wife. They assaulted her, then left the pub. In a panic, she rang her husband, Jack, to warn him what was coming.

Jack Collopy, a big, jovial ex-army man, was not worried. Soon a van pulled up outside his house in St Mary's Park and seven men got out. He recognised members of the McCarthy family – and John Ryan, Eddie's brother. When I spoke to him in 2002, he recalled:

> They were all out at the corner, with shovels and everything. I was into shooting and fishing. I went out to the car and got my gun and said to them to get the fuck out of it. They had already done enough damage to my wife. I went out with the gun just to frighten them away. It wasn't loaded.
>
> Johnny Ryan approached me and said to put the gun away. I said, 'I will in my bollocks.' One of the McCarthys was beating a shovel off the ground, drawing sparks. Suddenly, they wrestled the gun off me, and Johnny Ryan stabbed me in the gut with a screwdriver or a knife or something. Then I was stabbed in the shoulder. After I got stabbed, I got a slap on the head. After the attack, I was carried inside, and I remember saying to keep the pressure on the wound. I remembered that from my army days. Then I passed out.

His injuries were severe; to this day he suffers from epilepsy and one side of his body is weak. Despite naming all his attackers, no one was ever charged in connection with the assault. This led to open warfare between the Collopys and the McCarthys and Ryans. John Ryan became one of the focal points of the Collopy anger. The feud became nasty, with drive-by shootings and random attacks.

The Collopys were close friends of the Keane family, and Jack's sons Philip and Kieran became key members of the Keane gang.

Initially, the Keanes tried to keep aloof from the feud, but as time wore on they became attached to the Collopy cause, though never to the extent that it interfered with business.

All this was happening as Eddie Ryan's links with Hanley and the Dillons grew. He was coming under pressure to align himself with the Ryans and McCarthys in their war against the Collopys, but, like his bosses, he resisted this pressure for a long time.

However, in 2000, he began to distance himself from the Keanes. He began to think that he could do better on his own. Drugs worth hundreds of thousands of pounds were regularly brought into Limerick for distribution. Christy Keane ran out of places to stash the huge sums of cash that were flowing through his hands and regularly hid large bundles in his wheelie bin. The Keanes were coming to dominate the drugs trade on the north side and supplied as far afield as Clare, Galway, Cork and Kerry.

Mayor John Gilligan, who represented the people of St Mary's Park on the city council, said he was shocked when a senior garda visited the council to talk about the growing problem. The chief superintendent told Limerick City Council that, in six years, European police forces had intercepted drugs valued at €300 million destined for the mid-west region, to be distributed from Limerick.

The Keanes were turning over millions of euros distributing cannabis, cocaine, ecstasy and amphetamines throughout the mid-west. With this sort of money floating about, it is little wonder that Eddie Ryan decided he would cut himself in on a bit of the action and join his family in their feud. Initially, the Keanes were happy to let him do his bit of dealing. They even supplied him with some of his merchandise. But it changed their relationship with him, and it did begin to drive a wedge between the two sides. The distance widened when the Keanes ended up allegedly owing Ryan a considerable amount of money.

Michael Kelly told me: 'Eddie was being fed lies, things the Keanes were supposed to have said about him. And Eddie, being Eddie, he believed them. He was poisoned by them.'

Around this time the feud escalated once more. The cause was a fight between two schoolgirls. On 25 October 2000, a fight broke out between John Ryan's daughter and a niece of Christy and Kieran Keane. It happened in the yard of St Mary's secondary school in Corbally.

The following day, Anne Keane, the mother of one of the two combatants, went to collect another child from a primary school. Two of John Ryan's daughters were waiting for her. They laid into her viciously, knocking her to the ground and punching and kicking her. Then one of the girls produced a Stanley blade and slashed Anne Keane's face.

It was one up for the Ryans, but the score could not be left to stand there. That night, John Ryan was relaxing in his home in the Lee Estate, close to the Island Field. This was right in the heart of Keane territory. Unlike his brother Eddie, he had no distance between himself and his enemies. His peace was shattered that night when a number of shots rang out. He dived to the floor as his front window shattered.

When the shooters ran, Ryan rang Eddie, who came over immediately. He said that he would go up to Christy Keane and sort out the problem. He said that he wanted to give Christy 'a box'.

The brothers drove into St Mary's Park. Christy Keane was very close to one of his nephews, Owen Treacy, who was a major player in the gang. The Ryans drove straight to Treacy's house, but as they slowed down outside Owen Treacy came out with a gun and fired two shots at them, hitting the car. Eddie Ryan fired back as John Ryan accelerated out of the park. Now it was no longer punches in a schoolyard. It was war.

According to Michael Kelly, Ryan met with Christy Keane once more and straight away attacked him with his fists. All pretence of civility was gone. He told me: 'I have no evidence for this but I heard that the falling-out was over drug money. The Keanes owed Eddie £40,000, which they never handed across. I believe that is what happened. All feuds are drug-related.'

On the afternoon of Friday, 3 November 2000, Eddie Ryan

decided giving Christy Keane 'a box' was not sufficient. He would kill his former boss, now bitter rival. He got his handgun, loaded it and set out to kill yet again. He knew where Christy Keane would be – on the school run.

He was right: Christy Keane was in his van outside the Ignatius Rice secondary school on Shelbourne Avenue. Other parents were also there, waiting for the students to be let out. Christy Keane saw Eddie Ryan, and one of Eddie's sons, approaching him. Despite the recent assault he was still willing to talk. He lowered his window and put his head out to call. Ryan was walking rapidly towards the car. Then Ryan slipped his hand inside his jacket, pulling out his 9mm automatic pistol.

Lots of things can go wrong with a handgun. One of the most common problems is that the short barrel makes aiming a bit of a lottery. A standard short-barrelled handgun loses accuracy after a few yards. And after the kick-back from the first shot, the second can go anywhere. An experienced gunman will know this and will make sure of his aim. Eddie strode right up to Christy Keane's van and confidently rammed the gun at Christy's head.

Cold eyes stared into frightened eyes and Eddie pulled the trigger. There was a click. Horrified, Eddie pulled the trigger again. There was another click. The gun had jammed. Had he used a wrong-sized bullet? Had the bullets become damp in storage? There was no time to speculate. Christy Keane was already turning the key in the ignition and gunning the engine. Eddie's son banged on the window, cracking it in frustration. But it was no good. Keane sped off, driving along the pavement and scattering waiting parents. Ryan turned and ran. It had all gone disastrously wrong. Ryan knew the consequences of his failed assassination attempt. He was a marked man; barring a miracle, he would not see Christmas.

For once in his life, sense prevailed. Ryan left his pregnant wife Mary and went north to County Down, to stay with his mistress. He needed to be well away from Limerick to decide what his next move would be. He knew the Keanes would be planning their own.

But fate intervened before he got a chance to come up with a plan. Eddie's brother-in-law Patrick Collins died and Eddie decided he had to return home for the funeral. He had to be with his family.

Old friend Michael Kelly was one of those who called to the house to offer his sympathies. Kelly always saw himself as more than a gangster; he was a leader within his community. He had tried unsuccessfully to broker a peace between the Ryans and the Keanes and Collopys a few months previously.

When I interviewed him, Kelly remembered:

> I went out to the house and said to Eddie, 'Do you want me to sort this out?' He said that it was too late. I knew by his face and his attitude that he knew he did not have long left to live. He was a proud man and he would not admit that he had made a mistake. I said, 'Eddie, you are a sitting target. Don't go to the funeral.' But he wouldn't listen. It was the last conversation I had with him.

On the night of the removal to St John's Cathedral, Eddie's brother John urged him to wear a bulletproof vest. But Eddie refused. He felt that wearing the bulky Kevlar vest would be disrespectful. And who was going to target a mourner at a funeral?

Sunday, 12 November, was a wet night. The body was removed from the nearby funeral home to the church and there was a brief service. Afterwards, Eddie told his seven-weeks-pregnant wife Mary that he was going to have a pint before returning home. Together with his 18-year-old son Kieran, he headed through the rain for the Moose Bar, a comfortable, traditional pub on Cathedral Place, just a minute's walk from the church.

He got to the pub at 9 p.m. Several of the mourners had followed him in. Eddie settled at a small table just inside the front door, beside Mary Reddan and her daughters Deirdre and Majella. Mary Reddan was the sister-in-law of Jack Collopy. It had been here in the Moose that Eddie's brother John had assaulted Jack's wife, before setting out to assault Collopy himself, the incident that turned a small row into a bloody feud.

The Moose is not a rough pub. It is a modern, well-run establishment close to the city centre. Owner Pat Tobin, whose two brothers Adrian and John also run bars in the city, was on the premises. Unknown to him and his patrons, there was also a snitch on the premises. The Keanes had a number of lookouts in likely spots, waiting to pass on information on Eddie's movements.

Somebody slipped outside for a few minutes and made a call. Quickly, the Keanes put an improvised plan into operation. The first thing they needed was a car. They were prepared with that. They had stolen one the previous night from a pub at Murroe, a rural area about ten miles from Limerick, in the hope that Eddie's return to Limerick would give them an opportunity to strike.

They picked up a driver fairly quickly. Paul Coffey, 23, of Craeval Park, Moyross, and Derryfada, Clonlara, was an associate of the Collopys. No stranger to the law, he was on the run from Limerick prison. He had been given temporary release and had never returned. He was driving his girlfriend and one of their children home when he was flagged down by Philip Collopy.

Philip Collopy was the son of Jack Collopy; he had become a key member of the Keane gang. He was also a hardened gunman. He had been charged three years earlier with shooting at the car of a member of the McCarthy family, with whom the Collopys were feuding. The car contained a ten-year-old child; the driver was shot in the back, but survived. Collopy was not convicted of the shooting.

Now, aged 20, he was prepared to kill for his gang. He spoke briefly to Paul Coffey and told him he was needed to drive a car. Coffey said he would be back in a few minutes, after he had dropped his girlfriend and child home. He sped off and returned to the designated meeting spot a short time later, where he found Kieran Keane waiting with a number of men.

They went to the Keane coal yard in St Mary's Park and picked up the stolen car. The red Vauxhall Cavalier had been hidden there overnight. Coffey hot-wired the engine, then got behind the wheel. Collopy sat in the passenger side beside him, cradling a 9mm handgun. Keane got in behind. He was armed with a powerful .357 Magnum revolver. Collopy's weapon was the more modern. It could fire off multiple rounds in a fraction of a second and could carry a clip of more than a dozen rounds. But Keane's weapon had a reputation for one-shot stopping power. The .357 bullet was designed to cause maximum damage in a body: one shot, even off-target, is generally enough to do the job. The revolver only carried six shots, but that would be more than enough.

Coffey claimed that he did not realise what deadly business they were about until he saw the guns – and then it was too late to back out. The car pulled out of the coal yard and drove the two miles or so to Cathedral Place. Traffic was light and they were there in a few minutes. Coffey pulled the car into a yard across the road from the pub and Keane got out. He made a quick call to his informant inside, then swore under his breath before stepping back into the car. He was annoyed. He had been hoping that a close associate of Eddie Ryan would be in the pub, but he had just heard Eddie was there on his own, apart from his teenage son. He told Coffey to drive across to the pub and wait outside with the engine running. Keane and Collopy pulled balaclavas down over their faces and stepped out into the rain. It was time to go to work.

At around 9.50 p.m., Kieran Ryan, Eddie's son, stood up and walked to the toilet. It saved his life. At 9.53 p.m., patrons of the Moose who were facing the right direction were shocked when the door opened and two masked men stood silhouetted against the street light outside. Eddie Ryan had his back to the door and did not spot them initially. But they quickly drew his attention.

'You bastard! Come out, you bastard,' roared Keane. Then he pulled the trigger of his powerful revolver. Collopy took the cue and started firing straight away. The ear-splitting crack of the shots deafened those in the small lounge. The acrid smell of gunpowder filled the air, as patrons dived for cover. Proprietor Pat Tobin remembered in court: 'There was chaos and pandemonium. I realised we were being shot at, so I pressed the panic button.'

Outside, Coffey heard the sharp retorts and was in no doubt what was happening. 'I knew they were firing at someone down low or on the ground,' he said. The shooting frightened him so much he let the engine of the car stall and he had to quickly scramble with wires to restart it.

Inside, Eddie didn't have time to take any evasive action. Slug after slug hammered into his back and he slumped from his chair to the floor. Innocent bystanders also took stray shots, but the killers knew what they were doing and Ryan took most of the lethal dose of lead. Within ten seconds, it was all over. The two killers turned and ran from the pub, jumping into the waiting car.

'Drive! Drive!' shouted Keane. Coffey didn't need urging. With a squeal of tyres he shot off towards Garryowen and escape. But, as they pulled away, Philip Collopy wound down his window and fired one last fusillade at the pub. Seven needless rounds blasted the front of the pub. Luckily, no one was injured.

Inside the stolen car, Kieran Keane was jubilant. He kept shouting: 'Eddie is dead, Eddie Ryan is dead!'

Coffey drove the two killers to a nearby house, where he let them out. Then he drove to a deserted lane and torched the car, destroying valuable forensic evidence.

Meanwhile, back at the Moose, the stunned patrons were struggling to take it all in. The smell from the shots still hung in the air, and tables and chairs were scattered from the blind panic. Mary Reddan, 63, had been hit twice. Her 38-year-old daughter Majella had also taken two shots.

Afterwards, she said: 'I just could not believe what was happening. We were all absolutely numbed with fear – you would think it came straight out of *The High Chaparral*.'

Another witness recalled, in an interview with the *Limerick Leader*: 'There were at least six shots fired, if not more.'

In fact, it was a lot more. Seven bullets had lodged in Eddie's back, several penetrating his lungs. One bullet had ripped apart his spinal cord. In total, he had been hit 11 times. As he lay on the floor, consciousness fast fading, someone asked him where he had been hit.

'Everywhere,' he whispered, then he slipped away.

Eddie Ryan, gangland enforcer and hit man, was pronounced dead on arrival at Limerick Regional Hospital. He had lived by the gun; now he died by the gun. Both Reddans survived their injuries and made full recoveries.

Eddie Ryan's was the first death in what was to become a bloody litany, as Limerick's feud intensified and sucked more families into its miserable maw. The Garda investigation was as intense as Limerick had ever seen. The two killers were among those arrested and questioned, but neither was ever charged in connection with Ryan's death. The only one to face the jury was the driver of the getaway car.

Paul Coffey was charged with murder. The state maintained that, as he was part of the killing party, he was guilty of murder. Initially, he made a statement implicating both Keane and Collopy, but by the time the trial opened he had retracted that statement and there was no evidence against either gunman.

Coffey pleaded not guilty, but halfway through the high-profile trial he dramatically changed his plea to guilty of manslaughter. The court accepted this plea and he was sentenced to fifteen years, with the last seven suspended. The court took into account the fact that he had slight learning difficulties and that he had been a tool of the real killers.

Though Keane and Collopy escaped the law, the streets have their own way of dispensing justice. Within two years of the assassination of Ryan, Kieran Keane was caught in an elaborate trap. Members of the Ryan gang faked the kidnapping of Eddie's two sons, Eddie Junior and Kieran. There was a massive manhunt for them, involving hundreds of gardaí throughout the country. At the end of a week of intense speculation, the McCarthy-Dundon gang, associates of the Ryans, lured Kieran Keane to a house in the Garryowen area of Limerick, under the pretext of giving him news of the missing brothers. But instead he and his sidekick Owen Treacy were abducted. Keane was tortured then shot in the head. The gun jammed when it came to Treacy's turn, so they stabbed him a number of times and left him for dead. He survived seventeen stab wounds, and his evidence put five members of the McCarthy-Dundon gang behind bars for life.

Christy Keane was already behind bars, after being caught in possession of a sack of cannabis. Kieran Keane was dead. Philip Collopy became the leader of the Keane-Collopy gang. His rise mirrored that of Eddie Ryan ten years earlier. Like Ryan, he had shown a propensity for violence at a young age. He had been charged with a shooting offence when he was just 17. When he was 20, he had burst into the Moose and shot Ryan for his bosses, just like Ryan had burst into a caravan on a bleak January night seven years earlier to kill for his bosses. Collopy was a brutally efficient enforcer, both feared and respected by the hard men of the city.

But a moment of stupidity changed everything. At a party in 2009, Collopy, in a moment of macho bravado, decided to give an impromptu lecture on the proper use of a handgun to his followers. It was something he was an expert in. Limerick's gangsters had learnt a lesson from the afternoon when Eddie Ryan tried to shoot Christy Keane and was thwarted by a jammed gun. Several criminals, including Collopy, travelled to America for a week of intensive firearms training in a Florida shooting range.

As we have seen, the prank went terribly wrong: Philip Collopy shot himself. He was placed on a life-support machine but died the following day. Both of Eddie Ryan's killers had themselves died violent deaths.

But the life and death of Limerick's first hit man had more far-reaching implications than that. Ryan's death was the spark that ignited the smouldering feuds in Limerick, turning simple family bitterness into all-out war. The decade following his death saw the feuds claim more than a dozen lives – including several innocent people caught in the wrong place at the wrong time.

One of the victims was Eddie's brother John Ryan, killed by the Keane faction as he laid a patio one afternoon.

7

THE INNOCENT VICTIMS: KILLED FOR DOING HIS JOB

The Murder of Brian Fitzgerald

YOU DON'T NEED to be in a gang to be a victim of gangland violence. There is a smug feeling among those not in the know that most drugs wars involve gangsters shooting other gangsters; if we just sit back and wait, they will kill each other off, thus cleaning up the streets by a process of natural selection.

Nothing could be further from the truth. Gangsters do shoot each other, but they also shoot minor criminals who owe them money and people who cross them. More worryingly, they have no problem shooting members of the public who have nothing to do with their activities. You can take a bullet simply for being in the wrong place at the wrong time, or for doing your job.

Life is cheap to the gangsters. They don't care if an innocent bystander gets caught in the crossfire. It's not their problem. In fact, it adds to their reputation. That was the philosophy behind the murderous McCarthy-Dundon gang. Their arrival marked a new and terrible departure in Limerick crime. Much of the unsavoury reputation Limerick has enjoyed over the past decade can be laid at their door.

To understand the McCarthy-Dundons, and their impact on the city, we need to look at who they are. John McCarthy of Hyde Road, Prospect, a settled traveller, had a large family. One of his daughters, Anne, married a local man, Kenneth Dundon. He was a hard man, with a long list of convictions. At seventeen he had got two years for wounding with intent. It went downhill from there. By the '80s, he had pissed off enough people to make it sensible to get out of Limerick. The final straw came when he was shot after a row with a relative. Kenneth and Anne headed for London, where they reared their growing family of five sons. Four would eventually form the nucleus of the McCarthy-Dundon gang, while the fifth, Ken, kept his nose clean.

Kenneth Dundon Senior continued his criminal ways, clocking up convictions for assault occasioning actual bodily harm and robbery. Sons John, Dessie, Gerard and Wayne also gained reputations for violence and were constantly in trouble with the law. There was one incident in which one of the brothers glassed a man in a racist attack in a bar, simply because they objected to him drinking in their presence. Finally, Wayne went too far. In the course of a robbery, he threw an elderly pensioner, confined to a wheelchair, down the stairs. The British police deported him from the UK. He returned to Limerick and his brothers followed. This was in the late '90s.

Kenneth Senior remained in London. As violent as his boys, he reacted badly when his wife Anne took a lover. She started sleeping with Christopher Jacobs, a man she had met in August 2003 while in a dole queue. Kenneth found out and was furious. There was an angry confrontation with Anne in early October, after which he dragged her home. Jacobs, convinced she was being forcibly kept in the house, confronted Dundon and there was a punch-up. A few nights later, Dundon arrived at Jacobs' home and kicked in the door. He was armed with a knife, and he stabbed his rival repeatedly in the face, leaving him dead.

He then fled back to Limerick, but was arrested outside the courthouse in the city in 2005. He was convicted of manslaughter and sentenced to six years. On his release, he settled back into happy domestic life with his wife again, in Hackney, London. With parents like that, it was no wonder the boys ended up so violent and out of control.

In the late '90s, the Dundon boys teamed up with their cousins from their mother's side, the McCarthys. Settling in Ballinacurra Weston, on the south side of the city, they quickly began terrorising the neighbourhood. They also became involved in crime, beginning with robberies, but graduating to drug dealing and murder.

They brought the techniques and weaponry of the London underworld to small-town Ireland. Before they arrived, the drugs scene was ruled by the Keane-Collopy gang, engaged in a minor (but deadly) feud with their former allies, the Ryans. Knives, bats and axes were weapons of choice. The odd sawn-off shotgun was used, and occasionally a handgun. The weaponry was not sophisticated. Occasionally the handguns misfired because they were using ill-fitting or old bullets.

Once the Dundons arrived the weapons became more sophisticated. The AK-47 and automatic handguns made their appearance. Grenades and rocket launchers were eventually recovered by shocked gardaí. The level of violence escalated sharply.

It took a while before people noticed. In the beginning, it was gangster against gangster, and people tend to overlook that. On one occasion, the victim was a notorious hard man and violent thug, John Creamer.

It is thought that Creamer had taken part in the robbery of a jewellery store with his cousins the Dundons; on the evening of 11 October 2001, the 27 year old arrived in the estate to pick up his share of the takings. This is speculation; Creamer never revealed the full details of exactly what happened.

What is known is that he was struck by 15 bullets fired from an automatic weapon when he was ambushed at Hyde Road, Prospect, near the Dundon stronghold. He took shots to the head, neck, chest, left arm and leg. One bullet just missed his heart. He fell to the ground just outside his uncle's house.

'They have taken 15 bullets out of me, but there are still bits of bullets lodged in various parts of my body,' he told the *Limerick Leader* from his hospital bed two months later.

I don't know who did it, or why. It's just great to be alive, and I want to get on with my life. I don't want revenge or anything like that. They told me I'd be in intensive care for months but I was back in a ward in three weeks.

He had a selective but vivid memory of the shooting:

I was going to visit my uncle Kenneth Dundon, and the shooting happened near his house. I don't have a clue who did it. I saw the gunman and thought it was a joke. Then he fired, and I hit the deck. I tried to get up but I couldn't. He kept firing and was only about ten feet away from me. I collapsed. I was conscious through it all.

Doctors worked for 12 hours on him in emergency surgery at Limerick Regional Hospital in nearby Dooradoyle – a hospital that would soon become overly familiar with gunshot wounds. It took six more operations to remove most of the lead from his system.

Creamer eventually made a full recovery, but he could never identify his attacker – despite being only ten feet from him during the ordeal. However, the Gardaí are convinced it was the McCarthy-Dundon faction that shot him. It is thought the shooter could have been as young as his mid-teens. The gun used was eventually found in the possession of a Dublin gang with strong links to the McCarthy-Dundons, but no one has ever been charged in connection with the shooting of John Creamer.

Everyone knew it would not be long before the McCarthy-Dundons claimed their first life. No one knew the victim would be a completely innocent man, gunned down for doing his job.

*

Brian Fitzgerald was the affable and efficient head of security at Doc's nightclub, a popular nightspot near the centre of the city. It was a two-minute walk from the end of O'Connell Street and faced the river not far from where the Hunt Museum is now located. A big old stone granary had been converted into a pub and nightclub. The stone complex also housed the city library, the Enterprise Board and some Shannon Development offices.

Fitzgerald was a native of Limerick, born in 1968, making him 34 at the time his troubles began with the McCarthy-Dundons. Limerick is a rugby-mad city and Fitzgerald grew up with that tradition. A strong, athletic man, it was no surprise he began to play the game.

He was raised in the traditional working-class corporation estate of St Mary's Park, but when he was 12 the family moved to the more modern Lee Estate, a few minutes away. Brian had two brothers and two sisters. He attended the local schools, where his passion for rugby was encouraged.

When he left school, he got a job with Krups, the German appliance manufacturer, which had a big plant on the south side of the city for many years – a great source of employment. But the company pulled out of Limerick in the '90s, leaving yet another hole in the local economy. Brian had been with them for 11 years at that stage, and probably thought that was where he was going to remain for his working life.

He had married his childhood sweetheart Alice and they had two young sons. They had bought a modern, two-storey semi-detached house on Brookhaven Walk, Mill Road, Corbally. Mill Road is a long, winding cul-de-sac off the main Corbally Road. It is a lovely place to rear children. There is plenty of open space, the houses are roomy and the people are on their way up. It is a far cry from St Mary's Park or Lee Estate. Things were looking up for the Fitzgeralds.

Brian loved living in Corbally. It was very close to the Shannon and there are beautiful leafy walks along the banks of the river. He was a familiar sight, exercising his dogs. He loved pit-bull terriers and hoped to one day breed them. He was also a devoted dad and was regularly spotted with his five-year-old son Aaron, feeding the ducks on the river or playing in the park on Clare Street, just off the Dublin Road. In the evenings, he would often be out in the green area in front of his home with the children.

He also kept up his sporting interests. In addition to the rugby, he had broadened out to try powerlifting and bodybuilding, two sports he excelled at. He was a regular in many of the top gyms around town and was generous with advice to young lifters, helping them out with training programmes and diet advice.

But rugby remained his top interest. He was a member of St Mary's Rugby Club, lining out at number eight in their familiar blue and white colours; he also did one season with the Thomond club. In 1996, he was good enough to have a trial for Munster, which could have led to a professional career.

When Krups pulled out of the city, Brian was forced to look for other work. Big and strong, as well as honest and trustworthy, he found work as a bouncer and doorman at several city centre pubs and nightclubs, including the Newtown Pery on Thomas Street. But when he began to work for Doc's in 1998, he found his new home.

Doc's was the trendy place back then. Everyone went there. It attracted students, young professionals and the hip crowd. It was a well-regulated venue with a good reputation. Brian was a natural fit. Cool and level-headed, he was soon promoted from doorman to head of security. Now he was no longer doing casual shifts on the doors. He was back in full-time employment. The problems caused by Krups pulling out were behind him. Life seemed sweet again.

As one regular at the time told me:

> Brian was a very strict but fair security manager. He felt a great sense of responsibility towards the patrons of Doc's. The club is very popular with 18–21 year olds, and Brian knew he had to protect these young people from many ills.

Brian took his new position seriously. It wasn't just about keeping yobbos away from the club and throwing out drunks. Head of security carried responsibilities, and one of his responsibilities was to ensure that the club kept its good name. That meant no fighting, but more importantly, it meant no drugs. Back then,

Limerick did not have a major drugs problem. The heroin craze that had scoured Dublin barely touched the west, and even in Limerick you could count the number of users on one hand and leave fingers free for picking your nose. A bit of dope, a couple of ecstasy tablets, some speed, these were what young people were trying to score. LSD was available and some people experimented with it. But in general it was all soft drugs, no more harmful than the pints an earlier generation had downed.

Dealers mingled with the dancers, or hung around outside. A couple of pounds would get you your fix for the night. The drugs squad tried to keep a grip on the situation, but there were only four of them in a small office in Henry Street. Their lack of strength showed how seriously the problem of drugs was being taken in the city. What no one knew was that a drugs importer who had been supplying the Keane gang was now supplying the McCarthy-Dundons. He had the connections to get them whatever weapons they wanted, and he had the drugs that would finance their growing empire, as well as their campaign of violence and intimidation against other gangs and against the people of Limerick. The world was about to find out how dangerous the McCarthy-Dundons had become.

Early in 2002 some young men arrived at Doc's nightclub in hoodies. Brian Fitzgerald did not like the look of them. Experienced in his job, he spotted the warning signs and refused them entry. They looked like potential dealers to him.

The young men reacted badly, turning aggressive. They threatened him, but he didn't take it too seriously. If you worked the doors, you became used to people telling you to watch your back, they were out for you. But then the front of his house was raked with bullets. Such a thing had never happened in the gentrified surroundings of Mill Road.

The terrified family immediately went to the Gardaí. Brian revealed that not only had his house been shot up, he had also received a death threat. A man who identified himself as a gang leader told Fitzgerald that he would kill him because he had stopped drugs coming into the nightclub.

On the basis of the complaint by the Fitzgeralds, the Gardaí moved on the McCarthy-Dundons. A major player in the gang was arrested and charged with threatening the security man. But Brian Fitzgerald felt that the best way of ensuring the safety of his family was to strike a deal with the gangsters. It is speculated that he tried to negotiate for his life. He might have made a deal with the gang that if he did not press charges, they would leave him alone.

This is conjecture; what is known is that he did withdraw his statement, and the case of threatening and intimidation never came to court. Perhaps he thought that he was safe, that he could leave the fear behind him and get on with his life. If he did do a deal, the other side failed to hold up their end.

*

In the small hours of the morning of Saturday, 29 November 2002, a powerful motorbike shot out of the Corbally Road, then turned at the traffic lights down the dark Mill Road. It was just before 1 a.m. and traffic was light. The rider pulled into the shadows and waited. He was Gary Campion, described to me by prison officers and gardaí as one of the most evil men in the country. He is the only hit man to have been convicted twice for murder – which speaks volumes about his violence, and his lack of competence in his chosen profession.

Behind him was a big man with a bald dome of a head, James Martin Cahill. Born in Birmingham of Irish roots, he had been brought over to do a special job. The Dundons retained their links with the UK underworld and, for the job that was to be carried out that night, they wanted someone with no connection with the victim. It would make the subsequent investigation more difficult. Cahill waited patiently; he was being well paid for this night's work.

He had been approached and asked to come over to Ireland. The man who contacted him, he claims, was Anthony Kelly from Kilrush. Kelly is unrelated to the Kelly brothers of Southill, whose story is told elsewhere in this book. Kelly has a conviction for living off the earnings of a prostitute and has been forced to make a six-figure settlement after a CAB investigation. Kelly knew Cahill because, when he was 15, Cahill had spent some time in Kilrush on a holiday and got to know Kelly's sons.

The Dundons shelled out €10,000 – with half being paid upfront – to ensure that the job was done right; the money was divided between Campion and his passenger, Cahill. The going rate in Limerick for a professional hit was half that figure. An amateur hit, a simple shooting in the leg or a bad beating, was just a few hundred. But you got what you paid for.

The plan had been hatched weeks earlier and put into place meticulously. Cahill flew to Ireland a few days before the hit and met with his fellow conspirators. They went to Kilrush, County Clare, where Cahill claims they met local import/exporter Anthony Kelly.

Cahill also claims that Kelly showed him an automatic pistol and taught him how to use it. Automatic pistols have become one of the weapons of choice in Limerick. They are easy to conceal and can shoot – depending on the model – up to a dozen rounds in swift succession. They have one drawback – they tend to jerk upwards as they are fired. In the hands of an amateur, they can be wildly inaccurate. That is why several of the Limerick gangs have sent their hard men to Eastern Europe and the USA for specialist firearms training. The weapon Cahill was given for the hit was a 9mm automatic pistol.

'Put one in the cunt's head,' Cahill claims Kelly had said, laughing.

That Friday evening the man originally slated to ride the motorcycle arrived in Limerick from Dublin. He was late, as his bike was giving him trouble. When he heard that he was expected to be the getaway driver in a murder, he backed out. So Gary Campion was asked if he could step in. A notorious hard man, he willingly accepted the job.

Brian Fitzgerald's movements were well known to the gang. They had been watching him for weeks. That evening Dessie and John Dundon drove Cahill and Campion out to Brookhaven

Walk, Mill Road, and showed them where the Fitzgeralds lived. John Dundon pointed out some shrubbery where he said they could conceal themselves as they waited in ambush.

Then they went back into town, to Doc's nightclub. Cahill didn't know Brian Fitzgerald, so the Dundons pointed him out. Then Cahill and Campion left the club. They took the motorbike out to the Mill Road and pulled in to the side, hiding in the bushes as they had been instructed. Now it was a waiting game. It was after 1 a.m. They knew they had a few hours to wait, but they were being well paid for their troubles. It was Cahill's 28th birthday; he was celebrating it by ending another man's life.

*

Brian Fitzgerald had been enjoying a few days off. But that evening he was back on duty. Fridays were big nights in the club. Brian had his dinner, then bathed his two young sons and put them to bed. He stayed with them until they fell asleep. Then he got into his car and drove to work. It was about 8.10 p.m., his usual time. That left him in Doc's and ready for the night comfortably by 8.30 p.m.

The evening passed as usual. It was uneventful. The club opened, the people partied, closing time arrived and the party ended. By 2 a.m., throughout the city the nightclubs were closing, pouring their patrons out onto the cold and damp streets. In midwinter, people tend not to linger. They quickly dispersed, looking for taxis or chippers, or both. Doc's cleared out with the rest, but Brian and some of the staff remained behind to clear up. Friday is traditionally a busy night and the place had been thronged. It took over an hour to get the place in order. Glasses had to be cleared up, floors swept, the takings lodged in the safe.

Brian didn't know it, but his wife Alice was awake and waiting for him. She had woken at 2 a.m. to give one of the children a bottle and decided to stay up until her husband arrived home. He usually got home a little after three.

According to Caroline Daly, the bar manager at Doc's, a number of the staff left together at 3.15 a.m. Brian was among them. He gave them a lift home before turning for his own home. So it was about 3.50 a.m. when he pulled onto Mill Road and began to approach his house. He passed the motorcycle waiting in the shadows. According to Cahill, Dessie Dundon had phoned the hit team to warn them that their target was approaching. Though the roads were clear, Brian probably didn't spot the motorcycle slotting in a couple of car lengths behind him. He was not on the alert; he had done his part of the deal and felt the threat on his life had been lifted. They, on the other hand, were on full alert, thanks to Dessie's call.

Sitting inside, Alice Fitzgerald heard the jeep draw up and the door open.

Mr Fitzgerald pulled into his driveway and got out of his car. It was then he noticed that the motorcycle had pulled in close to him. He spotted the two men dismounting and immediately knew something was wrong. The bigger man, Cahill, was running towards him. Brian tried to keep the car between himself and the gunman, but Cahill was on him and armed. They struggled. In the melee, Brian managed to drop Cahill and he turned and ran for his life. But he had taken a bullet in the chest. Cahill had twisted his ankle but he got up and limped after the fleeing man.

Horrified, Alice was a witness to it all. She ran downstairs and heard her husband shout at his attacker, calling him a cunt. She saw two men in motorcycle helmets. One was stocky (Cahill). The other was slimmer (Campion). At one point, she rapped the phone on the glass to distract the attackers. One looked directly at her and she saw he had thick dark eyebrows that met in the middle. Many cultures see such eyebrows as a mark of evil, and they are the most distinctive feature on Gary Campion's face.

Alice desperately tried to dial for the Gardaí, but the phone was not working, so she had to get another handset. It was all delay.

Outside, Brian ran. He got 80 yards. A fit rugby player – fast but heavy – would cover that distance in perhaps twelve seconds, maybe a second or two longer. But Brian was in street clothes and haemorrhaging blood from his gaping chest wound. He was moving far slower than that, and faltering. He fell to the ground. Cahill walked up calmly to his prone victim, put the gun to the back of his head and pulled the trigger twice, applying the *coup de grâce*.

Windows lit up as shocked families were woken from their slumbers. The killer walked back to the motorcycle, got on behind the driver, then they revved up and were gone. They drove out of the city, but not far. Campion pulled down a laneway behind a garage and torched the getaway bike. Several witnesses reported the blaze. Then he took a taxi home to Pineview Gardens, Moyross. The taxi driver remembered Campion talking about visiting his grandfather, who was dying in hospital. Clearly, he wasn't too upset about his night's work.

Cahill left Limerick immediately and went to Dublin, from where he took the train to Belfast. After a few days he returned to the UK, arriving back in Liverpool.

*

By the time the first people got to Brian Fitzgerald, he was already dead. Alice had been out of the door within seconds. She ran to the car and saw that Brian was not there. Her initial thought was that he had been abducted by the two men. Then she looked up the road and saw the body on the ground.

Within minutes, the area was crawling with gardaí, and the blue lights of an ambulance were flashing. It was the start of the biggest murder investigation the city had seen since the murder of Garda Jerry McCabe.

Superintendent Willie Keane described the assassination as 'a most callous incident'. His detectives had recovered a number of 9mm shells at the scene but failed to locate the gun. The local detectives were joined by members of the National Bureau of Criminal Investigation from Dublin. Extensive door-to-door enquiries failed to generate any leads, but the investigators knew that the killing had been orchestrated by the McCarthy-Dundon gang.

Doc's closed for the weekend as a mark of respect, and a large crowd attended Brian Fitzgerald's removal to St Mary's Church, Athlunkard. More than 1,000 mourners attended the funeral on Monday, 2 December. The people of Limerick rallied behind the innocent man killed for doing his job. A trust fund was set up to provide for his family, and Sean O'Doherty, owner of Doc's nightclub, announced that their fundraising target was €100,000.

He also added, in an interview with the *Limerick Leader*:

We will continue our policy of ensuring that no drugs get into our premises and that everyone can have a good night out and a good time. We had this policy before Brian arrived, and it will continue after his passing.

A few days after Christmas, the club held a fundraiser for Brian's family. It was a sell-out. Brian's widow attended, along with his brother Ger, who told the *Leader*:

We didn't have any Christmas this year and the memorial night in Doc's just made us feel a bit brighter about things. I couldn't believe that so many people turned up. It was great. We sat down and had a few drinks and people told funny stories about Brian. We really enjoyed ourselves and it was good to be able to talk and laugh about him. I always knew that Brian had lots of friends, but we were all struck by the extent of his popularity. My mother told me the following day that she was delighted to hear all the nice things that people had to say about him.

In December, gardaí recovered what they believed was the murder weapon. Some time later, James Cahill was arrested on an unrelated charge. Gardaí believed they had the gunman, but he was saying nothing. For a while, it appeared that the investigation had stalled, even though the entire city knew who was behind the murder of the popular family man.

In 2005, the big breakthrough came: James Cahill decided to

confess. He was serving five years on a firearms offence and in May he contacted the Gardaí and told them he wanted to talk. He claimed that he was hearing voices in his cell and they were telling him to come clean. It is possible the callous killer got an attack of conscience. But it is equally likely that he got an attack of nerves. He knew he was a threat to the McCarthy-Dundon gang and his evidence could destroy them. Perhaps he feared that they would take him out before he was tempted. He appeared edgy to the gardaí who spoke to him and said that 'they' (presumably the McCarthy-Dundons) were trying to kill him.

Whatever the true motivation, he stuck to the version involving voices screaming at him. He said the voices only went away when he told the truth. He made a detailed statement to the Gardaí in May and a second in November, outlining his involvement in the Brian Fitzgerald murder. Some of his ramblings were incoherent. He claimed that gardaí and prison officers were trying to kill him. But, on the facts of the murder, the Gardaí had no doubts.

In November 2006, Cahill's murder trial opened in the Central Criminal Court in Dublin. He pleaded guilty. Cahill, whose address was given as Highfield Lane, Quinton, Birmingham, told the court he was willing to testify against the others involved in the killing. He was sentenced to life imprisonment.

Working with what Cahill had given them, the Gardaí began to build their case. Eventually, four men were charged with murder. The four accused of murdering Brian Fitzgerald at Brookhaven Walk, Mill Road, on 29 November 2002, were: Gary Campion (24) of Pineview Gardens, Moyross; John (27) and Desmond (23) Dundon, both from Ballinacurra Weston; and Anthony Kelly (50) of Kilrush. All four denied the charge.

Towards the end of October 2007, the trial opened. Cahill was the star witness for the prosecution and was escorted to the court by four armed members of the Garda Emergency Response Unit. He gave evidence for 40 explosive minutes. His account of the killing, given in court, is harrowing: 'I came out of the bushes as he was coming down the road. There was an argument by his jeep, and he ran into the road.'

He said that as Brian Fitzgerald tried to kick in a neighbour's door, he fired a number of shots over the roof of the car at him.

'After a while, I walked over and I shot him in the head.'

The trial, which lasted a number of weeks, was a sensation and attracted huge media interest. If the prosecution was successful, two key members of the McCarthy-Dundons would be convicted of murder, as would Anthony Kelly.

Cahill told the jury that he had been driven out to Kilrush and went to the home of Anthony Kelly, whom he knew. He said Anthony Kelly gave him a gun and showed him how to use it.

> He was clicking it back and showing me how to use it, the safety and that. He said that he didn't want to know what we were doing, but not to mess it up. He just said, don't mess around.

Cahill claimed that he had never used a gun before – just a shotgun for shooting rabbits. He said he had fired blanks once during an armed robbery, but aside from that guns were new to him.

He described the events of the evening of the murder: being driven to Fitzgerald's neighbourhood; identifying him outside Doc's; waiting for him to arrive home; and the scuffle that took place near his car.

He couldn't recall how many times he had fired, but he kept firing until the gun began to click. After the shooting, Cahill and Campion rode to where they had a red Mondeo hidden and Cahill took off. He had a shower, then drove to Dublin, leaving the car in Heuston Station. He got a lift across the city to Connolly Station, then took the train for Belfast. He left Campion to dispose of the motorcycle. In Belfast, Cahill met John Dundon. They flew out to Manchester, where they met Anthony Kelly.

Cahill's evidence was compelling, but soon his credibility took a severe blow. He admitted that he had made a statement about his involvement in the murder because the voices in his head told him he would only get peace if he came clean. The voices started when he was doing solitary confinement as part of his five-year sentence for possession of a machine gun. He claimed the gun had been used in a hit in Dublin for which he was paid €50,000.

He said the voices referred to him as a paedophile and a supergrass, and seemed to come from the television, asking him questions and answering him back. He started seeing a psychologist in 2005, but it wasn't helping: 'I was getting flashbacks. I could see the murder in pictures.'

He then astonished the jury by claiming he had been involved in six different murder plots by the time Brian Fitzgerald was killed. Five of the hits were in Ireland and one in the UK. However, evidence was produced by the defence to show that Cahill was a compulsive liar who had acquired the nickname 'Billy Bullshit' in his native Birmingham.

Detective Garda Darragh O'Sullivan told the court that Gary Campion, one of the four accused, told him that the state's star witness, James Cahill, had 'killed four or five people in England. He came over to Ireland and was doing hits.' He described Cahill as a 'mad man'.

'He's a serial killer. He should be signed away. He's involved in about five killings.'

The detective added that Campion denied any involvement in the murder and claimed that the burnt-out motorcycle was similar to his, but not his.

Detective Eamon O'Neill told the court that Anthony Kelly claimed to have had a meeting on the day of the murder with his accountant, but he had cancelled that because he forgot some vital papers. That night, he used his home gym and went to bed early.

The trial took an unexpected turn then, when the judge, Mr Justice Peter Charleton, directed the jury to acquit one of the accused. He said that the evidence of Cahill did not show John Dundon present at the time of the murder. But he reminded the jury that this decision had no bearing on the guilt or innocence of the other three accused.

As the trial neared its end, Sean Gillane, prosecuting, reminded the jury of one central, indisputable fact: 'A core truth that is unchallenged and unchallengeable is that James Martin Cahill, the chief prosecution witness, had shot and killed Mr Fitzgerald. Cahill is currently serving a life sentence for the murder of Mr Fitzgerald.'

He said that if the jurors worked backwards they could see that other facts sprang from this one central fact. There was enough truth in Cahill's evidence to spot the facts that were linked to that truth. He urged the jury not to discount Cahill's evidence because they were repulsed by him.

Conor Devally, for the defence, countered by claiming Cahill was a 'dangerous, dangerous' witness, who sought to please those who had authority over him – such as the Gardaí and the prison authorities – by telling them what they wanted to hear. He had changed his story to make himself more fascinating to the Gardaí and his psychologists.

The jury retired for four hours but came nowhere near a decision. So they were sent to a hotel for the night and the wait went on for the four accused, their families and the family of Brian Fitzgerald. When the jury returned in the morning, they did not take long to complete their deliberations. After another hour, they returned to the court. It was a mixed bag for the prosecution. Just one of the three remaining accused was convicted. Gary Campion was found guilty.

Both Anthony Kelly and Dessie Dundon were acquitted. Kelly, who had spent the last year in jail awaiting the trial, was now free to go. Dundon, on the other hand, was serving a life sentence for the murder of Kieran Keane, the head of the rival Keane-Collopy gang, so the acquittal made little difference to his life. The earlier acquittal of his brother was also academic; John Dundon was serving a four-year sentence for threatening a prison officer. Despite the result of the murder trial, two of the Dundons were off the street.

Outside the courthouse, Eugene O'Kelly, Anthony Kelly's solicitor, said that his client was grateful to the jury for upholding his innocence, but angry with the state for losing a year of his life 'on the word of a self-professed perjuring, perverted killer'.

The solicitor added: 'It is quite extraordinary that this man's freedom has been denied to him for the past year on the rantings and the ravings of a demented psychopath.'

Campion and Cahill are the only ones convicted so far of the murder. Senior gardaí indicated that the case would remain an open file; they believed that other people might eventually be charged in connection with Brian Fitzgerald's death. So far that has not happened.

Gary Campion got a life sentence. He was also awaiting trial on a second murder charge and would eventually become the only hit man in the state to be convicted of murder twice. But those were not his only brushes with the law. In 2005, he had been convicted of threatening to have a prison officer killed. He told the officer he had already shot people in Limerick for €10,000 and would have no problem spending twice that to have the officer killed.

Campion came from a family steeped in crime. His brother William is serving life for the brutal murder of a pensioner in Clare in 1998. Patrick 'Paud' Skehan was 68 and living alone in an isolated farmhouse near Bridgetown, County Clare, when William Campion and some associates broke into his house. They left the elderly bachelor beaten and unconscious, bound with cable ties and hanging upside down from the stair banisters. He died two months later from his injuries.

Campion's other brother, Noel, was associated with the McCarthy-Dundons too. A convicted armed robber, he was shot and killed by members of his own gang in April 2007 because he was trying to branch out on his own in the drugs business.

Cahill, who got his life sentence two years previously, was also mired in crime. In 1999, he had received ten years for stealing jewellery worth £300,000 from Hartmann Jewellers in Galway during an armed raid. But that conviction was overturned because the identification evidence was shaky. He had ten other convictions in Ireland and the UK for offences including possession of firearms, burglary, larceny, causing criminal damage, interfering with a car and assault causing actual harm. His claim that he was involved in up to six murders was probably fantasy.

Those were the two that were convicted. Those that got away were something of a rogues' gallery. Fifty-year-old Kilrush man Anthony Kelly had been coming to Garda attention for twenty years or more. He was one of the first targets of the CAB, set up after the murder of Veronica Guerin to go after the gangs where it hurts – their pockets. In 1997, he made a six-figure settlement with the CAB.

In 1984, he had been convicted of living off the earnings of prostitution. It was a set-up that would not have been out of place on Craggy Island. He drove a van around rural farms with a mattress in the back, offering a mobile brothel service. He did nine months for that. In August 2003, he survived an assassination attempt when his house came under fire from a gunman. He does have a respectable side: he is the director of an import business in Kilrush and travels regularly to the UK, the Continent and China for furniture and household goods.

Dessie Dundon, though less than half the age of Kelly, had a more impressive rap sheet. Aged 23, he was already serving a life sentence for the 2003 murder of gangland boss Kieran Keane. He played a key role in luring Keane to his death. A year earlier, Dundon had been found guilty of assault and sentenced to 15 months. He had attacked gardaí with blocks and a slash hook after they went to his house to retrieve ponies he had kidnapped from a circus. Prior to that, he had got nine months for larceny.

His older brother John, 27, was doing a four-year sentence for threatening to kill Owen Treacy, a witness to the Kieran Keane killing. He also threatened prison officers. He absconded to England before the sentence could be executed and had to be extradited back to Ireland.

*

As for the Fitzgeralds, they have had to cope as best they can. They have taken some solace in the support the people of Limerick have shown them, but their loss is enormous. Brian was one of the first completely innocent victims of the vicious gangland feuding. He would not be the last, as we shall see.

In a cruel twist of fate that shows how closely entwined events in Limerick can be, one of Brian Fitzgerald's cousins was also murdered. In May 2003 – just a month after Brian had been posthumously honoured with a Best of Irish award for heroism – Robert Fitzgerald, a cousin of the nightclub security head, was murdered in Cliona Park, Moyross. The 23 year old was a big, friendly man who was not a career criminal and had no links to the gangs. He had been in a bit of youthful trouble, but nothing more. As a garda said: 'He was a nice, likeable sort of chap. He only came to our attention over a minor issue and was not a major criminal or anything of the sort. He was very well liked in the area and very popular.'

Despite this, someone lay in wait for him as he returned to the home he shared with his grandmother and ruthlessly gunned him down. Several people heard the shots, but no one bothered to phone the Gardaí. That is the sort of place Moyross had become. It was six hours before his cold corpse was found, just yards from home. No one has been charged in connection with that crime.

8

BROTHERS IN ARMS

The Life and Crimes of Michael and Anthony Kelly

JEKYLL AND HYDE, the story of a good man with a dark side (or a dark man with a good outer veneer), could have been written about the Kelly brothers.

I knew them both personally, particularly Michael. He could be charming, friendly and informative, and was open about his failings and crimes. I interviewed them extensively, again particularly Michael, and I came to know the extraordinary mix of good and bad that made up his nature. This chapter draws on those interviews.

Anthony Kelly – who is unrelated to the Kilrush man charged in connection with the death of bouncer Brian Fitzgerald – is a big, affable man, a gentle giant. He has a round, friendly face on big shoulders and hands like small shovels. He smiles a lot and in the dangerous parts of Limerick he is liked and respected. But if you scratch beneath the surface you can find a different side to Anthony Kelly.

'He was very friendly and polite,' one senior detective from Cork told me. He had interviewed Kelly as part of a murder investigation in the southern capital. 'But he was the coldest man I ever met. I knew I was with a very dangerous man.'

Anthony Kelly and his older brother Michael are part of the reason Limerick has had to live down its Stab City nickname for the past few decades. They were the last of the ordinary decent criminals – bank-robbers and burglars – and they dominated the city throughout the '70s and '80s.

Then they went legit, setting up a security firm that many believed was a cover for a protection racket. Many more said they had gone straight and were providing good employment in their impoverished back yard. Michael even ran for the city council, topping the poll. The fairytale transformation seemed complete.

Then the taxman found some discrepancies and Michael was back behind bars. It broke him; he was out only a few weeks when, apparently, he took his own life. The business collapsed and Anthony found himself back in the ghetto of Southill.

He's still there, in a small house at the top of the estate. Inside it is neat and tidy. In the cosy sitting room, there is a big fish tank and an even bigger television. Large curtains fall from ceiling to floor and stretch from one wall to the other. He never opens the curtains in the front room. The curtains give an air of normality to the house. When you draw them, you see that they are hiding not a window but a double layer of railway sleepers – big balks of wood, about a foot deep.

'They could throw in a grenade, or rake the house with machine-gun fire, and I wouldn't be disturbed,' he grinned when I spoke to him in 2011.

The house is a fortress. But when the estate is quiet and certain people are off the streets, the sleepers go into storage and the living room becomes normal again. Being able to put such precautions in place is part of life in Southill.

In 2009, someone did try to fire through his windows. At least, that is how Anthony tells it. It was early one morning and his grown-up daughter had been involved in an incident with two local men. They arrived outside Anthony's door and produced a gun. In the ensuing melee, one of the men ended up shot in the leg. The two men disputed this version, saying that they were unarmed and the gun was produced by Anthony. The court believed Anthony.

At various times, Anthony has been charged with murder (after the stabbing to death of two brothers) and assault with a deadly weapon (after a humane killer from a slaughterhouse was used on a man). He has been convicted of numerous assaults and burglaries.

His brother Mikey, known as the 'Hard Man', had a reputation as one of the toughest street fighters in Limerick (though many would say that Anthony was the better fighter). He too was a suspect in the disappearance of a young man, was charged but not convicted of murder and spent years in jail on all sorts of criminal charges.

When you think of crime in Limerick, you think of the Kellys. Mikey was the older by five years, but in Anthony he found an eager and skilled apprentice. Mikey had the hard-man reputation, but people recognised the darkness in Anthony.

One of the employees of their security firm (and a distant cousin) summed up the brothers neatly. He said that Mikey had a tendency to lose his temper and shout a lot. But if you knew you were right, you could shout back at him and fight your corner. Anthony rarely ever raised his voice – but no one argued with him.

Jekyll and Hyde – it could have been the story of the Kellys.

*

A combination of misfortune and alcoholism plunged the Kelly family into hard times when the boys were still young. Michael found himself thrust into the role of bread-winner. He took delivery jobs and other odd work, but he supplemented this with thieving. He stole from the butcher he delivered for, he stole money from the local milkman and pilfered fruit and vegetables from the local shops.

Michael's father found out and took the young boy down to the Garda station.

'That strained our relationship,' Michael admitted to me. 'But I fed the family for two years. My father was drinking at the time. I gave him some money every week and he turned a blind eye to things.'

Michael also gave his mother money. While other members of the family remained in school and eventually got on in life, necessity was turning Michael into a career criminal. In his younger brother Anthony – five years his junior – he found a willing accomplice. The two grew into notorious trouble-makers.

Michael became known as Mucky John (John was his second name) because he had discovered the power of protection rackets. If you were painting a wall, you would have to throw him a few shillings, or you would come back and find the wall had been pelted with mud bombs. He even began to steal from his neighbours. One Christmas he managed to make off with the turkey from the house next door.

Anthony, being small, was agile and that fitted in with his older brother's plans. One favourite ploy of theirs was to stuff a sack into a chimney. As the house below filled with smoke and the inhabitants ran out, Michael would run in and take whatever was lying handy – a packet of biscuits, some coins, whatever came to hand.

But the cruel streak that was to characterise the grown man was beginning to emerge at an early age. At nine, he kidnapped the greyhound of a man who offended him and tied up the dog in the back of his house. The dog starved to death. Michael also got involved in lots of fights, losing out to bigger boys, but never backing down.

When he was 12, Michael carried out his first proper burglary. For a change, seven-year-old Anthony was not with him. Instead, he recruited one of his other brothers. His brother climbed onto the roof of a small grocer on New Street and slipped through a skylight. He opened the shop for Michael, who made off with cigarettes and sweets, as well as the contents of the till.

Michael might simply have been going through a stage of delinquency, except for one event that changed the course of his life. To solve the local housing problem, Limerick created the ghetto of Southill. Set on rolling hills on the south of the city, it could have been idyllic. Instead, it was an enclave of disadvantage. The houses were small, with no facilities for the young population. Hundreds of families – with no jobs, no security and problems with drink and drugs – were bundled together and ignored by City Hall.

'The move to Southill was the worst day of my life,' Michael recalled years later.

Within a year, he was drinking heavily, though still in his early teens. He had given up on school and was breaking into houses and shops regularly. He was a one-man crime wave and he was constantly in street fights. He came to the attention of the local gardaí.

In an attempt to get his life back on track, he followed his father's footsteps and joined the army. But the discipline rankled with him and he left within a year. It was 1973: now he was mature, tough, unemployed and angry with the world. The Michael Kelly Limerick came to know and fear was born.

By the late '70s, Michael Kelly was making a good living, alternating between house break-ins and armed robberies. He had a regular partner in crime, the teenage Eddie Ryan. They were not afraid to threaten people with knives, axes or hammers – whatever would get them to hand over cash. Violence was becoming a way of life, with theft of video machines especially lucrative.

Kelly's partner, Eddie Ryan, was as thuggish and violent as Kelly himself. In 1978, however, Ryan was convicted of manslaughter and sent away for five years, leaving Kelly alone; he began to rely more on younger brother Anthony.

He was also cementing his reputation as 'the Hard Man' – the toughest street fighter in Limerick. In 1976, he was jailed for assault. He got out and was sent back in almost immediately, again for assault. Then he got two years for robbing a petrol station close to his home in Southill. It was a crime of convenience, as he recalled when I interviewed him in 2002:

I was working in town at the time, and I'd get the bus home at 3.30. There was a petrol station beside the Galvone pub. If I was going out for the night and needed a bit of cash, I'd walk in and take a few bob from the till. That evening I took it all. I got two years for that job.

Between spells inside, Kelly resumed his thieving and his fighting.

Small feuds between families are a feature of life in Limerick, and Kelly became embroiled in a running dispute with a family of travellers – the McCarthys of the Cooperage, a halting site off the Dublin Road. The McCarthys were related to settled McCarthys in St Mary's Park, an old area of council housing that has spawned a lot of Limerick's criminality, and other McCarthys on Hyde Road (who later formed the nucleus of the notorious McCarthy-Dundon gang).

One day, one of Michael's brothers was beaten by four members of the McCarthy family. Michael sought them out and laid into them with fists and feet. He won the fight but the tensions escalated.

In 1982, Kelly stole a neighbour's car to carry out a robbery on a petrol station in Tipperary. He returned to the city and pulled into a petrol station to top up the car, before returning it to the neighbour. Needless to say, the neighbour never made a complaint. But Kelly had been spotted driving the missing car. That night, he was confronted in his local pub by a number of men, including Thomas 'Ronnie' Coleman, from Ballinacurra Weston.

Coleman used to go around town thinking he was a hard man. He used to take liberties, stuck glass ashtrays into people's faces. At the end of the night the band were playing my favourite song, 'Sweet Caroline'. I felt a hand on my shoulder and moved. I got it in the mouth. Someone smashed a pint glass into me. It was lucky I did move, because it would have got my throat if I hadn't turned. I got 157 stitches inside and out. I did not see it, and I did not make a complaint.

On his recovery (the scars remained until his death), Kelly became convinced Coleman had glassed him. This is something Coleman's family vehemently deny. Whatever the truth, it heralded the start of a three-month splurge of violence. Not all of the violence was down to the Kellys, but they were blamed for three of the four fatal stabbings that took place.

On 13 October 1982, someone stabbed Thomas Coleman to death at his home at Hyde Avenue. Twenty-four-year-old Coleman shared a caravan with his wife and seven-month-old son. Self-employed and described by neighbours as a quiet and inoffensive man, he was not a criminal, but was associated with some of the families that Kelly was feuding with.

The night of 13 October was cold and wet. The streets were dark and deserted. During the evening Coleman was disturbed by a knock on his door. The man outside identified himself as 'John Daly', and Coleman opened the door. A burly man with a knife was standing outside. He lunged at Coleman, stabbing him in the chest. Coleman sank to the floor as the man made his escape. As he fell to the ground, the dying man was heard to shout, 'Mikey Kelly!' A neighbour witnessed the attack but could not identify the assailant.

Coleman managed to pull himself upright and staggered to a neighbour's gate but collapsed again. He was pronounced dead on arrival at Limerick Regional Hospital.

The murder hunt was led by an experienced detective, Michael Browne. An abrasive veteran from Kerry, he knew every crook and hoodlum in the city – and was as tough as any of them. He had a chequered history with the Kellys over the years. They cordially hated each other, but he invited both brothers to his retirement party when he left the Gardaí. Anthony went; Michael declined.

Back in 1982, there were no mixed signals. Detective Browne surveyed the crime scene, the blood-soaked ground around the caravan door hidden from the rain under blue canvas, and he knew who he was looking for. Michael Kelly had been heard around town threatening to sort out Coleman after the alleged glassing incident. While gardaí busied themselves taking witness statements and collecting forensic evidence, Browne took some men with him and headed for Southill.

That evening, Kelly was on babysitting duty when the door of his home at Lilac Court was smashed in and raided by gardaí, including his old adversary Detective Sergeant Browne. Kelly told the gardaí he had never been involved in a fight with Coleman.

Kelly recalled the night of the arrest:

I used to rob places, hide the liquor in the house, in the washing-machine and all sorts of places so that the Gardaí wouldn't find it. At the time I was playing soccer with Southend United, the Southill team. I was training that night, with about 16 other lads. I came in from training at 8.30 p.m. and Jacqueline said she was going to the bingo and could I mind the child. I was in bed, with the child beside me. The next thing the door was off the hinges and the house was full of gardaí.

'Where were you tonight?' they asked. 'I was babysitting and training,' I said. They left, but an hour later they were back and they arrested me. Just as I was being arrested the wife came back and I told her to mind the child. I was brought to Edward Street Garda Station and made my statement of alibi. I said that I had never used a weapon in my life. But Michael Browne never checked my alibi.

Michael was placed in custody and charged with the murder of Thomas Coleman. The state was confident it had the right man. Coleman, in his dying breath, had identified his attacker. But, aside from that, their evidence was non-existent. And Coleman could not be put on the stand. But at least one hard man was off the streets.

Barely two months passed before there was another vicious stabbing in the city. This time it was a double tragedy: two young brothers lost their lives in an altercation at the Treaty Bar in Thomondgate, a short walk from the city centre. And another Kelly – Michael's brother Anthony – was in the frame. The *Irish Times* informed its readers on Monday, 13 December:

'An inter-family feud is believed to have led to the death by stabbing of two brothers in a public house in Limerick at the weekend.'

Two members of the McCarthy family had been viciously hacked to death in a gory fight that spilt out onto the street. But that is only scratching the surface of the full story. It began much earlier. The simmering feud between the Kellys and the McCarthys had steadily escalated over a number of months. At the subsequent murder trial, Pa McCarthy admitted as much.

He said that, on 27 November, Kelly bumped into Sammy McCarthy in the Treaty Bar. Words were exchanged, and the two men went outside to an alleyway and squared off. Pa spotted them leaving and followed.

'I just went down to see what was happening. I thought Anthony Kelly was going to have a fight with Sammy. I wanted to separate them.'

Cross-examining, Senior Counsel Patrick MacEntee said that Kelly was then confronted by a number of McCarthy brothers. 'Are you suggesting that what you were doing was really about mediation, about trying to make peace?'

'That is what it was about,' said Pa McCarthy.

In the end, there was no fight. Anthony Kelly struck Sammy McCarthy with his fist and ran off, saying that there were too many of them.

'I will come back later and I will not be on my own,' he said.

Later that night, the McCarthys were drinking in the Tudor Lounge, a local pub, when Anthony Kelly arrived with a hatchet. He attacked Sammy. Pa ran to his brother's assistance and punched Kelly on the head. Kelly responded by hitting him twice on the head with the back of the axe. He fell to the ground under the blows, and as he lay there he raised his hands to try to protect his face.

Pa's sister, Anne O'Brien, remembered the night vividly. She later told the court at Anthony Kelly's murder trial that her brother Sammy was very drunk that night. He came over to her

and she got up and danced with him. After the dance, she sat down and he went back to the bar. Moments later she heard him shout: 'Anne, save me!'

She turned and saw her brother staggering, practically crawling.

'There was a man chasing him with a hatchet. It was in his right hand. I saw him [Sammy] getting hit on the left shoulder with the back of the hatchet.'

She grabbed at the man with the hatchet to try to stop him, but he turned and struck her in the eye with his fist. She called out to another of her brothers, Tommy, who was standing at the bar with a friend, Eugene Glasheen. She then ran from the pub. When she came back in, she was told that a third one of her brothers, Patrick (known as Pa), was injured in the ladies' toilet. When she checked, he was bleeding from the forehead and hand.

On seeing what had happened to her brothers, she went to another bar where she knew her brother John was drinking. They returned and took Sammy back to her mother's house on Colmcille Street in St Mary's Park. From there, they went up the street to her brother Tommy's house. Eugene Glasheen and Sean Moloney, two friends, were also there.

At the trial, she was asked by barrister Patrick MacEntee, who was representing Anthony Kelly: 'Would I be right in saying they were having a council of war? They were discussing revenge?'

'They were discussing what happened,' Anne O'Brien replied.

The four brothers – Pa, Sammy, Tommy and Christy – along with Glasheen and Moloney, bundled into a car and drove off. They were heavily armed. There were two slash hooks, a wicked-looking knife and an iron bar in the car. But the men were spotted by gardaí and pulled over. They told the disbelieving gardaí that they were on their way to the hospital to get Sammy checked out after the injuries he had received in the bar fight earlier that evening. But the bleeding had stopped, so they were returning home. Asked about the slash hooks, they said that those were for cutting holly as Christmas was only a month away.

Gardaí believed they were actually on a hunt for Anthony Kelly.

'Were they going to beat him up or kill him?' Barrister MacEntee asked Anne O'Brien.

'They would not be up to killing,' she said.

Pa told the court that they were not looking for Anthony Kelly that night when they were stopped by the Gardaí. But under cross-examination he changed his story and admitted that they hoped to give Kelly a beating.

'But we were not a killer pack out to track down Anthony Kelly for the purpose of murdering him,' he said.

Asked why he had not gone to the Gardaí after being attacked with a hatchet, Pa McCarthy said: 'I did not want to tell the police what Kelly had done to me. I had heard about the Kellys and that they were dangerous. If I had involved the police, I would not be able to walk the streets. I was in dread of my life.'

A fortnight would pass before the McCarthys met Kelly again. On 11 December, Kelly was with his girlfriend Elizabeth Roche. They went out for a drink at Hassett's Bar, a popular pub on Hassett's Cross, about 20 minutes from the centre of town. On a busy road, the pub was between the traditional old areas of Thomondgate and St Mary's Park and the new council estate of Moyross. It was on the north side of the city, well away from Kelly's usual stamping-ground.

As they left to go out, Kelly strapped a knife to a string attached to his waist. He assured Ms Roche that he was not looking for trouble, just taking a precaution. They met some people at Hassett's Bar, including Ms Roche's aunt, Pauline Ward; the group persuaded him to join them for a few scoops at the Treaty Bar. The Treaty Bar is an old traditional bar close to the Treaty Stone on Thomond Bridge, a quick stroll from the city centre. Kelly was reluctant because he did not want to bump into the McCarthys, but he accompanied his companions.

They arrived at the Treaty Bar and settled down around a table. The night was growing late and it was approaching last orders. The door of the pub opened and in walked Sammy McCarthy. He appeared to be drunk, but he spotted Anthony Kelly and immediately left. A few minutes later, just before closing time, he returned with two of his brothers, Tommy and Pa.

Publican Michael Higgins, the joint owner of the premises, was at the door as the three brothers arrived. He was trying to keep people out as the pub would be closing shortly. But Tommy McCarthy pushed past him, throwing him off balance, and the three brothers forced their way through into the pub.

The sequence of events from then on is open to interpretation. Many people gave evidence, but, as some of them were closely connected with the victim, their evidence could have been tainted. And many people, mysteriously, were using the toilets and missed the entire altercation. One retired detective joked to me: 'They were all in the toilet when the row broke out. It must have been the biggest toilet in Ireland!'

It seems that Tommy picked up a stool and rushed at Anthony Kelly, striking him on the back of the head. At least two of the McCarthy brothers appear to have been armed with stones, while the third also had something in his hand.

Kelly evaded the first assault, then jumped onto a seat or bench in the pub and acquired a knife – either the one around his waist, or another one. He began shouting and roaring at his attackers, saying: 'Come here, ye bastards!' He was swinging the knife wildly.

According to Pa, as his brother Tommy entered the pub, Kelly spotted him and went for him, swiping at him with a knife, but this contradicts many of the other accounts. Tommy fought back and Pa lifted a stone he found on the floor of the pub and hit Kelly several times on the head.

'He had nearly taken my life two weeks previous with a hatchet,' he told the court.

However, the likelihood of finding a stone on the floor of a city centre pub was remote, so it is far more likely the stone – described in court as a lump of masonry – came in with the McCarthys.

Pa said that someone grabbed him from behind at that point and he saw Kelly stab Tommy with a knife, once.

Tommy was staggering, and blood was pouring from his side. I broke loose and ran for Sammy. He was trying to lift himself off the ground. I took him outside the door and ran back but I could not get in. Then the police arrived and arrested me.

Asked in court why he had gone to the Treaty Bar that night, Pa said that he had gone with his wife and his brothers, Sammy and Tommy, for one last drink before closing time. He denied that they had gone there because Sammy had told them Kelly was inside.

'What was to stop you all from retreating when you saw Anthony Kelly in the pub?' he was asked.

'Why should we retreat like that?' he answered.

He said that no member of the family had brought a knife or a weapon to the pub that night.

We were not looking for trouble. After I had helped Sammy, who had been stabbed, I went back to save my brother Tommy's life, but I could not get back in the door. I went across the road to where Sammy was lying, and the police came and arrested me.

Thomas Anthony Dillon, who was in the bar and knew the McCarthys, gave the court a different account of how the fight broke out.

Tommy picked up a stool and ran towards Anthony Kelly. The next thing I remember is Kelly was on the ground and three people were standing over him. One had something in his hand and hit Kelly on the back of the head.

Mr Dillon said that he caught hold of Tommy's arm and said: 'For fuck sake, Tommy, it's three to one.' Tommy told him: 'Tony, it's none of your business.'

'Everything was breaking out,' said Mr Dillon. 'Glasses were flying, and tables. Everyone was screaming about the women.'

Later he saw Tommy on the floor of the pub, bleeding.

Elizabeth Roche told the court that when she was getting ready to go out that night with Kelly she had seen him tying a knife to his waist with a piece of string. When he stood, the knife was hidden by his jumper and coat.

'I asked him what he was doing with it, and he said he was not going to use it,' she added.

She described their move from Hassett's Bar to the Treaty Bar: '[Anthony] said that he did not want to go to the Treaty Bar because there could be trouble. He said he had been threatened by the three McCarthys some time before.'

Ms Roche remembered Sammy McCarthy hitting Kelly on the back of the head.

> I think he fell back onto a seat then, I am not sure. All I saw after that was Anthony getting on top of a seat. He had a knife. He had one with him that night. I don't know if that was the knife he had.

She said that Kelly was attacked by three people without provocation and was not looking for trouble.

Ms Roche's aunt, Pauline Ward, said that three men attacked Kelly. Moments later she saw him with a knife in his hand and tried to get it off him.

> I said, 'Anthony, give me the knife. It is dangerous.' He did not answer. He was pure wild. He was standing up on a seat with his two hands in the air, and he kept screaming words I did not understand.

Another witness, Janette Crawford, said that after the row broke out she saw Anthony Kelly standing on a bench with a knife in his hand. It had a black handle and was about seven or eight inches long.

'I saw him jump off the seat. He was shouting something about "Get out of the way," and he was swinging the knife back and forth,' she said.

She added that, before Kelly jumped off the bench, Tommy McCarthy was walking towards the door. Kelly ran towards him.

'That is when he stuck the knife in Tommy.'

She said Kelly stabbed Tommy in the lower right-hand side of his back.

'I saw Tommy walk a little bit, and then he fell to the ground.'

Patrick O'Riordan was one of the barmen on duty that night. He said that he saw a man holding a bloodstained knife after the fight broke out.

'The fight was so violent I did not attempt to intervene,' he told the court. He added that the man with the knife was enraged and frightened.

Joan Griffin remembered being in the bar when Sammy, Tommy and Pa McCarthy came into the pub: 'Tommy took up a stool and ran towards Anthony Kelly. I saw Sammy with something in his hand, and he was swinging it.'

Martin McCarthy, a cousin of the three brothers, said that he saw his three cousins swiping at Anthony Kelly. He gave witness that:

At closing time Tommy and Sammy rushed towards Anthony Kelly. They were swiping at him. The next thing I seen was Tommy staggering and falling to the ground. He seemed to be all blood.

Afterwards Kelly jumped up on a seat with a knife in his hand. He started swiping the knife and swinging it. He jumped down after five minutes and threw the table up towards Tommy, who was on the ground.

Tommy Connors said he saw Sammy, Tommy and Pa involved in some 'digging' (punching) in the pub: 'Sammy was on a chair kicking someone and Tommy was fighting, but I couldn't see who he was fighting with.'

Then a man he had never seen before jumped on a chair with what appeared to be a knife. He saw Tommy pointing his fists at this man and Sammy kicking him. He didn't see what Pa did, but he was aware that Pa was also involved in the attack on the man.

Catherine Coady's account was at considerable variance with the others. She said that Anthony Kelly was sitting among a group of women when he was attacked. But she didn't think the attack was unprovoked. She said that she had heard Kelly threatening one of the McCarthy brothers at the Treaty Bar a little earlier. She was at the bar chatting to Sammy when Kelly approached from behind and said to Sam: 'I will get you for what you done to me, and for what the rest of you done to me.'

He spoke calmly and did not appear to be in a temper, she said. Sammy replied: 'Go away and fuck off. I came here for a quiet drink and I want no trouble.' Kelly then walked over to the bar. She did admit that Sammy, who was a friend of hers (and his brother was married to her cousin), was drunk and was talking foolishly at the bar.

From the conflicting accounts there is a thread of consistency. It appears Kelly was sitting at a table with a group of people when Tommy McCarthy struck him from behind with a stool. The other brothers joined in the attack. Kelly managed to evade the initial attack and got a knife – probably the one he brought with him that evening. He stood on a seat and began to swing wildly. Then he attacked two of the brothers. Sammy was stabbed first, under the armpit. He was dragged outside by his family. Then Tommy was stabbed, in the back. He fell on the floor of the bar.

Mr Higgins, the proprietor, said that after the fight – which lasted only minutes – he heard someone shouting at him to call an ambulance. He saw a man bleeding near the jukebox. That was Tommy. Sammy was being attended to by his family.

Ambulances were quickly on the scene, as were the Gardaí. Kelly immediately fled with Ms Roche. Pa McCarthy was arrested briefly. Both brothers were removed to Barrington's Hospital, a small hospital within a mile of the scene. Sammy died at 12.30 a.m., while Tommy lingered on a further hour before dying.

The scenes in the hospital were chaotic, as the family converged on the casualty unit. Garda William Cummins was on duty that night; he described the scene as the two brothers lay dying as 'bedlam'. Relatives crowded the hospital and were in a very excited state. He told the court:

> I tried to placate them as best as I could. When Tommy was brought in the McCarthys got very troublesome. There was total bedlam in the waiting room. They were trying to go from the waiting room into the casualty unit. John McCarthy broke a glass door dividing the two.

He needed the assistance of the hospital porter and a number of nurses to calm the situation down.

Later that night three of the brothers – Pa, Christy and John – set out to find Anthony Kelly. They broke three windows of a house in Keyes Park, but it was the wrong house. They had come prepared – there were impromptu weapons in their car. But they would not have found Kelly; he did not go home that evening. He went to the house of an uncle, James Kenny, on Swallow Drive.

Mr Kenny told the court that he asked what had happened at the Treaty Bar. He said that Anthony replied: 'What would you do if you had your back to the wall and you were attacked by three people with a weapon? You would have to defend yourself.'

Kelly and Ms Roche stayed the night, then left around noon the following day. Gardaí subsequently found a knife – thought to be the murder weapon – behind a couch in the sitting room of Mr Kenny's house.

Kelly went from there to the home of one of his brothers, James Joseph Kelly. He told his brother that one of the McCarthys had hit him with a brick and he had also got a 'belt of a stool'.

Kelly went on the run and was at large for a number of days as the McCarthy family prepared to bury their dead. On Tuesday, 14 December, the bodies of the two were taken from Cross's Funeral Home to St Munchin's Church, almost across the road from where they had met their deaths. A large crowd was waiting. The following day, requiem mass was celebrated at noon, then the large cortège wound its way to Mount St Lawrence cemetery, where the brothers were laid to rest.

The *Limerick Leader* reported that the Gardaí were particularly anxious to interview one man:

'We are following a definite line of enquiry,' said an investigating officer. A feud is being blamed for the tragic deaths. While the Gardaí have been taking statements from witnesses they are still trying to piece together what exactly happened. It is understood that one brother came to the aid of the other when the fracas, which spilt out onto the street, broke out.

'There was blood all over the place. It was really tragic,' a garda revealed.

Murder squad detectives from Dublin have been brought to the city to help gardaí in Henry Street under Superintendent Albert McDonagh . . . Gardaí believe that the motive for the killings is linked to a vendetta between rival factions in Limerick.

*

As the Gardaí investigated the deaths of the McCarthy brothers, violence continued to plague the city. There was another fatal stabbing, this time on Christmas Eve. A young Libyan student was the victim.

There had been a lot of mindless thuggery in the city that night, with drunken youths breaking windows and causing mayhem. But Garda strength on the streets was almost non-existent. Trainee pilot Abousef Abdussalem 'Saif' Salim, who was based at the industrial estate at Shannon Airport (about ten miles from Limerick), was out with his girlfriend, Mary King. They were with another couple in a city centre pub. When they left the Courtyard Bar at closing time, they went to the taxi rank on Thomas Street, close to a popular chipper. The area was always crowded and there was some scuffling going on when they arrived.

While they were there, a local man, Paul Duffy (25) of Moyross, began to call Mr Salim a 'nigger' and a 'bastard'. Mr Salim said something in Arabic and Mr Duffy punched him in the face. Mr Salim fought back.

Ms King tried to intervene, then saw her boyfriend staggering back, a bloodied screwdriver impaled in his head. He had been stabbed. She held him in her arms, while a companion removed the screwdriver from his head. Mr Salim lingered four days on a life-support machine, then died.

Duffy, who denied murder but pleaded guilty to manslaughter, said he had consumed at least ten pints that night. He was at the taxi rank when he said Mr Salim pushed against him.

> I think I hit him to get away. I knew I had a screwdriver in my inside pocket. I remember swinging it at him. I could swear I thought I hit him in the arm or chest. There was a crowd there and they were screaming.. I walked away.

He said that he never intended to cause serious injury to Mr Salim. He was convicted and jailed.

Mr Salim's death was the third violent stabbing incident in less than three months – and the fourth fatality. The newspapers misreported it as a riot, and Limerick quickly became known as 'Stab City'. Newspaper columnists, radio commentators and comedians took up the cry and the city has not been able to live it down since. Mr Salim's death was also a heavy economic blow to the region, as the Libyan Civil Aviation Authority decided to stop sending students to Shannon to train, costing the region an estimated £1 million.

However, the Gardaí were getting on top of the situation. In late May 1983, Anthony Kelly was finally arrested and charged with the murder of Sammy and Tommy McCarthy. He was remanded in custody.

Then, in June, Michael Kelly was brought to trial for the murder of Thomas Coleman. On Wednesday, 29 June 1983, the trial opened at the Central Criminal Court in Dublin. It lasted three days. Kelly was defended by Senior Counsel Patrick MacEntee.

The prosecution outlined their case. Kelly had harboured a grudge against Coleman for a number of years; this was exacerbated by the incident in which Kelly had been smashed in the face with a pint glass. Kelly had blamed Coleman for this and had threatened to kill him. The man who stabbed Coleman was big and burly – like Kelly.

However, MacEntee reminded the jury that the only witness to the attack had failed to identify Kelly as the killer. He said:

> All you know from the evidence is that when the door of his home was opened he shouted 'Mikey Kelly' as he was stabbed. The only other eyewitness to the murder was a neighbour who did not purport to identify Kelly as the killer.

It was not enough. After deliberating for just twenty-five minutes, the jury of seven women and five men returned a verdict of not guilty. Michael Kelly, now 27, was a free man. No one else was ever charged in connection with the death of Thomas Coleman.

Michael Kelly maintained his innocence up to his death. I spoke to him a number of times and he claimed that he was framed by friends of Coleman, who wanted him off the streets.

'I know who killed him,' Kelly told me.

> I met the killer in town one day after I was acquitted, and I said to him, 'Why didn't you tell the truth? You could have ruined my life.' He just shrugged. A short time later he left for England and has not come back. I suppose he got frightened, once he knew I knew.

In all my interviews with Kelly, I found him to be straight about what he had done and not done – but not to the point of incriminating himself. This story of the killer fleeing to England does seem a bit fortuitous to me.

Kelly was back on the streets, but a few months later Anthony's murder trial opened. It lasted more than a week. State pathologist John Harbison said that both brothers had died of haemorrhage as a result of the stab wounds inflicted in the fight with Anthony Kelly. Sammy had bled to death as the knife had severed an artery near his armpit. Tommy had bled out from a severed vein. Forensic scientist Maureen Smith told the jury that she had examined the knife recovered by the Gardaí from Kelly's uncle's house and had found no blood on it. She did, however, find bits of hair and scalp on the piece of masonry recovered from the pub. They were consistent with having come from Kelly's head after a blow.

Mr Justice Ronan Keane instructed the jury that they could return a verdict of murder if they felt Anthony Kelly had set out to kill the McCarthys. But they could return a verdict of manslaughter if they felt he acted in self-defence and went too far. It was also open to them to decide he had acted with reasonable force in self-defence.

'There is no doubt that the McCarthys were the aggressors,' he added. 'At least one, and possibly two, had a stone. There is evidence that the third had a weapon as well.'

The jury deliberated for more than four hours, but returned with a verdict of not guilty. Smiling, Anthony Kelly turned to his legal team and shook hands. His ordeal was over. But he was not a free man. At the time of the double killing he was on the run from other charges, so, when he was acquitted of the murders, he still had to return to prison to serve out the remainder of that sentence. However, his freedom was not far off.

In the space of three months, both Kelly brothers had been accused of vicious stabbings, in which three men had been killed. Yet both brothers had left the courts free men. The McCarthys were understandably bitter, and for a while there was a sharp escalation in the feud between them and the Kellys, though no more lives were lost. One Southill resident remembers:

The McCarthys were cruising around shooting at the Kellys and the Kellys were cruising around shooting at the McCarthys. I remember one day seeing a man with a shotgun, a close associate of the Kellys. He was fed up of having his door shot in. He had got word that the McCarthys were on their way up, so he went out to meet them. Sure enough, the car came around the corner with the McCarthys and he shot out the back window.

I believe one of the McCarthys was a born-again Christian. They fired in the window of his house with a sawn-off shotgun. He showed me the wall where it was peppered with the pellets, and the outline of his head was on the wall. He was an innocent man who wasn't involved in the feuding at all. But he was living in Southill, and the rest of the McCarthys were living in St Mary's Park.

It was all right when they were hitting each other, but they once destroyed the house of an old couple. They got the wrong house. That feud made guns normal. It helped to make guns acceptable, though thankfully no one was seriously injured in any of the shootings.

It took a decade, but the McCarthys and the Kellys finally ended their feud with a public peace deal in the early '90s. But the bitter dregs of the violence remain. To this day, you cannot mention the Kellys without seeing the faces of the McCarthys darken over. But the violence of previous years is now consigned firmly to the past.

However, the Kellys did not go away. Their colourful careers continued and both brothers were suspects in serious crimes before they finally went straight. But neither ever faced a murder charge again. Throughout the '80s the brothers operated as 'ordinary decent criminals'. They held up places, burgled houses and made a good living. They also pursued their various feuds with undiminished zeal. In time, they came to dominate the criminal landscape in Southill. They ruled the estate; nothing went on without their say-so.

Michael Kelly had operated for years with a partner, Eddie Ryan. They were effective armed robbers, travelling all over Munster to ply their trade. Security systems were more primitive then and firms took fewer precautions about their cash. Armed robberies were a crime of the '70s and '80s, and Kelly and Ryan were good at them. Often they would steal a car and drive to Tipperary or the Midlands, to carry out the robberies with impunity.

Michael Kelly claimed that the partnership broke up over drugs. This was one business that the Kellys never got into to any extent. Michael claims that they never touched drugs. This might or might not be true. But it is known that they were never heavily involved in the trade. At most they only dabbled.

After breaking up his partnership with Ryan, Kelly did not stop committing crimes. He had a young family to feed and, just like when he was a child, he did it through whatever dishonest means were at his disposal.

Then he had an epiphany.

He claimed that he had, finally, learnt his lesson and was determined to go straight. He told me that there were two reasons for his decision: the death of his father and the influence of the curate in Southill, Father Joe Young. Father Young was a charismatic but controversial figure. He threw himself into the life of the community and could be quite forceful, particularly when it came to the hard men like Kelly. He was also sports mad and was heavily involved in the local soccer club.

In 1985, Michael Kelly was doing three years in the familiar surroundings of Limerick prison. He had spent a decade behind bars and had met all the country's top criminals. This time his offence was that he shot at a neighbour's house. He had been told that the occupants of the house had attacked his young brothers, so he took his shotgun and went calling. He told me:

I went up to their house. I ran up and kicked in the door. They ran out the back. I was going to go through the house after them when I saw a movement behind an upstairs curtain. I pointed the gun and was about to shoot when I remembered that the mother and daughter were in the house. So I pulled the shot as I fired it.

That was his story; the Gardaí charged him with discharging a firearm with intent to endanger life. He was sentenced to ten years, with the final seven suspended. While doing the three-year stretch he got an unexpected visit from Father Young. The news was bad – his father had passed away. Kelly was devastated – and unsure whether he would be allowed out for the funeral.

'On the day of the burial I spent all the morning on tenterhooks. I found out later that Joe [Young] had followed Michael Noonan [Justice Minister] around the country until he got permission for me to get out.'

Kelly got three days' compassionate release.

'The funeral was very emotional for me. I held my father's hand and I said that what I could not give him in life I would give him in death. And I have never done anything wrong since.'

On his release in 1987, Kelly began to go straight. He stayed out of trouble and began to help Father Young with the management of Limerick Football Club, as well as becoming involved in community initiatives. He admitted to me that going straight was a struggle:

There was a time we were living on £10 a week. I wanted to go back to robberies to try and provide for us in the only way I thought I could, but Majella [his wife] was so strong. She said she preferred being poor and honest than rich and dishonest. She was right, and we struggled on. I was bad to her as well. I often took my frustration out on her.

But she stuck by me through thick and thin. We had two little boys and then she fell pregnant again, this time with twins. I was on the edge, ready to go back to crime. Then one of the twins died when he was six weeks old. I suppose it made me realise that there was more to life than money.

Michael continued to work in the community and set up a few businesses, including a cleaning business.

But there was a dark side to all this: it became known that if you kept on the right side of the Kelly brothers, problems were solved for you. A young artist had his bicycle stolen. It was his pride and joy – and only form of transport. An expensive racer, it was worth as much as a small car. The artist worked with a cousin of the Kellys on a Community Employment Scheme. He mentioned the stolen bike – it was returned the following day. If Michael or Anthony put the word out on the street, the young bloods listened.

It went further. The Kellys, particularly Michael, began to see themselves almost as community workers. If a granny was beaten up by young thugs, Michael proudly told me, he would go out and beat up the youngsters. For certain elements of the community, the Kellys became the police.

In 1988–9, he helped supervise the Garda Activity Programme. He was becoming rehabilitated. But he still needed to earn a crust. In 1991, he set up a security firm, M&A Kelly Security, with his brother Anthony. It became quite a big concern, employing a number of people. But often the sign was enough. No one was going to mess with the Kellys.

Rumours circulated that the security firm was a front for a protection racket. In the early '90s, I attended a residents' meeting of a new estate near Moylish, close to the Institute of Technology, but also just a stone's throw from Moyross – literally. Every night windows were broken on the estate. Michael Kelly was invited to address the meeting, to pitch his security business. He promised signs, and patrols every evening.

After he left there was, to put it mildly, a vigorous discussion. Some people felt that Kelly was behind the vandalism, to make hiring his security firm more attractive. In the end, the estate did not hire security and the petty vandalism continued. The longer the vandalism continued the less likely it was that the Kellys were behind it; they had lost the contract, so where was the benefit to them of continuing the attacks? However, not everyone saw it that way.

Former mayor and Southill resident Joe Harrington told me:

To be fair to them, they had businesses, cleaning businesses and so on. They took on fellows that no one else would take on and gave them a chance. There was a question mark over whether they were using these fellows for other jobs, criminal jobs, but I don't think so. They seemed to be doing well out of their businesses, and they were legitimate. Their security business did very well. They were able to do things that ordinary security firms were not able to do. And they were doing so without paying their employees too much. They had a name for not paying too well.

Locals began to turn to the Kellys, and Michael loved that. Occasionally, his enthusiasm overflowed. Once, he spotted an elderly woman being spat upon by a youth. The woman had suffered a couple of break-ins, and Kelly decided to take the matter in hand. He beat the youth so badly he ended up in hospital.

Kelly's reputation in Southill was growing. But he found it difficult to shake off concerns about his security company. It wasn't helped by the fact that a number of fires coincided with the termination of security contracts. Rathbane Golf Club cancelled their contract with M&A Kelly and, shortly afterwards, the clubhouse was damaged in a fire. The same thing happened to a garage in Roxboro. Both fires were started deliberately, but there was no evidence to link them to Kelly.

At its peak, the security firm employed 60 people. However, it began to lose contracts as the rumours flew. By 2003, they were down to one client.

Although Kelly had picked up no convictions since his release from prison, the Gardaí were not convinced he had left his violent ways behind him. In 1996, Sean Mescall was abducted and severely beaten. Gardaí believed that Kelly had supplied the heavies to carry out that beating. He denied it.

By the turn of the new millennium, whether they realised it or not, the security business of the Kelly brothers was in terminal decline. There were too many rumours, too many unanswered questions. But, nothing daunted, Michael Kelly decided to take the next step on his road to reform. He decided to get involved in local politics.

This was not such a bold step as might appear. Many former criminals feel the urge, as they grow older, to become legitimate businessmen and members of the community. They clean up their acts and crave respectability. In Colombia, the huge drug baron Pablo Escobar, responsible for scores of deaths, successfully ran for parliament.

Kelly set his ambitions lower: he ran for the city council in the elections of 1999. As he explained to me:

> I've been 19 years out of trouble, concentrating on old folks and youth. Three mothers of young children with a tendency to crime and joyriding approached me. I said that the behaviour of their kids could not be tolerated. They said that there was nothing for the children and that I should run for election to do something about it. So I decided to go for it.

He appeared on the election list as a company director and ran as an independent. He ran a laid-back campaign and did not spend much, concentrating on his own patch of Southill. But it paid off. He topped the poll, securing more than one in four first preferences. He was deemed elected on the first count and became an alderman of Limerick.

The forty-three-year-old father of eight (through two marriages) was delighted with his success, but soon found the polite diplomacy needed to succeed in City Hall was a far cry from the rough and tumble world he was used to. But he was determined to learn the ropes; he attended every meeting, made regular contributions and never skived off early after signing for his expenses.

John Gilligan, an experienced local independent, told me that Kelly was trying his best to fit in:

> He was never vindictive, never aggressive, though that is what people might have thought to look at him. I never saw him lose his temper, which is more than I could say for myself! He made his point and he made it strongly. He would be persistent and

211

he would not kowtow to anyone. But he was never overtly disruptive.

This enthusiasm led him to make some naive mistakes, but Kelly was enjoying himself and even contemplating a run for the Dáil. But his empire came tumbling down in 2001. His past hadn't caught up with him – the CAB had. They announced that they were probing Kelly's affairs. Kelly said he welcomed the investigation; it would put to rest all questions about his legitimacy.

That was his public stance. But he and Anthony also picketed in the city centre, carrying posters saying: 'Stop the Garda Vendetta Against the Peacemaking Alderman Michael Kelly and Family'.

The probe took a year, at the end of which Kelly was charged with tax offences. Kelly, his own man to the end, decided to represent himself, firing his legal team at the start of the proceedings. But he was feeling the pressure and reluctantly stood down from the city council in November 2002.

The case opened in January 2003 and Kelly was charged with twenty-seven offences, including eight VAT and income tax offences, seven summonses against his company Crestwin Ltd, trading as M&A Kelly Security, and twelve breaches of the Social Welfare Act. He pleaded not guilty. By now, he had a new legal team in place.

Halfway through the trial he changed his plea to guilty to eight breaches of the Social Welfare (Consolidation) Act, but maintained his innocence on all other charges. On 13 March, the trial came to an end and Judge Michael Reilly was ready to give his verdict. It was a dramatic day. Kelly had a heart attack that morning and was rushed to hospital. But he signed himself out, against medical advice, to hear the verdict.

He was sentenced to eight months in prison, then rushed back to the hospital, where his condition was described as 'critical but stable'. He was released on bail pending an unsuccessful appeal, but eventually returned to jail after a two-decade absence.

He was a much changed man. Before, he had been the toughest nut on the block, capable of dealing with any trouble. Now he was heavy and moved slowly, any exertion leaving him breathless because of his heart condition. The time went hard with him.

A few weeks after his release in April 2004 his fall from grace seemed to overcome him. He had been a city councillor and a company director. Now he was back living in his mother's house, on whatever money his brother could spare for him. His marriage had broken up, his business was a memory. Unable to take what life had become, he got his hands on a handgun and put a bullet through his brain.

On Friday, 14 May 2004, at around 7.30 a.m., a shot rang out in the house. Michael's shocked mother was the first at the scene, and Anthony, living at the top of the estate, was down within minutes. Gardaí were quick to arrive and Michael, still alive, was rushed to the regional hospital; he was then transferred to Cork University Hospital, where they had expertise in head injuries.

It had all the hallmarks of an attempted suicide, with one problem; Michael was not holding a gun. There was no gun in the small bedroom.

Anthony spent the next five days by his brother's bedside, as doctors battled to save his life. A bullet was lodged in his brain and could not be removed. They kept him in an artificial coma, hoping he would stabilise. After five days, they took him off the medication to see how he would react. Anthony told reporters:

Mikey is heavily sedated. There has been no change in him at all. There is a bit of a reaction when he sees light in his eyes. The bullet is still in his brain, but they are going to take him off the medication on Thursday or Friday to see how he is – that will be a big day for him.

Anthony rejected the idea that Michael had tried to take his own life.

Mikey didn't shoot himself; my mother didn't shoot Mikey and

I didn't shoot Mikey. Somebody came into the house and shot him. The gossip mongers are out, stories have been flying around like confetti. This is very hard for our family. We are still fighting for justice for our brother Damien, who died in Spike Island in 1994, and then this happened. It is a very tough time.

Damien was a younger brother of Michael and Anthony who died from hanging while in custody on Spike Island in Cork. The family always rejected the suicide verdict in that case.

Anthony insisted that an intruder had shot Michael, adding:

I will not be run out of Southill by anyone. Over my dead body will I leave Southill. I don't care if I get killed myself. Two weeks prior to this I was under siege in O'Malley Park from another family in Southill. Last Tuesday night there was shots fired at me – there are constant threats to my family. But they won't force me to leave my home in Southill.

Gardaí did investigate the shooting, but leant towards the attempted suicide theory. They believed that a family member had removed the gun from Michael's hand to avoid the stigma of suicide. For this reason, the Kellys refused to cooperate with the Garda investigation.

'We won't talk to or help the Guards – all we get is hassle off them. They have never helped us,' said Anthony.

Michael lingered a month, but finally passed away peacefully exactly five years to the day after the great moment of his life, his election as an alderman to Limerick City Council. His family immediately called for a full murder investigation. Anthony told the *Limerick Leader*:

When I came into the bedroom that morning with my mother, we found Mikey lying there, there was no gun there. Somebody shot him. It was a peaceful death. All his family were with him. He is not in pain any more. His children were at his bed: James, Shane, Gerard, Michael, Louise, Anthony and Michelle.

But even in death Michael Kelly was a controversial figure. The question of the missing gun continued to trouble many. Some of the papers were quite harsh in their treatment of the former criminal. One paper, the *Star on Sunday*, suggested that one of Kelly's brothers had taken the gun and hidden it, then concealed it in the coffin with Michael to get rid of the evidence of a suicide. Anthony was the brother in the frame; he was the first on the scene after his mother alerted him to what Michael had done.

The family were incensed. What happened next gripped the nation for a day. I was in bed asleep when I heard loud banging on my door. It was around 7 a.m. on Monday, 11 July 2004. I looked out and a group of Kelly's brothers were in my garden, calling me down. Anthony was among them. They told me that they were going to exhume Michael's body to prove that there was no gun in the coffin. I was to open the coffin, because no one would believe them if they did it themselves.

Reluctantly, I joined them at the graveyard. It was about a month after Michael's funeral; several of his brothers were digging into the clay. Within minutes, the Gardaí arrived and a tense stand-off followed, lasting several hours. The Kellys were insisting on digging; the Gardaí were insisting on a proper exhumation order. Every now and then a garda would look away and a Kelly would dart in with a shovel.

At lunchtime, the Kelly family applied to City Hall for an exhumation order. It takes several weeks for an exhumation order to be processed, but the paperwork was fast-tracked and the order granted that afternoon. At 5 p.m. the media and all non-family members were asked to leave the cemetery. The gardaí erected a tent and took over the job. After an hour and a half, the coffin was removed and opened. Michael's wife Majella was at the graveside and his mother Rita was nearby. His oldest brother James, along with Detective Sergeant Declan O'Brien of the National Bureau of Criminal Investigation, examined the coffin and confirmed that there was no gun. An hour later, Michael Kelly's remains had been blessed and reinterred. The grave was restored; the crowd had drifted away. The drama was over.

*

Anthony Kelly still lives in Southill. He lives in splendid isolation at the top of the park. Because of the efforts of the regeneration scheme, many of the houses around him have been torn down. His days as a career criminal are in the past, but he continues to have brushes with the law. In 2009, he was fined €63.49 (the maximum fine) for running an illegal shebeen at the back of a house at 9 Lilac Court, Keyes Park. The court heard that the shebeen had 'all the appearances, vestiges and attributes of a bar, and the ambiance of a bar'. The premises had a full bar counter, several taps, TV, a fully stocked stand-alone fridge, kegs, slabs, several bottles of varied spirits, a dart board, a pool table, a game machine, alcohol advertisements, and ladies and gents toilets.

I have had a pint in the shebeen, and it was a very basic bar. It never seemed particularly busy and was not a money spinner. It did seem like a sociable place to hang out and have a drink, though.

Anthony's most recent brush with the law was more serious. He was charged with being in possession of a semi-automatic Glock pistol with intent to endanger life at O'Malley Park on 28 October 2009. A 27-year-old man, Michael Lynch, had been shot in the back during an altercation outside Anthony Kelly's home on the morning of 28 October.

Kelly denied having held the gun, or having shot at the man. He said that a number of people attacked his house. One of them must have fired the shot that hit Lynch. The trial lasted a number of weeks, at the end of which the jury acquitted Anthony Kelly. Afterwards, he said he was 'happy and relieved'.

In May 2011, Anthony Kelly was remanded on a burglary charge. He was charged alongside his 23-year-old daughter, Jessica. They were accused of breaking into a house at the Goody Student Village, Castletroy, shortly before midnight on 6 April.

Both were remanded on bail. The charges were eventually dropped when Anthony was able to show he had a legitimate reason for being at the scene. One of Michael Kelly's sons has been convicted of possession of drugs with intent to supply.

Going straight has not been easy for the Kellys, the original hard men of Limerick.

9

THE MOST EVIL MAN IN IRELAND

Gary Campion, the Only Irish Hit Man to Have Been Convicted Twice of Murder

When you shoot a man, he drops down. He doesn't go flying backwards. It doesn't matter if it's a shotgun or a nine mil, that stuff you see in the pictures is pure crap. I never saw anyone move more than a few inches in my life. I'll tell you another thing. If you shoot a man in the back of the head, a funny thing happens. His two eyeballs will pop out of the front of his head and just hang there on stalks – ha, ha!

Gary Campion, quoted in *Inside Man*
(Philip Bray and Anthony Galvin)

GARY CAMPION IS the only Irish hit man to have been convicted of two gangland murders – though his death toll could be a lot higher. He and his brothers, Willie and Noel, were described to me as the most evil people in Ireland. That description came from a leading Limerick politician; several months later, a prison officer used the very same words. Several of the hit men in this book could vie for that title, but there is no doubt that cold-blooded killer Gary Campion would be in the top rank of them. As I write, he is doing life for two murders, but there is a lot of his story that will never get told.

The three brothers grew up in Moyross. Everyone on the

housing list in the '70s tended to get shunted out there. Limerick had one of the highest percentages of single mothers in the country, and Moyross quickly became an estate with a large number of kids growing up without the influence of a father figure. It was not uncommon to find several children in one house each sharing one mother, but having separate fathers.

Historically, Limerick had a shortage of secondary school places. One in twelve children finished primary school – and finished with education. There was no secondary school place for them and they dropped out of the system at the age of 12. Most went back on the list for the following year; but bizarrely they were not given priority, so they still faced the one-in-twelve odds. If you lived in Moyross (or Southill, or any of the other large corporation estates), the odds rose to one in four. A quarter of the children were not given their constitutional right to an education.

It is small wonder that crime and delinquency thrived in Moyross. When I began working at the *Limerick Leader* in the '90s, I remember Moyross as a war zone. Every night gangs of marauding teens patrolled the estate, stoning windows, breaking into empty houses to use them as drinking dens and firebombing other houses. Cars were stolen and joyridden through the estate. Hardly a night passed without the fire brigade being summoned to put out another car or another house. Frequently, the firemen, and the gardaí who accompanied them, were stoned and assaulted.

Moyross is nowhere near as bad now, but this was the Moyross the Campions moved to in the late '80s. They had been from Southill, the other big problem estate a number of miles away on the other side of the city. When they moved out of Southill, locals lit bonfires and held impromptu parties. 'People were glad to see the back of them,' one garda told me.

When the Campions arrived in Moyross, the only people who had money were the drug dealers, and these were the role models for kids who wanted to succeed. The Campions decided they wanted to be the kings of Moyross. And the way to the throne was through violence.

Gary Campion was just fifteen – and already had criminal convictions – when one of the most vicious murders in the history of the state took place at an isolated farmhouse not far from the city. At that time, his older brothers had begun a crime spree, stealing cars and driving out to the countryside to commit burglaries. In 1998, three men broke into the house of 68-year-old farmer Paud Skehan near Bridgetown, County Clare.

The terrified pensioner was beaten badly by the intruders on the night of 9 April. They beat and tortured him until he passed out from the pain of the sustained attack. When a neighbour found him the following day, he was hanging upside down, blindfolded and bound with television cable and a tie. Dressed only in his shirt and underpants, his hands were tied behind his back and his head was covered in blood. He was moaning softly. His body had been doused in paraffin and the intruders had obviously threatened to set him alight before he passed out.

The injured man lingered for several weeks, but eventually died of his horrific injuries. William Campion was convicted of the murder. His young brother Noel was suspected of being one of his two companions on the night. Those were the sorts of role models Gary Campion had as a teen. Even then he had a name for being trouble.

Some gardaí later speculated that Gary had been taken along that night and that that was the reason for the viciousness of the assault. His older brothers were blooding him. However, I have spoken to people who know Campion and they assure me that he was not involved in the attack on Paud Skehan, though he was no stranger to antisocial behaviour.

'He was into everything: robbing cars, a bit of thieving, drugs,' said a garda.

In 2000, Gary Campion and another man abducted two young men in Moyross. They forced the two men to strip and were thought to have been about to shoot them when gardaí arrived at the scene, possibly saving two lives.

By the time he hit 20, Gary was a regular in Limerick prison and a man with a reputation for aggression and violence. At that point, the Campions aligned themselves with a fledgling new gang, the McCarthy-Dundons. These thugs brought a new level of violence to the streets of Limerick. They used automatic pistols and machine guns, and thought nothing of killing to further their aims. With the traditional forces of the Keane-Collopy gang at war with the Ryan faction, the McCarthy-Dundons were trying to use the opportunity to take control of the multimillion euro drugs distribution industry.

In the Campions, they found eager henchmen – though henchmen who had a tendency to get caught. In 1999, Noel Campion was jailed for fourteen years for the armed robbery of a petrol station (though the final six years of the sentence were suspended).

In 2002, the gang was trying to get drugs into a local nightclub, Doc's. But the doorman there, Brian Fitzgerald, was having none of it.

The McCarthy-Dundons decided to send a message to the city that they were not to be messed with. They planned Fitzgerald's murder with military precision, hiring James Cahill to do the dirty work. Gary Campion was his motorcycle driver.

A month later Campion is suspected of having been back in action. This time he went back to the old pattern of his family – breaking into houses in the countryside outside the city. It was New Year's Eve, and 39-year-old bricklayer and part-time car salesman Sean Poland had returned to his home at Blackwater, Ardnacrusha, County Clare, with his partner. Blackwater is only five minutes out from the city suburb where Brian Fitzgerald had been murdered, but it is in the countryside and is quiet.

Poland had sold a car to a gang member earlier that week for €1,000, and the gang decided to pay him a visit and get a full refund. It is believed that Gary Campion was in the party that came knocking at the door that evening. When Poland opened the door, he was immediately shot in the abdomen with a shotgun and fell to the ground dying. The intruders stepped over his body in the hallway and tied up his partner, Joanne Lyons, before ransacking the house.

Clearly, life had no value for this new breed of thug. No one has ever been charged in connection with the murder of Sean Poland, but his death, following so soon after that of Brian Fitzgerald, showed clearly that completely innocent people were in danger from the gang wars.

Meanwhile, Campion pursued his criminal ways. It would be four years before he was charged with the killing of Brian Fitzgerald and another year before his conviction. But he continued to get in trouble.

On Thursday, 1 May 2003, Campion is believed to have tried to kill a man in Moyross. It was about 10 p.m. and getting dark. Two men burst through the front door and confronted Joseph 'Dodo' McCarthy, opening fire on him. McCarthy, 32, was a criminal with a number of convictions, but he was not associated with any of the three main gangs fighting for control of the city. The gunmen opened fire at point-blank range and hit him, but miraculously he was still alive when he was rushed to Limerick Regional Hospital. Although he remained in a critical condition for several days and in intensive care for several weeks, he survived the assassination attempt. In fact, he made a full recovery – and is now doing hard time himself for manslaughter.

Five days later, the hit man is believed to have struck again. It was Monday, 6 May and the victim was Robert Fitzgerald, a big, friendly 23 year old who was not a member of any of the gangs. He lived in Cliona Park, Moyross, with his grandmother, Mary Fitzgerald, and was a cousin of the nightclub bouncer whom Campion had helped assassinate. Although he was not a criminal, some of his friends were in the Keane-Collopy gang, and that was enough to mark him down for death.

Moyross was on full alert after a number of incidents, including a few gangland murders. There was a heavy Garda presence in the estate and CCTV was monitoring the streets. Despite this, the gangs proved they could act with impunity under the close scrutiny.

That night, Robert went to a number of pubs in the city. He ended the evening at a party on College Avenue, Moyross. This was very close to his home in Cliona Park. During the party, Robert had a row over a woman with a man who was associated with the McCarthy-Dundon gang. A little after 1 a.m., he phoned a friend and said he would drop over to see him, but he never arrived. He remained at the party for well over an hour more. But, around 3 a.m., he got a phone call and decided it was time to call it a night. He left the party and set off to walk the short distance home.

The shooting appeared to have been carefully planned. The killer waited in a narrow passage that leads from College Avenue to Cliona Park for his victim to arrive. As Fitzgerald entered the passage, his killer opened fire with a semi-automatic handgun. Perhaps Fitzgerald realised his danger at the last moment, for one bullet hit him in the back, indicating that he had tried to run. The second bullet went through the back of his head, killing him instantly.

Hours later, the Gardaí received reports of shots being fired between 3 a.m. and 3.30 a.m., but no reports were received at the time. Gardaí patrolling the park also failed to notice the shots. Two fully armed patrols and an unarmed one were in the area when the shooting occurred. But it was not until the following morning that the body was discovered. No one was ever convicted of shooting Robert Fitzgerald, but the Gardaí suspected that Gary Campion might have been the gunman.

Around the same time, Campion is believed to have taken against a young man in the neighbourhood. There was no reason for his campaign against Wayne Waters, except he just didn't like the guy. He bullied and threatened him, making more than one attempt on his life. The young man grew so depressed and terrified that he eventually took his own life.

In 2004, Campion was behind bars yet again, a guest of the state at Limerick prison. I was told by a prison officer that there was a scuffle on one of the wings; Campion was at the centre of the trouble. Three prison officers rushed in to restrain him. As he was being restrained by the three, he turned on one of them, John Ryan, and stunned the officer by saying:

I have shot people in this town for €10,000, and I'd have no difficulty spending €20,000 to have you blown away. It wouldn't be my first time. If it's the last thing I do, I'll get you and your family. Ryan, you still have to go out that Dublin Road every evening.

This was a chilling reminder to the prison officer that Campion knew where he lived. He had two years added to his sentence for the threat. The threat wasn't idle either; on one occasion Campion had firebombed the home of a prison officer on behalf of his brother Noel.

In July 2006, Noel Campion was released from prison and immediately began to try to muscle his way into the lucrative drugs business. But things had changed since 1999; he had to deal with the ferocious McCarthy-Dundons. His ambitions brought him into conflict with his old allies. Also, while in Portlaoise prison, he had come under the influence of a senior member of the Keane gang, so was thinking of switching sides. This decision would prove costly.

Knowing the dangers, Noel Campion arranged a holiday to the USA – a working holiday. He and some of his associates spent a week in Florida, training on a weapons range. The new weapons were more difficult to control than the old-fashioned sawn-off shotgun. With a sawn-off shotgun you fairly much aim in the rough direction of your target and you will hit him. But with a semi-automatic pistol accuracy is far more important – and more difficult to achieve. In addition, the semi-automatic can fire several shots a second. When you pull the trigger, the recoil from the first shot tends to throw the barrel up, meaning that the second and subsequent rounds pass harmlessly over the target. That is why there were so many botched hits in the late '90s and early 2000s, until the gangsters learnt how to use the new weapons.

Gary was not able to join Noel on the working holiday; he was in prison, not being released until 14 September 2006. But he did join his brother in switching sides. However, it was a while before this became obvious in the criminal underworld. The Campions were now firmly entrenched on the Keane-Collopy side, but old friends and associates in the McCarthy-Dundon gang still trusted Gary Campion. After all, he had killed for them, hadn't he?

Fat Frankie Ryan, 21, from Delmege Park, Moyross, was a key man for the McCarthy-Dundons in Moyross. He had a list of convictions for public order offences, robbery, theft and traffic violations. He was also suspected of being involved in some of the many shootings in the city. He was a hard man with a good future in the gang. On the evening of Monday, 17 September 2006, he was driving his Toyota between Pineview Gardens and Delmege Park. A 17-year-old friend, Erol Ibrahim, was in the passenger seat beside him.

At the side of the road was Gary Campion. Now a father of two, the twenty-three year old had been released from prison just three days previously and had contacted Ryan with a view to getting straight back into the crime game. They were old friends. Ryan was glad to see him. Campion got into the back seat of the car and Ryan pulled out. He would not have let Campion sit behind him if he had any doubts about his friend. This was just a meeting to catch up and plan future operations. But, unknown to Ryan, he was about to become the victim of a vicious double-cross.

Campion had switched sides – though probably not out of loyalty to his brother. Gary Campion was a lone wolf, a vicious thug who let money dominate over all other concerns. The reason he had switched sides was that the Keane-Collopy faction had offered him a large fee to shoot his old friend. They had made a number of attempts on Ryan's life (in revenge for the murder of criminal David Nunan, which Ryan had been involved in). None of these attempts had been successful. So they decided to hire the most ruthless killer in the city.

They had hired him on one previous occasion. Philip Collopy, a hit man himself and acting leader of the gang after the death of Kieran Keane, had come up with an audacious plan to wipe out several of his enemies in one go. He needed a man with no qualms about shedding blood, so he went to Campion.

A group of people would be attending a party; Collopy wanted Campion to burst into the party and open fire. 'Kill everyone,' was the chilling instruction. Campion was handed a loaded Sig automatic pistol with a full clip of 15 rounds. However, the Gardaí were tipped off about the plan; they seized the gun in a search a few days before the party.

'The plan was to kill everyone at the party and Campion would have had no difficulty in doing that at all,' a garda told me.

But this time, his second job for the Keane-Collopy gang, there were no gardaí on hand to prevent him carrying out his contract. As the car picked up speed, Campion opened his jacket and took out a handgun. He put the gun to the back of Ryan's head and pulled the trigger. The noise of the shot filled the car, as Ryan slumped forward, blood flowing from his mouth and nose. The car kept moving; Campion calmly reached forward and took the wheel, guiding the car to the side of the road. Then he jumped out of the car and wrenched open the front passenger door. Leaning across Ibrahim, he fired a second shot into Ryan's head to make sure.

Erol Ibrahim stumbled out of the car and began pleading for his life. He promised he wouldn't rat on the young hit man. Unbelievably, Campion seems to have accepted this. He turned and ran, leaving a witness who had seen everything.

'If anyone rats on me, they are dead,' he shouted as he ran.

Within a day, he was in Cork, lying low. But he was arrested within a week of the murder. His first words to arresting Detective Sergeant Patrick O'Callaghan were: 'Who ratted me out?'

Then he went on a rant: 'If you'd let me out longer, I would have killed more people. Fucking scumbags is all ye are. I'll clean up Moyross, not ye.'

He never got the chance. Gary Campion has been behind bars since September 2006. While awaiting trial for the murder of Ryan, he was charged with the murder of bouncer Brian

Fitzgerald. He was convicted of the murder of Frankie Ryan, then he made history by becoming the first hit man to be convicted of two hits, when he was given a second life sentence for the hit on Fitzgerald. He will probably spend the next two decades or more behind bars. But that hasn't stopped him getting into trouble.

In July 2007, detectives launched a major investigation into drug dealing in Limerick prison – and when they searched Gary Campion's cell they discovered heroin with an estimated value of €2,300. The heroin was found in a knotted bag that Campion had concealed in his clenched fist during a search of his cell by prison officers. A follow-up search resulted in 73 knotted bags of heroin being found. These knotted bags were known as 'street deals'. Campion had four years added to his two life sentences for the drugs.

Meanwhile, his brother Noel was in trouble. Now it was known that he had switched sides his life was in danger. Shortly after the Frankie Ryan murder, Noel Campion went to pick up his daughter from school. He was shot at, but escaped. Not long after this he ordered a pizza, but instead of a pizza a gunman arrived and shot into his house. In retaliation, the Campions responded by firebombing two houses – including the family home of the late Frankie Ryan.

Noel Campion, now 35, got a reprieve of sorts when he was jailed for a short time in late 2006, but on his release he was back in the firing line. On 22 March 2007, he had a lucky escape when a gunman opened fire on him while he was walking through Moyross. The gunman fired twice but missed and ran off. But it was obvious Campion's luck would not hold forever.

This didn't stop Campion getting into trouble. At the end of the month, Limerick City Council officials descended on his home in Pineview Gardens after they learnt that the married father of two was keeping six horses in illegal stables at the premises. The horses were seized and he had to fork out €6,000 for the return of the animals. At around that time, local Fianna Fáil politician (and later Defence Minister) Willie O'Dea was walking about the estate. O'Dea, who always tops the poll in Limerick, was campaigning for the May general election. Campion confronted him and began shouting abuse at him over the seizure of the horses.

On 26 April, the sun shone down strongly on the bright, clear spring morning, though the air was a bit chilly. The local District Court was sitting in the new building overlooking the Curraghgower Falls on the River Shannon. That day, Noel Campion was facing minor traffic charges and he was making his way towards the court for the 11 a.m. sitting. A friend was taking him on a powerful Suzuki motorcycle – Campion was riding as pillion passenger. Because he was going to spend the morning in the court he had decided not to wear his bulletproof vest that day.

They left Moyross and headed through Thomondgate towards the city centre. It was 10.40 a.m. Unknown to them, two men were loitering near a phone box at the junction of Inglewood Terrace, Treaty Terrace and High Road. The motorcycle approached the junction, then stopped when the traffic stopped. Suddenly, a man in a red hoodie stepped from the phone booth. The gunman opened fire and the motorcycle immediately shot forward, crashing into the car in front of it. The motorcycle driver was thrown forward, going through the rear window of the car. Campion was thrown to the ground.

As shocked onlookers dived for cover, the gunman continued firing on Campion as he tried to stumble from the scene. Severely wounded, he fell to the ground less than 15 yards from where the motorcycle had crashed. He had been hit three times. One shot had hit him in the back, and he had been hit once in each side. Had he been wearing the bulletproof vest, he would not have suffered anything more than bruises.

The man in the hoodie ran from the scene to nearby Canon Breen Park, where he got into a waiting Volkswagen Passat, which immediately took off. The car had been stolen in Galway. It was later torched in Delmege Park, Moyross.

An onlooker told the *Limerick Leader*:

I heard the six shots: bang, bang, bang, bang, bang, bang. They were like mad wallops. I ran upstairs. I knew they were gunshots and there was a girl standing over the man screaming. He was just lying there on the ground still wearing the motorcycle helmet.

One of Noel's sisters, 23-year-old Mary, had been shopping in the city centre and was in a taxi on her way home when she came across the shooting. Noel Campion was taken to nearby St John's Hospital, but was pronounced dead shortly afterwards.

That night, there were celebrations in Ballinacurra Weston, stronghold of the McCarthy-Dundon gang. A bonfire was lit and there was a drunken party. Even the children joined in, chanting: 'Whack, whack, Noely got it in the back!' A number of phone calls were made to members of the Campion family taunting them about the death.

The kings of Moyross had been overthrown. Noel Campion was dead, and his brothers Willie and Gary were behind bars doing life for murder. Limerick was finally rid of the most evil men in the city. But there would be others to take their place . . .

10

THE INNOCENT VICTIMS:
SHOT IN HIS BROTHER'S PLACE

The Murder of Noel Crawford

ON THE EVENING of Sunday, 17 December 2006, Noel Crawford put down the paper and prepared to go out. He folded the paper carefully, leaving it open on the story he was just reading, obviously intending to pick it up again later. The story concerned a recent gangland assassination in Dublin. Notorious gangster Marlo Hyland, a drug lord who controlled the Cabra district, had been gunned down.

What horrified the country was that there was a plumber doing a job in the house when the assassins attacked. Anthony Campbell was a young man who had never put a foot wrong. He was just doing his job, trying to earn a few bob for Christmas. And the gunmen blew him away with Hyland. A completely innocent young man had his life snuffed out because he took a job in the wrong house.

Noel Crawford left his house in O'Malley Park, Southill, and walked across the park to the house of one of his sisters. A gentle, hard-working man, he was a father of six, though he was separated from his wife and from the mothers of his other children. By all accounts, he was a good father, a devoted son and a considerate brother. Nobody says a bad word about Noel Crawford.

At one point, Noel was stabbed in the hand during an incident in a pub. He recovered and forgave his attacker, often chatting to him as if nothing had ever happened. That was the sort of man Noel Crawford was. The family believe that if he had survived his shooting, he would have forgiven his attacker.

Noel left school early and worked all his life. From the age of 14 he held down a number of jobs. These included security work and retail jobs. At one stage, he managed a garage in Shannon. Now he was a floor manager at Heaton's department store. He lived alone and kept the house in immaculate condition. He had a file keeping track of all his bills and never let one fall behind.

I conducted personal interviews with members of the family, which are quoted below.

'He would pay a bill before he would buy himself a dinner,' said his brother Paul.

'He was very quiet,' added his mother, Mary. 'If anyone was fighting him, he would never fight back. If you went into a pub with him, you would need earphones!'

Although he was softly spoken, Noel could talk for Ireland. He loved chatting and after a few pints there was no shutting him up. He loved hanging out with his family, especially his sisters. He would do anything for them. That night, a day shy of his 40th birthday, he called in on his sister Ann. Around ten o'clock she told him that she needed to go out for an hour, to call on a friend up the road, and he agreed to stay in the house. He wasn't quite babysitting, as Ann's daughter was in her teens, but he was keeping an eye on things. He chatted to the teenage girl and had a can or two. He knew his sister's hour could last a lot longer than that. It was long after midnight when she returned; she had watched a movie with her friend.

Noel left the house and walked down the road towards his parents' house. His brother Paul lived with them. If Noel was the white sheep of the family, then Paul was its black sheep. Several years younger than Noel, Paul had been in and out of trouble for years, starting with joyriding as a teen.

232

'I began hanging out with the wrong people and working with them,' he said. 'You get sucked in. It is easy to join a gang but not so easy to get out of one.'

Paul Crawford is coy about what he was involved in, but the Gardaí believe he rose to become a key figure in the McCarthy-Dundon gang. He admits himself that he worked with them, but maintains that he was never an important cog in the organisation. It didn't matter; perception can often be more important than truth. Everyone believed Paul was a major figure and a dangerous man. The Keane-Collopy gang, bitter rivals of the McCarthy-Dundons, saw Paul as a figure they needed to eliminate. As Noel reached his parents' house, intending to cross the estate to where he lived, he had no idea that he was about to fall victim to forces that had been gathering like storm clouds over the past several months.

As Paul was seen as an increasingly important figure in gangland, a number of attempts had been made on his life. He had been shot at least four times in the previous few months, with numerous shootings outside the house he shared with his parents. It was all orchestrated by the Keane-Collopy gang and by rivals in the troubled Southill estate.

In July, Crawford had escaped serious injury when shots were fired at him while he was sitting in a car with a woman and child. A fifteen-year-old boy, one of Crawford's nephews, was hit twice in the fire. He suffered minor injuries, but made a recovery. From that point onwards the shootings became more frequent and more indiscriminate.

On one occasion, Paul was walking through John Carew Park, at the bottom of Southill, when a gunman had accosted him and pointed an automatic weapon at him. The gun jammed and Crawford had a miraculous escape.

'He aimed a machine gun at me, but it jammed and I got away,' he said.

In early November, someone opened fire on the house with an automatic weapon. Seventeen bullets slammed through the window, shattering ornaments inside and narrowly missing the family. One bullet passed clean through the wall of the living room and was recovered from the far wall of the kitchen on the other side. It was a terrifying experience. Four youths were arrested by the Emergency Response Unit following a car chase.

Two days later, on 5 November, a young nephew of Noel and Paul was playing outside in the tiny garden in front of the house. Paul and Noel were with him. A gunman approached on foot and fired at Paul. The shot missed, but five-year-old Jordan Crawford was shot in the thigh.

'They came in here to get me, to finish me off. They wanted me dead and shot my nephew. There is a hit out on me. They want me dead,' said Crawford.

In addition to his parents' house, the homes of relatives of his in the Corbally area had also been targeted. That was the storm that was gathering around the Crawford family, reaching its climax in the early hours of that December morning.

It had all begun a number of hours earlier. On the morning of Sunday, 17 December, a local woman, Jennifer Fitzgerald, reported that she had been kidnapped. No one is sure of the exact circumstances. The Crawford family believe that she had been doing something her own family would not have approved of, suggesting she made up the story to cover herself. It may be true, it may not. In any case, Paul Crawford was an easy scapegoat. When she said she had been kidnapped by him, she was believed. Her brother Jonathan, aged 17 at the time, was furious. He began to put a plan in place to take his vengeance.

He went to the Island Field, stronghold of the Keane-Collopy gang, for a gun. He didn't get it there, but picked it up from a house in Garryowen, where it was being stored in a dog kennel. He got the gun and took a taxi late that night to O'Malley Park. He went to a house not far from the Crawfords and got ready for that night's action.

There was a 15-year-old in the house, Michael O'Callaghan. He knew the area well and was going to guide Fitzgerald to the Crawford house.

The two men got to work making a petrol bomb. Their plan

was to throw a petrol bomb into the back of the house, then rush around to the front and shoot Paul as he ran from the house. But they were persuaded to leave the petrol bomb behind. They left the house a little after 2.30 a.m.; Michael O'Callaghan led Jonathan Fitzgerald down the short distance towards the Crawford house. He pointed out the house, but did not go the full way. Fitzgerald was on his own at the end.

Meanwhile, Noel Crawford had left his sister's and walked down towards his parents' house. He had to pass that before turning and crossing the estate to his own home. It was 2.30 a.m. and he was not planning on stopping. Everyone would be in bed. His mother had retired before midnight with one of her grandchildren. The house looked quiet.

Paul saw Noel coming down the road. It was late and he knew that Noel would be in talkative mood. Paul decided to close the door so as not to attract his brother.

I said to myself to lock the door and he would not see me, but he spotted the light. I went out and we chatted for about ten minutes. I remember he was saying that he could be killed crossing the estate. That was the way he was thinking, almost like he knew something was going to happen. He said that life begins at 40. He didn't know it would end for him.

Mary Crawford, Noel's mother, remembers the days leading up to that December as some of the tensest the family had ever lived through. The shootings and the injury five-year-old Jordan had suffered were taking their toll.

'I almost forgot that Noel was going to be 40 on Monday. I hadn't even bought him a card. We had nothing planned, but I am sure he would have been over for a few drinks that night,' she said.

The papers wrongly reported that Noel was celebrating his birthday when he was having a can with Paul. But he was just making his way home; any celebration would have been the following day.

'We were ten minutes chatting and then I heard my phone ringing. It was upstairs charging. So I ran into the house to answer it,' remembers Paul. The phone was a hang-up. As soon as Paul answered, it went dead. The most likely caller was an associate of Fitzgerald. The plan was simple: the phone would ring and Paul would step out to answer it, bringing him into the line of fire. They did not know that the phone was upstairs charging. Paul stated:

> I heard two bangs. I looked out the box room window and I saw a fellow going up the road in a hoodie. I roared out the window: 'You are a big man.' He said, 'Yeah.' I didn't think anyone had been hit. I went downstairs. I tried to open the porch door, but Noel was leaning against it. As I got it open, he fell to the ground. He said, 'Help me.' I phoned 999.

Who knows what thoughts passed through Paul's mind in those bleak moments. The scenario was all too familiar. Twice people had been injured in failed assassination attempts on Paul Crawford. Now his brother lay dying in his arms. He might have had nine lives, but the people around him didn't.

Within minutes, the Gardaí had arrived; the ambulance followed swiftly. Noel was taken to the regional hospital, where surgeons struggled to save his life. But the bullet had entered his abdomen and passed out through his back, doing massive internal damage. He died in the small hours of the morning.

At 4 a.m., the night was shattered as shots were fired at a nearby house. Gardaí believed the shots were fired in retaliation for Noel's murder. The house that came under fire was the house Fitzgerald and O'Callaghan had left earlier that night on their black business. Gardaí believed that Paul and one of his brothers had fired the shots. Paul denies this. He did get into a car and drive around the estate (he was spotted), but he says he had nothing to do with the shots. However, he does credit those shots with helping secure a conviction against his brother's killers.

The shots kept them in the house and they were there when the Gardaí raided the house the following morning. If the shots had not been fired, they would have snuck out of the house and set themselves up with alibis.

The following morning tensions were running high in Southill. The pain is still raw as Paul talks about it. As a crowd of sympathisers gathered around his mother's house the following morning, not everyone was sharing the grief. Some people were taking pleasure in the death and, according to Paul, one person behind a curtain pointed an imaginary gun at him and mouthed that he would be next. That, at least, is his version:

I went up to the people that were involved in Noel's murder and they were giving me the gun signs and laughing at me, so I went mad. Who wouldn't? I'm human too. So I said what anyone would say. I said, 'I'll kill ye.'

Investigating gardaí did not see the gestures. But they did hear Crawford shouting: 'My brother Noel is dead, you are all dead too.' He shouted it at a group of people nearby, then pointed to three houses and said: 'That will be done tonight, children and all, and that one, and that one.'

Crawford was immediately arrested and brought before the City Court on a charge of threatening to kill one of his neighbours. He was denied bail and remanded in custody pending a hearing. Three days later, on the morning of his brother's funeral, he again applied for bail to attend the ceremony. It was a last-ditch effort and the case was heard minutes before the funeral mass was due to begin at the Church of the Holy Family in Southill. Crawford, 32 at the time, told the court he had made the threat because he was in a state of shock after his brother's death.

The woman who had made the initial allegation, Elizabeth Sparling, attempted to withdraw her statement, but the Gardaí said this was the result of intimidation. Ms Sparling told the court that she now believed she had nothing to fear from Mr Crawford or his family, whom she had known all her life. She said she made the initial statement while under stress and no longer believed that Crawford posed any threat to her.

Detective Garda Dave Burke, who heard the threat being made, said that he was concerned that there had been intimidation in the case. He described Paul Crawford as a leading member of the McCarthy-Dundon gang.

'In my view, Paul Crawford and his gang have caused such fear in the community that decent people like Ms Sparling, who has never been in court before, feels she has to come down here and withdraw her statement,' he said, adding that Ms Sparling's life was now in danger and that she was afraid that she or her family might be injured if she did not withdraw her statement.

The court was told that her home had been shot at five times and that seven shots were fired into her house just hours after Noel Crawford had been murdered in the same estate.

'She has been bullied by the McCarthy-Dundons to withdraw her statement,' the detective concluded.

Judge Tom O'Donnell refused bail and also refused to make an order allowing Crawford to attend his brother's funeral on compassionate grounds. The judge said: 'If the prison authorities decide to release him on compassionate grounds, that is their decision. It is not within my remit.' The prison did not release him.

Though it was hard on Crawford, the judge and the authorities had good grounds for their concern. The presence of an acknowledged player in the city's feuds would have made the situation very tense and could have led to violence. Noel Crawford was not the first person to have been targeted for being related to Paul Crawford. With that background, it was no surprise that Judge O'Donnell took the decision not to allow him to attend Noel's funeral.

Paul was devastated: 'I missed his layout and his funeral. He died over my sins.'

At the funeral mass the local parish priest, Father Pat Hogan, said that the killers had separated themselves from dignity and self-respect by their actions. He told the congregation:

> They might wish each other happy Christmas, but they know they have a man's life on their hands. They have caused a man's death. They may joke and laugh with each other, but they will never wipe away the goodness and the non-violence and the harmlessness that was in Noel Crawford. Noel was a good man, highly loved by his family and well spoken of by people in this community. In the words of someone who knew him well, 'He wouldn't harm a fly.'

He called for the family and friends of Noel to resist the temptation to seek revenge.

> Noel died at his parents' front door, a place where he had every right to be. His death can give rise to understandable anger, maybe even thoughts of: how do we get justice? How do we get even? But we have to remember that the great people of our community were the people who were able to carry great suffering and injustice with tremendous strength and patience. The family are entitled to be angry, but we cannot allow ourselves to be contaminated by the shame, guilt and evil intent in those who caused Noel's death.

Floral tributes filled the church. Afterwards, a horse-drawn carriage removed the remains. A single bouquet was placed on the coffin as Noel Crawford was laid to rest in Mount St Oliver cemetery.

Gardaí were quick to distance Mr Crawford from any suggestion of criminal activity by stating publicly that he was not the intended target of the gunman. Superintendent Frank O'Brien, leading the investigation, told reporters:

> We believe that the killing is related to an ongoing feud, but we believe that Noel Crawford was killed only because of a family

association. We are not aware of any involvement by Noel Crawford in any feud-related activity. We would not regard this man as being actively involved in criminal activity. Noel Crawford was a hard-working man with a number of children and we have no knowledge that he was involved in any sort of criminal activity that would put him at risk.

As the murder investigation continued, Paul Crawford spent the next several months behind bars, finally being released at the end of May 2007. Gardaí were immediately on the alert, both for some retaliation from him and for some fresh attempt on his life. Just days before his release, shots had been fired at his parents' house – an apparent warning to the gang member to stay away from the Island Field and the Keane-Collopy heartland when he got out.

On his release, in an unusual move, he was banned from four estates in Limerick, including Southill, where he lived. So he moved in with a brother in Cork. The *Sunday World* ran a big spread about the commuting gangster, who drove up to Limerick each day to run his drugs empire, then retired in the evening to a suburban estate in Cork.

'They say I was a drugs lord. I was driving around in a '93 Mondeo,' he said. 'My mother needed a loan to bury my brother.'

Paul's big fear was that his family would blame him for what had happened to Noel. He had not been able to attend any of the funeral and had been imprisoned within hours of his brother's death. After his release, he says he used to drive up from Cork and meet family members in Supermac's for a meal, then spend a few hours mooching around one of the local shopping centres before heading back again.

'We do not blame Paul,' said his mother. 'We blame the guy who pulled the trigger. And we got justice.'

A number of arrests were made over the following months and years, but it was a slow process. From the beginning, the Gardaí knew who they were looking for, but they had to build a watertight case. Finally, on Wednesday, 3 June 2009, someone was charged with the murder of Noel Crawford. The accused was the teenage Michael O'Callaghan; initially he could not be named because of his age.

By now 17 years old, and originally from the south side of the city, he was arrested in County Clare. He was given free legal aid. His solicitor, John Herbert, said that the boy's mother was still alive, but there was minimal contact between them. The boy was remanded to St Patrick's Institution.

Then, in June, a man was extradited from the UK to face a murder charge. Jonathan Fitzgerald, then 20, of South Claughaun Road, Garryowen, Limerick, was also charged with a number of unrelated thefts. He was just 17 at the time of the murder. His accomplice was just 15.

The murder trial opened in January 2011. Michael O'Callaghan (of Pineview Gardens, Moyross, Limerick), charged with murder, could be named by this time, as he was 19. He denied the murder charge, but pleaded guilty to manslaughter. As he was only 15 at the time of the killing, this plea was accepted by the state. Fitzgerald denied the murder charge.

Mary Crawford, mother of the victim, gave harrowing testimony of the night she lost her son. She shook and sobbed as she took the oath in the Central Criminal Court in Dublin. She said that her son Paul was still up when she went to bed with her grandchildren on the night of Sunday, 17 December. She woke some hours later to hear his phone ringing, then she heard two loud bangs. She ran downstairs and found her other son, Noel, lying on the ground. She said that she knew immediately he was gone and there was nothing she could do for him. She added that Noel did not live in the house and that she had not even known he would be calling around that evening when she had gone to bed.

The court had heard earlier about what the two brothers had been doing and about how events unfurled.

A single bullet had struck Noel in the stomach, exiting through his back. The second shot had missed him, hitting the front window of the house. The Gardaí had not recovered the gun, but they had several witnesses placing the accused in the area with a gun at the time of the shooting.

David Duggan said that he had been helping Noel Crawford celebrate his 40th birthday. But Mr Duggan said that O'Malley Park could often be like the 'Wild West' and that it was not uncommon for shots to be fired into the air at night. The Crawford house had been shot at at least twice not long before the night of the murder. Because of this Mr Duggan was not initially concerned when he heard the two shots ring out. He didn't realise his friend had been hit.

Under cross-examination, Paul Crawford denied knowing Jonathan Fitzgerald. He did admit that shortly after the shooting he 'went off for a spin' with a number of other people. Some of those people were serious criminals, now doing time for violent crimes. He also admitted that he and one of the men he was with got out of their car at the top of the Southill estate. Gardaí had seen them. However, he denied shooting at a house at the top of the estate at 4 a.m., later on the morning of the murder. The house that was shot at was where Jonathan Fitzgerald was found by gardaí some hours later.

Ann Crawford said that she had left her brother Noel minding her children in her home in Southill at around 10 p.m. on the Sunday night, while she went out to watch a film in a neighbour's house. That night had been an active night; before she went to watch the film she had seen her brother out at her gate watching a stolen car being raced around the estate.

'He just liked watching,' she said.

After she returned home, Noel had left and gone to their parents' house.

She said that when she heard bangs around 3 a.m. she immediately phoned Noel. His phone must have been answered automatically as he fell, and she could hear her sister Olivia screaming in the background that their brother had been shot.

The chief prosecution witness was Laura Kelly, who testified via a live video link from Westminster Court in London. She said that Jonathan Fitzgerald and another man, Michael

O'Callaghan, had come to her home in O'Malley Park shortly after 2 a.m. on Monday, 18 December 2006. She overheard their conversation. They were planning an attack on a nearby house.

She said that she heard them discussing the attack. Both men were wearing bulletproof vests and they were making a petrol bomb. She did not approve of that and asked them to leave her house. They left. A few minutes later, she heard two shots ring out. Moments later, both men returned to her house, banging on her door to be let in.

'They were kind of jumping,' she said. 'Jonathan Fitzgerald said: "I got him. I got him. I got Paul Crawford."'

She added that, about an hour after the killing, her windows had been shot in. Fitzgerald and O'Callaghan had left the house, but returned during the night, while she was sleeping. When gardaí called at the house at 7.50 a.m. on the Monday – more than four hours after the shooting – both men were there.

Fitzgerald had instructed Ms Kelly and her partner, Jonathon Kiely, to say that they had come in after 4 a.m. They felt intimidated by Fitzgerald and initially told that lie to the Gardaí. However, a month into the investigation, Mr Kiely changed his statement and told the truth about what had happened that night and when Fitzgerald and O'Callaghan had visited the house. Ms Kelly also changed her statement, but she took two years to finally admit the truth. She only made an accurate statement when she moved out of Limerick.

Over the course of the trial the prosecution argued that Jonathan Fitzgerald had a good motive for wanting to kill Paul Crawford, the intended victim of the shooting. Fitzgerald's sister Jennifer had been kidnapped on the Sunday morning before the shooting and he blamed Paul Crawford for that.

'That abduction arose out of an ongoing feud in the city to which members of each family have links,' Detective Sergeant Denis Treacy told the jury. 'Retaliation is the norm in these incidents. It's expected and very common.'

The defence countered that Paul Crawford had many enemies,

there had been previous attempts on his life and it was someone else who had fired the fatal shot.

Detective Treacy told the court that Fitzgerald's teenage accomplice, O'Callaghan, had been questioned after the killing. Within a month, he had admitted his involvement. He said that he had not actually been with Fitzgerald when the shots were fired, but he had been with him just before. Being originally from O'Malley Park, he knew his way around the estate. He led Fitzgerald down the hill and pointed out the Crawford house. But he didn't go all the way to the house with him.

'He said he was sorry about what happened to Noel Crawford, that it wasn't meant for him,' the detective said. 'He said Jonathan Fitzgerald had meant to shoot Paul Crawford, the victim's brother.'

Detective Treacy added that Noel Crawford and his mother were both 'thoroughly decent people'. He confirmed that it had been a gangland hit and said, 'This incident on the night arose directly from the abduction.'

After hearing all the evidence, the judge reminded the jury that the fact that the wrong man was shot did not absolve the shooter.

'Mistaken identity or shooting at one individual, missing and hitting another, does not absolve someone from responsibility,' Mr Justice Barry White told the jurors.

The jury found Fitzgerald guilty of murder. He was given a life sentence. His accomplice, Michael O'Callaghan, who pleaded guilty to manslaughter, was sentenced to seven years. The court heard that his father, Gerard Power, had been stabbed to death when O'Callaghan was just three. His mother had alcohol problems.

'His upbringing was in a dysfunctional family. His family moved out of Southill in mid-2006 when Michael became involved in serious feuding in the city,' said Detective Treacy. O'Callaghan was shot in 2006; later that year, he was involved in shooting a man in Moyross, for which he was convicted of assault. He moved in with an 18-year-old cousin in Moyross when he was just 14.

'During that period he became very involved in criminal and gangland activities in Limerick,' stated the detective. He added that gardaí would frequently spot O'Callaghan – from the age of 14 – walking around with criminals and wearing a bullet-proof vest.

In a victim impact statement, Mary Crawford described herself as a 'broken-hearted mother'. She said that it was her son's 40th birthday when he was 'callously' shot. 'It was to be a day of great joy,' she said. 'But it was the day he died.' She said the pain that followed was indescribable and that she would pray for those who had lost children but had not yet got justice.

*

The murder of his brother changed Paul Crawford. I met him on a warm summer's day – one of the handful in the summer of 2012. He was in a small grotto to the Virgin Mary at the back of O'Malley Park, Southill, and he was clearing rocks. The grotto had been renovated and cleaned up, and the field beside it was being cleared for a five-a-side pitch. He was working beside the parish priest, Father Pat Hogan, and a couple of his neighbours.

'Older lads like me are a role model for the young guys,' he said. 'They could see me up at the top of the park with a hurley laying into someone, and they will copy that. Maybe if they see me down here clearing a field for the kids, they will copy that too.'

This was a different Paul Crawford from the snarling face leering out from the lurid pages of the *Sunday World*. The reason for the change is simple: Paul Crawford has seen at first hand the devastation that visits a family when an innocent man is gunned down by mistake.

He was a completely innocent man. He was only killed because he was my brother. But the papers never say that. Because I have done bad things, they forget that he was innocent. He never did anything wrong. He didn't deserve to die.

Paul claims that the death of his brother forced him to re-evaluate his life.

> It is a night we will never forget. When he died, they killed us as well. We all died with him. Christmas will never be Christmas to us any more. Christmas is gone. On Christmas Eve, Noel would come over and fix all the bikes and buggies that were there for the kids. Those sorts of things we will miss.

Paul was also surprised at the lack of support both within the community and within the criminal underworld.

> Nobody helped me or my family when we needed them. When Noel died, they were like, 'Fuck him, he's nobody.' But no one had the right to come to my parents' house with a gun and do what they did to him, no matter what I had done.
>
> It took me to lose my brother for me to open my eyes. You have to experience it to realise it. Now all I want is to do something right to pay back my brother for his loss. All I want is the chance to let people know it's all fun and games until you lose someone you love. I would swap my life now to have him back, but I know that can't happen. I could kill someone for Noel, but two wrongs do not make a right.

As I write, Paul claims that he is trying to lead a quiet life. He just wants to be left alone to get on with it. He claims he is no longer involved in criminality. He has become involved with the local soccer club and cleared a small field for five-a-side games. Other projects he has become involved with include repainting the homes of some of the elderly residents of O'Malley Park.

Southill is a different estate from what it was ten, or even five, years ago. Many people have moved out and the city-wide regeneration programme has changed the estate. Boarded-up houses are gradually being demolished and people are being given grants to move out. There are fewer than half the houses left compared to when O'Malley Park was first built in the early '70s.

One other thing has changed: it is far quieter now. There are still troublesome families, drug deals still go down in the alleyways and stolen cars race through the park at night. But the shootings are a thing of the past – though the Crawfords are taking no chances. Paul still looks over his shoulder.

'I won't pull my car up beside someone. I will pull up a bit ahead, in case they are trouble. But things are a lot quieter,' he said.

Mary Crawford's house has bulletproof glass in the windows and a reinforced front door. The curtain in the front room still has a bullet hole and there are buckshot dimples on the walls. But the Wild West days of 2006 are gone. Mary Crawford, originally from the rural town of Dromcollagher, is determined she will not be forced out by the events of that traumatic year.

'I am not going anywhere,' she said. 'I am here 43 years. This is my home. My memories are here.'

11

THE INNOCENT VICTIMS: SHOT BECAUSE HE LOOKED LIKE HIS NEIGHBOUR

The Murder of Shane Geoghegan

WHEN THE MCCARTHY-DUNDON gang gunned down innocent security head Brian Fitzgerald, there were lessons that could have been learnt. The first lesson was that the high-profile murder of an innocent man brings a lot of heat on a gang and makes normal business difficult to transact. The second lesson was that the Gardaí would not stop searching until they found the killers.

The McCarthy-Dundons are known for many things – viciousness, brutality, thuggishness, avariciousness. But one thing they have never been known for is brains. They learnt nothing from the earlier killing.

In November 2008, they did it again – they gunned down an innocent man. This time his connection with the gang and their affairs was even slimmer than Brian Fitzgerald's. Fitzgerald had stood in their way; Shane Geoghegan had never even crossed their path. But he looked like a guy they wanted dead, and they shot him by mistake. It was a murder that horrified Limerick and once again brought the gangland drugs wars out of the slums and into the peaceful suburbs.

The victim was Shane Geoghegan, a 28-year-old rugby player

who held down a good job and was described by all as a decent and friendly man. Shane grew up in the city, where his parents, Tom and Mary, ran a nursing home on O'Connell Avenue. They lived in Kilteragh, a sprawling estate in Dooradoyle, a good part of Limerick. Shane had a brother, Tom, and a sister, Kate, who tragically died from cancer at the age of 11.

He went to the local Crescent College comprehensive, a large school in Dooradoyle run by the Jesuits. The Jesuits have had a school in Limerick, on and off, since the sixteenth century. In 1973, they moved from O'Connell Avenue (The Crescent) to a green-field site in leafy Dooradoyle. The new school was a big one, with plenty of room for expansion and lots of sports facilities. Initially, the school was boys only, but within a year it went co-ed. The school now has close to 1,000 pupils and is one of the best in Limerick.

Jesuits have a reputation for an intellectual and character-forming education, churning out rounded individuals who generally do well in life. The Crescent comprehensive is no exception. It is also a sport-mad school, with rugby, hockey, track and field and GAA teams regularly lining out in the school colours. Shane, a big lad, thrived there. The school's rugby coach, Chris Cullinan, remembered him well, telling the *Limerick Leader*:

> He started out as a winger and then moved to the front row, when he was with us in Crescent. He played in both our junior and senior schools cup sides. We reached the semi-finals of the Senior Cup on both occasions. He was very much a team player. He loved the craic and the camaraderie of the game.

The coach said that, in his final year, Shane was over-age for the senior cup. Instead of quitting to concentrate on his studies, he helped coach the under-13s. 'That was the kind of guy he was,' said Mr Cullinan.

After leaving school, Shane trained as a fitter and got a job with Air Atlanta at their aircraft maintenance facility in

Shannon, about ten miles from Limerick. He also maintained his interest in rugby, playing for both Old Crescent and Garryowen, winning an All Ireland League under-20 title. He was a good player, but, more importantly, he was a good leader on the field, a natural motivator. He became a fixture on the Garryowen Thirds and his contribution on the field was recognised when he was made captain.

Shane had a long-term girlfriend, Jenna Barry, and the two bought a house at Kilteragh, Clonmore, Dooradoyle, close to the school where he had spent many happy hours and the home where he had grown up. They were planning on getting married. The couple hadn't been in their new home long, but were enjoying the peaceful residential estate. It was close to the modern Crescent Shopping Centre and only a ten-minute drive from the centre of town. It was also close to the Garryowen pitch.

On 8 November, Shane Geoghegan lined out as usual with Garryowen. He led them onto the pitch for their match against local rivals Shannon. It was a close game, which Garryowen lost. But no one was too bothered; the real game was that evening, on the television. Ireland was playing Australia and the excitement was intense. Limerick loves rugby and the whole city would be indoors, either in homes or pubs, for the game.

Shane joined some friends at a private house and had a few beers while he was watching the international. They stayed, socialising, after the game. It was after 1 a.m. when he finally made his way back towards his new home in Kilteragh.

A burly, bearded man of a certain age, Shane had no idea that he closely resembled a neighbour – one who was not such an innocent man.

*

John McNamara was reputed to be a leading member of the Keane-Collopy gang, bitter rivals of the McCarthy-Dundons. The Keane gang were in disarray and losing the feud. Several leading members were either dead or behind bars – but that did not stop the savagery of their opponents. McNamara had been targeted before. On 23 August 2006 – a little over two years previously – up to 20 shots were fired at his car and home, but he escaped without injury.

Not all of the gangsters remain in the enclaves of Southill, Moyross and St Mary's Park. McNamara lived in Dooradoyle, in the same estate as Shane Geoghegan. He had lived there since 2006, and his house was only four doors up from Shane's. Known as Johnny Mac, he was a big man with a beard.

The drug dealer, who has only one eye, was identified at the subsequent murder trial as the intended victim that night. It was Shane Geoghegan's bad luck that he bore a superficial resemblance to the real target.

*

As the evening blended into the early hours of the following morning, Shane knew it was time to return home. It was a little after 1.30 a.m.; he was making his way across a green area in Kilteragh, only moments from his house. His attention was caught by a flickering figure in his peripheral vision. As he turned to look, he was shocked to see two young men walking towards him, one carrying a gun. The men had arrived earlier that evening and were lying in wait. Their getaway car, a dark Renault, had been stolen a few weeks earlier in preparation.

Shane turned and ran, but the gunman followed, shooting. The other man hung back, near the getaway car. Shane managed to get to a nearby house on Clonmore and tried to go into the back. But some of the shots had caught him in the upper body, and he was losing the race for life. He took three direct hits and, inevitably, his strength failed him. He was cornered in the garden of the house he had reached. The gunman caught up with him and finished him off with a shot to the back of the head. It was the ninth shot he had fired and four had struck his victim. Then he was off, disappearing into the night.

The roads of Dooradoyle are not patrolled nightly like those of Southill and Moyross, and there was nothing to hinder his escape. The dark Renault Espace revved violently and the killer was gone. The car was later burnt out in Rosbrien, not far away.

As Shane lay bleeding to death in the darkness, it brought to 17 the number of fatal shootings in Ireland that year. He was the 14th victim of the murderous gang war that started with the killing of Kieran Keane in 2002. Several of the deaths had been innocent people caught in the crossfire.

Shocked residents phoned the Gardaí as the shots rang out in their estate. Members of the Armed Response Unit were on the scene quickly. They knew at once they were too late to do anything. The area was sealed off and the body covered until morning, when state pathologist Dr Marie Cassidy attended to examine the body before it was removed to the regional hospital for the post-mortem examination. The reaction to the brutal murder was one of horror; Garryowen cancelled their weekend fixtures as a sign of respect.

As in the case of the murder of Brian Fitzgerald, people were stunned that the feud had stretched its tentacles into the middle-class suburbs. But there was one vital difference. Brian Fitzgerald had stood up to the gangs. He was killed because he said no to drugs in his nightclub. Shane Geoghegan had no connection, however tenuous, with the gangsters. He had never had any contact with them and was probably not even aware that one of his neighbours was involved in the deadly drugs trade. If Shane could be a victim, anyone could be a victim.

Over the coming days and weeks, people expressed their horror. The local paper, the *Limerick Leader*, opened a book of condolences, which was signed by thousands. Politicians jumped on the band wagon, calling for legislation to bring the gangs into order. Mayor John Gilligan, who also opened a book of condolences at City Hall, summed up the mood when he described the murder as a new low.

Mayor Gilligan, from St Mary's Park, knew many of the main players well. He told the *Leader*:

An innocent person has been murdered by people who have nothing to offer the city, only brutality and tears. We always knew what these people were capable of doing, but they generally went out and murdered one another. Now they are murdering people without even checking to see if they are murdering the right people. It just goes to show how callous these criminals have become and it does mark a new low for our city, a city that is hanging its head in shame.

He was referring to a rumour that had spread through the city that the killer had phoned his paymasters just before the shooting and expressed doubts about whether he had the right target. The gang boss told him to shoot anyway. The story was apocryphal, but was widely believed. It may not have been true, but it summed up the gangs' attitude. Everyone knew they didn't care who they killed.

Like the murder of Veronica Guerin several years earlier, the brutal killing became a rallying point for politicians looking for tougher anti-gang laws and citizens expressing their outrage. Even the Taoiseach became involved; Brian Cowen and Justice Minister Dermot Ahern met with the Garda Commissioner about the growing problem of gangland violence in Limerick. This followed growing opposition criticism of the government and calls for decisive action in introducing tough new legislation.

Limerick TD Jan O'Sullivan, Labour, said that the murder was 'shocking beyond belief' and called for electronic surveillance to be used to secure convictions. Fine Gael's Michael Noonan said he had known three generations of the Geoghegan family and he was 'absolutely appalled' at the killing.

Dermot Ahern described the murder as 'an absolutely awful crime committed by scum', while Willie O'Dea said it was 'unspeakable'. He told the *Leader*:

There's a palpable sense of shock right throughout the community from last night. It is a horrific case, a perfectly innocent young man, a well-known local rugby player from a well-known local family, obviously mistaken for someone else and shot down. It's unspeakable.

But he struck a note of optimism:

> There's no more successful units than the detective unit in Limerick at detecting serious crime and putting away serious criminals, and I've every confidence that the Gardaí in Limerick will track down the people responsible for this and take them off the streets for many a long day to come.

Statistically, Minister O'Dea was right. The detection rate for murders in Limerick is very high. You might get away with it in Dublin, but not by the Shannon. And gardaí were taking this one very seriously.

Superintendent Donoghue went on *Morning Ireland* to say:

> This certainly was a tragic case. At this stage of our investigation we see no reason as to why Shane Geoghegan would have been targeted or would have been killed in this way. Until we find out who killed him and why, anything beyond that is speculative.

He said that about 40 officers were directly involved in the investigation, but they needed the public to come forward to help. He added:

> It is important in all of these incidents to say we're merely policing on the community's behalf, and there are people in the community in Limerick and society generally who have information in respect of crime.
>
> We have a sighting of a dark blue or black Renault Espace in the area, and we are certainly anxious to talk to anyone who would have seen that car in and around the estate on that night, or indeed any vehicle matching that description that would have tweaked anyone's interest in the preceding days or weeks.

The next few days were filled with people's poignant reactions to the killing, as Shane's family prepared for the funeral. A Garryowen RFC spokesperson told the *Limerick Leader*: 'We are absolutely shocked and saddened by Shane's tragic and untimely death. He was a fabulous young man and a talented, committed and honest player.'

Fine Gael councillor Richard Butler said to the *Leader*: 'We are all shocked that something like this could happen in a lovely community where hard-working, decent honest people live.'

This was the nub of the shock: the location of the killing. It was the 14th homicide since 2000 linked to the Limerick feuds, but this killing brought the feud to the suburbs. Mr Geoghegan's remains reposed in his mother's house, while friends, colleagues and family gathered to pay their respects. It was not the first tragedy to hit the Geoghegan family. Shane's younger sister Kate had died of cancer when she was just 11 and his grandmother, who ran a nursing home in the city, had been killed in a car crash in France some years earlier. Shane was survived by his girlfriend Jenna, brother Anthony and parents Tom and Mary. He was laid to rest in Mungret cemetery. A few days later, Garryowen Rugby Club also organised a special mass in his memory. The chairman of the club, Ger Clarke, told the *Leader*:

> Shane was a young fellow making his way in life and playing rugby with Garryowen. He was a lovely human being. It is not something that any of us know how to deal with. Our concern is for his family, his friends and the players.
>
> The level of shock and trauma that they are going through is something I haven't seen in a long, long time.
>
> We are doing as well as we can in the circumstances, but our only thoughts are with Shane, who we miss dreadfully, and his family.

People noted the eerie similarities with another innocent victim,

Brian Fitzgerald. Both men were shot at point-blank range close to their homes, in quiet and respectable estates. Both men were shot in the early hours of the morning by assassins who waited in the darkness. Like Fitzgerald, the early indications were that Shane Geoghegan tried to run from his attackers, but could not get away from the bullets. Both were big men, described by those who knew them as loving and valued members of their communities. But the most important thing that they had in common was that they were innocent victims gunned down by the McCarthy-Dundon gang.

*

There was one other similarity, which many people did not immediately spot. Both had been killed by professional hit men. That would make the job of the Gardaí a lot more difficult. The man they were looking for would not be from Limerick and would have no connection with his victim.

Gangs have been using hit men for years – and loaning them out to other gangs in other cities. As Garda detection methods become more sophisticated, the use of hit men will increase. I remember sitting in a small living room of a corporation house in a more respectable part of Limerick. The tearful parents told me about the death of their young son, killed because he got involved in a row with one of the city's several shadowy gangland figures. The boy was completely innocent and lost his life in a trivial dispute. At the time I met them, another of their sons had been shot at, by an associate of the man accused of murdering their first son. The family didn't know whether their second son had been shot as a warning to back away from doing anything about the first killing, or if the intention had been to kill him.

'What sort of a monster would shoot someone he doesn't know and who has never done anything to him?' I mused.

'He was paid to do it,' said the mother. 'He was paid €800.'

Eight hundred euros. That was the fee five years ago to have someone shot in Limerick. In other parts of the country, it probably varied slightly, but like the price of a pint those variations were not significant: €800 to have someone shot, no guarantee of a kill. It could be a kneecapping, a warning, a death . . . It cost a lot less just to have someone injured. I spoke to one man – from a respectable family in a working-class part of Dublin. He had been attacked and the Gardaí had not prosecuted his attacker. So he paid €250 to have his attacker beaten, on the anniversary of the attack; the man was hospitalised.

He told me that within two years of carrying out that little job the hired heavy was dead himself, taken out in a gangland hit as he was working out in a local gym. It's a dangerous world, and life is cheap. If you know where to look, you can have someone's leg broken, or have them kneecapped, or have them shot in the head. Dozens of gangland murders in the past few years show the truth of this.

You might get someone shot or even killed for small money, but the really professional hit men can command five-figure fees for a contract. And some of them work regularly. The reason they can command those fees is that most gangland activity is driven by the drugs business and there is huge money floating around. Some gangs are making in excess of €100,000 a week.

But you don't need to pay big bucks to the professionals. There is another method, as former McCarthy-Dundon gang member Paul Crawford explained to me when I interviewed him in 2012:

> Lots of guys try to go straight in jail. But when you come out you have nothing. You went in and you had a relatively new car, you had a girlfriend. Now you have nothing. And a guy you know comes up in a flashy car and gives you a kilo of coke or heroin and tells you there is no rush paying him back. So you are back dealing.
>
> A couple of months later you are getting back on your feet, but you still owe for that bag. And he says to you, Johnny down

the road is causing me problems. You'd be doing me a great favour if you whacked him. And you think, why not? It will knock a couple of grand off what I owe for the drugs.

Sometimes bad debts, or other forces, turn men into killers. There was more than money involved when a Dublin crook was persuaded to take on the Dooradoyle shooting.

Gardaí charged a suspect, Dubliner Barry Doyle, in February 2009. He was a young man from a family steeped in criminality. His brother Paddy was one of the most notorious hit men in the capital. Like the Campions in Limerick, they seemed to have turned murder into a family business.

Paddy was by far the worse of the two, being responsible for several murders in Dublin before fleeing to Spain's Costa Del Crime. He was assassinated himself, possibly over a drugs deal gone wrong. His life story is the stuff of fiction. It is also the reason that Barry agreed to shoot a man in Limerick – and shot Shane Geoghegan by mistake. He believed that he was avenging his brother's death.

*

Paddy Doyle was at the heart of a feud in Dublin that had cost close to a dozen lives. As vicious as the feud between the McCarthy-Dundons and the Keane-Collopys, it tore apart Crumlin and Drimnagh, and sucked in criminals from surrounding areas. Like the Limerick feud, it was, at its heart, about drugs.

Declan Gavin and Brian Rattigan were friends growing up together in Crumlin. They entered the drugs trade together. But when they fell out, it was murder. Thugs with pedigrees, such as Fat Freddie Thompson and Paddy Doyle, sided with Gavin.

Doyle, unlike some of the other members, was a genuinely tough guy. He had been in trouble since he was a child. Violent and dishonest by nature, he also had a certain discipline which made him more dangerous. An experienced amateur boxer, he didn't need a gun in his hand to inflict hurt. There is something about men who have trained as fighters. They carry themselves with a confidence that can make them very intimidating. In addition, Doyle worked out regularly and used steroids to build up a hard and strong body. At 6 ft 5 in. he was a big man. Apart from the occasional line of coke, he didn't abuse his body. He was polite and calm, but had killer eyes. He was a good man to have on the Gavin side.

When Gavin was murdered in 2001, Fat Freddie Thompson became the leader of the Gavin faction, with Paddy Doyle his lieutenant. On St Patrick's night the following year, Paddy Doyle was one of a pair of assassins who broke into Brian Rattigan's house, shooting him in his bed and leaving him for dead. Against all the odds, Rattigan pulled through and made a full recovery. But his time out recovering left the field to Thompson, and now his gang was a serious threat. In Paddy Doyle, Thompson had a loyal lieutenant who was ready to kill.

In time, the Rattigan gang forged strong links with the Keane-Collopy gang in Limerick. The Thompson gang forged equally strong links with the McCarthy-Dundon gang. Over the course of the next decade, the gang is thought to have been responsible for at least 15 murders. Their enforcer and hit man Paddy Doyle was directly involved in at least four murders, and possibly a few more.

He moved around a lot, often sleeping in a different place each night to avoid rival gangs. As his notoriety grew, he also began to indulge in childish disguises. He got a woman's wig and took to driving around in drag. Once he had the dress and wig on, he felt his enemies could not spot him. Tall and slim, with the leanness from his boxing days, he passed as a striking, if slightly masculine, woman.

He tried to live a normal enough life outside of his criminal activity. A father of two, gardaí who knew him described him as more personable and respectable than the average criminal. He dressed better, carried himself with an air of confidence and was polite. But they remember that he had cold eyes. He seemed to look through you.

Though he was taking crazy precautions for his safety and was rightly paranoid about everyone, he did not lighten his workload. He was still the enforcer. He was still a trigger man for hire. In November 2005, he showed just how effective a trigger man he was. He went on a killing spree.

His first two victims were from his own gang. That was part of what being an enforcer was about. They were Darren Geoghegan, the gang's money man, and his assistant, Gavin Byrne. Doyle was a very close friend of Geoghegan. They had been friends since childhood and hung out together a lot. But business is business.

On the evening of 13 November 2005, Geoghegan and Byrne were in a car when Doyle got into the back seat. He pulled out a Sig Sauer automatic pistol and shot Byrne twice in the back of the head. Without pausing he spun towards Geoghegan and put two bullets in the back of his head as well. The speed with which he did this is shown by the fact that neither man even had a chance to begin turning.

Within two days, Doyle was busy again. This time his victim was Noel Roche, a leading member of the Rattigan gang. He shot him during the course of a high-speed car chase along the Clontarf Road.

In the days after the three killings, Doyle knew he was a marked man, with a rumoured price of €60,000 on his head. He became increasingly paranoid. After a month, he fled to the UK. From there, he went on to Spain, basing himself in Marbella. Doyle fitted right in with the international crime set.

He enjoyed all the trappings of his wealth, thinking nothing of paying €20,000 a year for private parking near the harbour in upmarket Puerto Banús. Some people lived a year on less, yet Doyle could pay it for parking. He maintained his criminal links; it is thought he was involved in planning the murder of mother of two Baiba Salute back in Dublin. In 2007, he travelled to Amsterdam to carry out a hit for a British gang.

But on Monday, 4 February 2008, Doyle was shot dead by an assassin with a machine pistol. He was shot 15 times. There were many suspects. The British gang who hired him for the Amsterdam hit were furious because he killed the wrong man. He had insulted a Russian Mafia boss. And he had been involved in a botched drug deal involving Turkish gangsters. Take your pick. Spanish investigators leant towards the Turkish gangsters.

Whatever the truth, Doyle was one of the most vicious killers Ireland has produced. He was completely ruthless and was quite comfortable shooting even good friends, if the money was right. Doyle was a new type of killer: he killed for money. And he had no conscience about it. He was a monster.

*

But even monsters are loved by their families. Barry Doyle, when he was hired to carry out a hit in Limerick, was told that the man he was going to kill was involved in the murder of his brother Paddy. Paddy had been seen in the company of members of the McCarthy-Dundon gang in Spain before his death. After his brother's death, Barry, who was also in Spain, came home and joined up with the McCarthy-Dundons. He was told that John McNamara – a leading member of the Keane-Collopy gang – was involved in his brother's murder. It was completely untrue, but it helped get him onboard.

Barry Doyle's trial opened in February 2011 and was jinxed from the start. A jury was sworn in and returned the following day for the trial only to be discharged by Mr Justice Paul Carney. He did not go into the reasons, but a new jury was sworn in and the trial got under way. The accused, with addresses at Portland Row, Dublin, and Hyde Road, Limerick, pleaded not guilty to murder.

Barrister Tom O'Connell told the jury that Doyle had admitted to shooting Shane Geoghegan by mistake in a series of video interviews with the Gardaí:

> He admitted that he fired seven or eight shots. He admitted following Shane Geoghegan into the back garden of a house in Clonmore, shooting him in the head. He told the Guards the

gun jammed and that he pulled back the slide two or three times, which is confirmed by the finding of the two undischarged casings on the street outside. He admitted that he never met Shane Geoghegan before, that Shane Geoghegan was an innocent man, in other words not the intended target, but a case of mistaken identity.

Jenna Barry, Shane's girlfriend, said she last saw Shane about two hours before his death. She left him at a friend's house and went home, visiting his mother briefly on the way. 'I texted him to see was he coming home just before 1 a.m. He said he was on his way. He'd be home in a minute,' she testified. 'I heard a series of loud bangs. I heard two outside the house. It sounded like fireworks to me. It was around Hallowe'en.'

However, when the couple's two dogs didn't stop barking and seemed 'unusually tense', she looked out of the front door onto the cul-de-sac. 'I saw someone run towards a car. The wheels were screeching and someone was shouting "Drive".'

She saw a young, hooded man get into the car. She dialled 999 and reported the incident. 'I texted Shane. I told him: "I think there's been a shooting,"' she added.

Dramatic testimony was provided by Victoria Gunnery, a former girlfriend with whom Barry Doyle had had a child. She said that he told her he would have his phone off on the evening of the murder because he had a job to do. He turned his phone back on at 1.30 a.m., and when she texted asking him why the phone was off he told her to read Teletext in the morning. When she read that a man had been murdered, she called him a scumbag. She said that Doyle went to Turkey for a few weeks and phoned her, asking how the papers were reporting the murder.

'I said, "They know it's you because they say it's a very close associate of Patrick Doyle." He said they had no proof,' she continued.

'I just said to him, "That was an innocent man." He said, "If it wasn't an innocent man, there wouldn't be so much hype."'

263

Detective Sergeant Mark Philips of the National Bureau of Criminal Investigation told the jury he interviewed Doyle after his arrest. A series of 23 interviews were carried out. On the 15th interview, Doyle changed his story; he no longer denied killing Shane Geoghegan and admitted his involvement.

'Yeah, I shot him,' said Doyle. 'I seen someone walking across the estate. I got out of the car and shot him. He ran. I chased him around the back of the house. I shot him again.'

He said that the rugby player was halfway across the road when he fired at him first, but that he then ran into one of the back gardens. 'I was looking around the cars . . . I heard heavy breathing,' he said, confirming that he then chased the deceased into the garden. He said that Mr Geoghegan was 'on the ground, up against the wall' when he shot him twice in the head.

Detective Sergeant Philips said: 'When we had completed our interview with Barry Doyle, he took a set of white, plastic rosary beads from around his neck, threw them on the interview table and asked us would we give them to Shane Geoghegan's mother.'

He agreed that he regretted the shooting and that he would turn back the clock if he could.

However, the video interviews were challenged by Doyle's defence team. It was put to the Gardaí that Doyle had been offered a deal: if he admitted to the murders, his girlfriend Victoria Gunnery, who had been taken in for questioning, would be released. Their young child had a heart condition.

Barrister Martin O'Rourke said: 'This was inducement . . . using his girlfriend and the mother of his sick child as bait.'

Summing up at the end of the trial, Barrister Sean Guerin, prosecuting, said that Shane Geoghegan was 'inoffensively and entirely innocently' walking home when he had been gunned down. 'There's no question that it was murder,' he said. 'The question is: was Barry Doyle the person who committed the murder?'

He said that there were many consistencies between the statements made by Doyle in custody, with what witnesses saw and what forensic investigation uncovered. Referring to Shane Geoghegan's jacket, which had a bullet hole in it, he said: 'Even after all the evidence, if you still have any doubt, put your finger in the hole in that jacket and you'll believe.'

Defence barrister Martin O'Rourke suggested to the jury that all the details supposedly supplied by Doyle in his video interviews had been given to him by gardaí during those interviews. He said it was the defence's case that there was psychological pressure, coercion and inducement, and that his client was the victim of threats and promises. He said that Doyle's solicitor had done a deal with the gardaí securing the release of Ms Gunnery. 'Do the right thing. Don't keep Vicky away from the young one any longer than she has to be,' he quoted from a memo of the interview. 'What could that mean other than "Tell us what we want to hear and Vicky will be released"?' he suggested. 'There's the threat and the promise.'

The jury retired to consider its verdict. The jinx of the trial struck again: one of the jurors had to be excused because his father became seriously ill. The eleven remaining jurors deliberated for two and a half hours, but failed to reach a verdict. It was Friday afternoon and the judge sent them home for the weekend. On Monday, the judge told them they did not have to reach a unanimous verdict; he would accept a ten–one decision. They deliberated all day, even through lunch. They took just one brief smoke break.

At one point, they requested the judge to resolve a question for them. They asked for clarification on what constituted murder and what level of involvement was needed.

'The state's case is that Barry Doyle was the gunman. How much more involved can you get?' replied Mr Justice Paul Carney.

The jury then asked about joint enterprise. This was the involvement of other conspirators in the murder. 'You're not concerned with other people not before the court,' replied the judge.

At lunchtime on Tuesday, one of the jurors informed the

judge that he had a pre-booked flight to catch. He had informed the court at the start of the trial that he had the flight booked and had been assured that the trial would be well over in time for him to make it. The judge excused him, reducing the jury to ten.

By Wednesday morning, the jury was facing its fourth day of deliberations. However, the loss of the second juror meant that the option of a majority verdict was no longer open to them; it had to be all or nothing. By the end of the day, the jury had been deliberating for more than 15 hours. It was one of the longest deliberations in the history of the state. And it was fruitless.

The jury approached the judge with another question. 'The jury would like to know how to proceed if we believe it will never be possible to agree a unanimous verdict,' asked the foreman.

'You fill in the words "cannot agree" on the issue paper and sign it,' replied Mr Justice Paul Carney.

'Can I request a pen?' asked the foreman, ending the marathon session.

The judge thanked the jurors and discharged them from jury service for the rest of their lives.

Shane Geoghegan's family and girlfriend, who had attended every day of the four-week trial, sat silently with their heads bowed while the 25-year-old accused smiled at members of his family, who had also attended the entire trial. But he was not home free; the jury's failure to reach a verdict would not let him off the hook. The former bricklayer, a father of three, was sent back to jail until a new trial could begin.

The second trial began in January 2012. April Collins, the partner of gang leader Ger Dundon and the mother of his three children, told the court that she had heard the murder being planned.

Ger Dundon, John Dundon, Barry Doyle and some others were present the night before the murder. 'John Dundon was saying he'd everything sussed out about John McNamara and that it was time to make the move,' she said, adding that Dundon said, 'I've the gun and car ready and everything ready to go.'

She overheard John Dundon describing John McNamara (the intended victim) to Doyle. She said that Dundon said to Doyle: 'The gun is there, you kill him.'

She said that after the murder: 'We met John Dundon and Barry Doyle. John was saying John McNamara was dead.

'John Dundon phoned someone. Then he asked Barry Doyle to describe the man he killed and Barry described him. He said he was big, the way John described him.'

At that point, Doyle was convinced he had shot the right man. This is in stark contradiction to the rumour floating around Limerick that he knew before he pulled the trigger he had the wrong man.

The jury – again reduced to eleven – deliberated for four hours, spread over two days, returning a unanimous verdict of guilty. Doyle was given a mandatory life sentence.

It was a terrible fall from grace. Although Barry was from a deprived area of Dublin, those who knew him said that he showed early promise. He was a good-looking young man who excelled at sport, was a good student and was skilled with his hands. He was particularly good at Gaelic football. After school, he apprenticed as a bricklayer, but never qualified as he became immersed in gang culture.

Someone who knew him told the *Irish Times*:

In many ways he was a golden child. He genuinely did have it all. When people who he knew then heard his name on the television the first time he was in court for the killing in Limerick, they were stunned. It stopped you in your tracks; to think that all he had going for him and yet that's what he ended up doing. But it was the brother that dragged him down into the gutter, everyone knows that.

Paddy Doyle had significant contacts in Limerick, having met some of the McCarthy-Dundon gang in prison. The Doyle brothers spent time together in Spain, where Barry was introduced to many of the gangsters his older brother hung out with. Barry first met members of the McCarthy-Dundon gang at his brother's home near Malaga. When Paddy was shot dead, Barry Doyle continued the relationship with his brother's Limerick associates.

Up to that point he was not a criminal. His only convictions were for driving offences and public order matters. Yet he threw in his lot with the McCarthy-Dundons and was soon dealing drugs on the streets of Limerick. Gardaí believe that a number of factors turned him into a killer. He was a fully fledged and loyal member of the gang, and he believed he was gunning down a man who had conspired against his dead brother.

In an unusual move, Barry Doyle was sent to Mountjoy to serve his life sentence. Gangland figures are normally sent to Portlaoise, or to a special wing in the Midlands prison. But Portlaoise was out, because Brian Rattigan was serving there. Rattigan had been shot by Paddy Doyle, and his brother killed by him, so Barry Doyle's life would be in danger if he was there. And the Midlands prison was also out. It housed members of the McCarthy-Dundon gang. If Barry Doyle agreed to give evidence against his co-conspirators, some of them ran the danger of being convicted of murder. So they might decide to kill him and remove the danger.

After the verdict, Superintendent John Scanlon said that while the Gardaí were pleased with the decision of the jury, other people were involved in the killing of Shane Geoghegan and the case was still under investigation.

'This is not a moment of triumph. This is an ongoing investigation that will continue,' he said in a statement to the press, adding that the murder had left 'a lot of decent people traumatised', but the conviction was proof 'that the law will win out'.

The murder of Shane Geoghegan is still an open case. On

18 August 2012, John Dundon of Hyde Road, Limerick, was charged with the murder at the Special Criminal Court. At the time of going to print the trial is listed for June 2013. Others may also be charged. The Gardaí are patient. And they never close a murder file . . .